Comments from Readers and Reviewers

"Love your *Parachute* books, I am on my third one in my thirty-year career, with the 2012 version, and can't believe how much better each one gets, plus they stay so timely and relevant through all the changes over time!"

—Anthony DeLisi

"The new edition of the best-selling job-hunting book *What Color Is Your Parachute?*, in addition to the tried-and-true advice for job seekers Dick Bolles has provided for close to forty years, has new information on job-search productivity, job clubs, and how to organize and manage your job-search. *What Color Is Your Parachute?* is deservedly the world's most popular job-hunting book, with over 11 million copies sold in 26 languages.

This 2011 edition is as relevant today as when it was first published. Dick Bolles insightfully stays on the cutting edge of job searching, and the book is full of new and updated suggestions, along with the classic advice that continues to hold true today."

—Alison Doyle, About.com Guide

"[One of] the 100 best and most influential [nonfiction books] written in English since 1923, the beginning of TIME . . . magazine."

—TIME.com

"I graduated college in 2008, wallowed hopelessly in career frustration, and later received the best career advice of my life . . . which was to read your book *What Color Is Your Parachute?* Today, I am happily employed in a job that is the envy of my peers. I'm living proof of the power of your book and I recommend it to everyone I meet. It will eternally be the gift I give to recent graduates. Thank you for writing your book! I cannot begin to describe how much I have enjoyed it."

—Whitney Moore

"Anyone looking for career direction advice or solid information about how to find the job that's right for them should begin their search with Richard Bolles's classic book, *What Color Is Your Parachute?* It's been named one of the most influential books of all time for a reason—it has probably changed the course of more people's lives than almost any book except the Bible. Richard updates the book every year so it is always relevant."

  —Eric Wentworth

"Dick Bolles is effectively the 'inventor' of career management as we know it today."

  —Tom O'Neil

"If you go into the bookstore and find the section on jobs, careers, or networking—the reason that section even exists is because of Dick Bolles. His book, *What Color Is Your Parachute?*, has helped many people find their true passion at work. Plus he is a great man."

  —G. L. Hoffman, JobDig

"Dick Bolles is the last person on earth who needs my recommendation. Everyone knows his value to the world of career development. My recommendation/gratitude is for his friendship. He's a wonderful human being, joyful, resilient, and generous."

  —Ellen Jackson

"Dick Bolles is clever and witty and has some superb ideas. . . ."

  —Karen Elizabeth Davies

"I want to recommend Dick for the hard work he has put in both as an author and as a coach. The amount of influence Mr. Bolles has had on the people in career transition, such as myself when the dot-com bubble burst, is immeasurable. . . . His sage wisdom has forever changed my life, and I insist that all future employees read the *Parachute* book."

  —Devin Hedge

"I just wanted to tell you how grateful I am to you and your book, *What Color Is Your Parachute?* I graduated from a four-year university in May, and I had no clue what I wanted to do, or how to look for a job. Like any kid, I thought I knew the best way to do things and that I didn't need anyone's advice, but after a few months of unemployment I realized that this wasn't true. My dad had given me a copy of your book, but after a few months of nothing, not even an interview, I really read it, did the exercises, and trusted in what you were saying. I didn't believe that I would find MY job, the perfect job for me. But I did, at a nonprofit that does cleft lip and palate surgery missions to China and Africa. This job has literally every single attribute that I listed, and I wouldn't have known what attributes I needed in a job unless I had done your exercises. I'm sure you get probably hundreds of emails a week saying the same thing, so I'll keep it short—I just wanted to say that I owe my happiness in my job to you and my dad. I recommend your book to EVERYONE, including strangers."

    —Heather Smith

"How can any of us in the career and employment industry not only recommend Dick, but . . . thank him (and the Good Lord) for single-handedly creating the industry we love and cherish? I know, for sure, I would not be where I am today if Dick and his parachute hadn't led the way. No, *What Color Is Your Parachute?* is not the Bible. But it may be a distant second :-) I know I speak for every single person who works in the career/employment industry when I say . . . "THANK YOU, DICK" for all you've done. You are one of those very few people who truly is 'a legend in your own time.'"

    —Jay Block

"I DON'T HAVE A PARACHUTE OF ANY COLOR."

What Color Is Your Parachute?

A Practical Manual for Job-Hunters and Career-Changers

2013 Edition
Revised and Updated Annually

RICHARD N. BOLLES

TEN SPEED PRESS
Berkeley

This is an annual. That is to say, it is revised each year, often substantially, with the new edition appearing in the early fall. Counselors and others wishing to submit additions, corrections, or suggestions for the 2014 edition must submit them prior to February 1, 2013 using the form provided in the back of this book, or by e-mail (dickbolles40@gmail.com). Forms reaching us after that date will, unfortunately, have to wait for the 2015 edition.

PUBLISHER'S NOTE
This publication is designed to provide accurate and authoritative information in regard to the subject matter covered. It is sold with the understanding that the publisher is not engaged in rendering professional career services. If expert assistance is required, the service of the appropriate professional should be sought.

Published in the United States by Ten Speed Press, an imprint of the Crown Publishing Group, a division of Random House, Inc., New York.
www.crownpublishing.com
www.tenspeed.com

Ten Speed Press and the Ten Speed Press colophon are registered trademarks of Random House, Inc.

Jacket author photo by Glenn Jones.
Jacket people illustrations (left to right) copyright © iStockphoto.com/4x6; iStockphoto.com/enjoynz; iStockphoto.com/Illustrious.
Photo of Marci and Dick Bolles copyright © 2011 by Christine Vargas Yates.
The drawings on pages viii–ix, 79, 80, 146–47, and 227 are by Steven M. Johnson, author of *What the World Needs Now*.
Illustration on page 180 by Beverly Anderson.

ISBN: 978-1-60774-147-3 (paper)
ISBN: 978-1-60774-146-6 (cloth)
ISBN: 978-1-60774-148-0 (electronic)
ISSN: 8755-4658

Printed in the United States of America

Cover design by Patty Benson of Goodsite Web Solutions, Santa Cruz, CA, and Katy Brown
Back cover design by Colleen Cain
Interior design by Betsy Stromberg and Colleen Cain

10 9 8 7 6 5 4 3 2 1

Revised Edition

The wonderful actress
Anne Bancroft (1931–2005) was once
loosely quoted as saying
about her husband, Mel Brooks,
*My heart flutters whenever I hear his key
turning in the door, and I think to myself,
Oh goody, the party is about to begin.*

That is exactly how I feel
about my wife,
Marci Garcia Mendoza Bolles,
God's angel from the Philippines,
whom I fell deeply in love with, and married
on August 22, 2004.

What an enchanted marriage this has turned out to be!

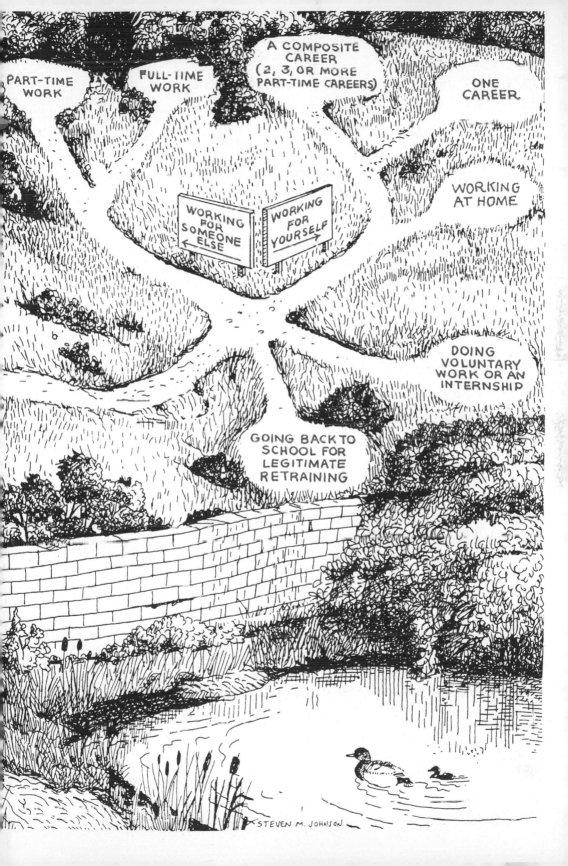

The 2013
Table of Contents

THE BASICS FOR JOB-HUNTERS AND CAREER-CHANGERS

THE PINK PAGES

Preface I'm Desperate: How Can a Book Help?

April 20, 2012

Well, this isn't really a book. It's more of a yearly journal. A journal rewritten every year for the past forty-one years.

I'm not normally an argumentative man. But I have my moments. Case in point: people say to me all the time, "Oh yes, I read your book." I ask what year. "Oh, 1978," they say. Or "1993" or "2002" or even "2010."

I reply, "Oh, so you haven't any idea what's in *Parachute*, today?" They look at me as though I were mad. "No," they argue, "I told you: I read your book."

"But it's changed its shape and content," I say. "It's morphed into something very different, over time. The 2012 edition is quite different even from the 2011."

"Oh come on," they say. "I know you don't really rewrite it every year. Revise it, maybe. Update a few addresses, and websites, and that sort of thing."

"No, actually you're wrong," I say. "I rethink the whole book, I rewrite it, I drastically change it, every single year." They stare at me: "You're kidding." No, I'm not.

Some of my readers know this. That's why ten million copies have sold to date; many go out and buy each new edition. And read it. I kid you not. You can see some of their comments, just inside the front cover.

Why rewrite it every year? Well, the restless job-market keeps changing. My restless mind keeps thinking of better ways to explain things. And I keep discovering new and better strategies for job-hunting or career-changing. New entries, new ideas, new events, every year. Sometimes I want to issue weekly bulletins.

The most important answer to the question with which I began—how can a book help?—is simply this. Blogs, websites, and apps dealing with job-hunters are too brief to describe a whole system. They are more like seagulls, dipping into the sea of truth wherever they will. A tidbit here. A tidbit there.

Sometimes very valuable truths. Very helpful truths. But not a whole, coherent system. It takes a book to do that. It takes a book to lay out a holistic view of job-hunting and career-changing, and show how things are all interconnected. That's what this book tries to do.

Is it hard for me to do this, every year? No, I love it! I love helping people. I love being an author.

An author's dilemma is easily stated: How much is too much information? How much is too little? I think there is too much information floating around out there—particularly on the Internet—and if you try to include it all, this book would turn into a ten-volume encyclopedia. So it is my responsibility to sift it down, and talk only about the most essential truths. But (a big "but") I must first gather as much of the information as possible here on my desk, before I sift it down to what seem to me to be the essentials.

In other words, I define an author's task to be that of a fisherman: cast a wide net, haul in a large catch, but then pick out only the best fish from all those taken in the net.

That said, this book demands a lot of you. Mostly in the way of thinking, and rethinking, what you thought were essential truths in job-hunting. But the rewards are comparable. Use it, and good health!

I will close, here, by noting that I didn't get here, alone. I do not stay here, alone. I am not inspired, alone. I am not able to write, alone. So, I am filled with gratitude. First of all, I am enchanted by every moment of my life with such a wondrous woman as my wife, Marci. I am so grateful for her. Then I am grateful for the family that loved me and played with me. I had a wonderful Mother and Dad. I had great siblings: one brother (Don), one sister (Ann). They're all dead now. I'm the only survivor from those generations. So, that's why I'm grateful for those who still live: my four grown children and their families: Stephen, Mark, Gary, and Sharon, plus their most-loving mother, my former wife, Jan, who shares in all our family gatherings; and my former stepdaughter, Dr. Serena Brewer, whom I helped raise for twenty years; she is now a wonderful physician in the town of Butte, Montana. I'm grateful for Marci's grown children, Janice and Adlai, with their families. They are as dear as if they were born to me.

I want to express my gratitude also to my dearest friend (besides Marci), Daniel Porot of Geneva, Switzerland—we taught together for two weeks every summer, for nineteen years; then there is Dave Swanson, ditto; plus my international friends, Brian McIvor of Ireland; John Webb and Madeleine Leitner of Germany; Yves Lermusi, of Checkster fame, who came from Belgium; Pete Hawkins of Liverpool, England; Debra Angel MacDougall of Scotland; Byung Ju Cho of South Korea; Tom O'Neil of New Zealand; and, in this country, Howard Figler, beloved friend and co-author of our manual for career counselors; Marty Nemko; Joel Garfinkle; Richard Leider; Dick Knowdell; Rich Feller; Dick Gaither; Warren Farrell; Michael Robinson; Chuck Young; Susan Joyce; and the folks over at Ten Speed Press in Berkeley, California, now an imprint of the Crown Publishing Group of Random House, plus Crown's head, Maya Mavjee, who has been very kind to me.

My original publisher, Phil Wood, is gone now. He was my publisher for almost forty years; he was a dear man, and I owe him more than I can say for helping *Parachute* find its audience, and for letting me have great control over the annual editions. *Parachute* would never have sold ten million copies, if it were not for him.

I much appreciate my current friends over at Ten Speed: Aaron Wehner (publisher), George Young, Kara Van de Water, Lisa Westmoreland, and Betsy Stromberg.

My especial thanks to my readers—all ten million of you—for buying my books, trusting my counsel, and following your dream. I have never met so many wonderful souls. I am so thankful for you all.

It is not fashionable these days to talk about one's faith, but I'm going to do it anyway. I am very quiet about my faith; it's just . . . there. But it is the source of whatever grace, wisdom, or compassion I have ever found, or shared with others. I have all my life been a committed Christian, a devoted follower of Jesus Christ, and an Episcopalian (I was an ordained priest for fifty years). I thank my Creator every night for such a life, such a wonderful mission, as He has given me: to help millions of people make their lives really count for something, as we all go spinning through space, here on Spaceship Earth.

Dick Bolles
dickbolles40@gmail.com
www.eParachute.com
www.jobhuntersbible.com

A GRAMMAR AND LANGUAGE NOTE

I want to explain four points of grammar, in this book of mine: pronouns, commas, italics, and spelling. My unorthodox use of them invariably offends unemployed English teachers so much that instead of finishing the exercises, they immediately write to apply for a job as my editor.

To save us unnecessary correspondence, let me explain. Throughout this book, I often use the apparently plural pronouns "they," "them," and "their" after singular antecedents—such as, "You must approach someone for a job and tell them what you can do." This sounds strange and even wrong to those who know English well. To be sure, we all know there is another pronoun—"you"—that may be either singular or plural, but few of us realize that the pronouns "they," "them," and "their" were also once treated as both plural and singular in the English language. This changed, at a time in English history when agreement in number became more important than agreement as to sexual gender. Today, however, our priorities have shifted once again. Now, the distinguishing of sexual gender is considered by many to be more important than agreement in number.

The common artifices used for this new priority, such as "s/he," or "he and she," are—to my mind—tortured and inelegant. Casey Miller and Kate Swift, in their classic, *The Handbook of Nonsexist Writing*, agree, and argue that it is time to bring back the earlier usage of "they," "them," and "their" as both singular and plural—just as "you" is/are. They further argue that this return to the earlier historical usage has already become quite common out on the street—witness a typical sign by the ocean that reads, "Anyone using this beach after 5 p.m. does so at their own risk." I have followed Casey and Kate's wise recommendations in all of this.

As for my commas, they are deliberately used according to my own rules—rather than according to the rules of historic grammar (which I did learn—I hastily add, to reassure my old Harvard professors, who despaired of me weekly, during English class). In spite of those rules, I follow my own, which are: to write conversationally, and put in a comma wherever I would normally stop for a breath, were I speaking the same line.

The same conversational rule applies to my use of italics. This book is a conversation: I'm sitting down with you to tell you what I know. Conversations have rhythms. You emphasize a word here, you speak a word softly, there. There are pauses. The speed of a sentence sometimes changes from the previous. All of this is difficult to reproduce in print, if all the text looks equal. So I use italics, I use dashes, I use parentheses, I use color, etc. to reproduce in print—as much as I can—the rhythms of natural speech.

Finally, some of my spelling (and capitalization) is weird. (You say "weird"; I say "playful.") I sometimes like writing it as "e-mail," for example, but other times I feel like writing it as "email." Fortunately, since this is my own book, I get to play by my own peculiar inclinations and playfulness; I'm just grateful that ten million readers have gone along. Nothing delights a child (at heart) more, than being found at play.

—Dick Bolles

P.S. Speaking of "playful," over the last forty years a few critics (very few, actually) have claimed that *Parachute* is not serious enough (they object to the cartoons, here, which poke fun at almost everything). On the other hand, a few have complained that the book is too serious, and too complicated in its vocabulary and grammar for anyone except a college graduate. Two readers, however, have written me with a different view.

The first one, from England, said there is an index that analyzes a book to tell you what grade in school you must have finished, in order to be able to understand it. My book's index, he said, turned out to be 6.1, which means you need only have finished sixth grade in a U.S. school in order to understand it.

Here in the U.S., a college instructor came up with a similar finding. He phoned me to tell me that my book was rejected by the authorities as a proposed text for the college course he was teaching, because (they said) the book's language/grammar was not up to college level. "What level was it?" I asked. "Well," he replied, "when they analyzed it, it turned out to be written on an eighth grade level."

Sixth or eighth grade—that seems just about right to me. Why make job-hunting complicated, when it can be expressed so simply even a child could understand it?

THE BASICS FOR JOB-HUNTERS AND CAREER-CHANGERS

It was the best of times,
It was the worst of times,
It was the age of wisdom,
It was the age of foolishness,
It was the epoch of belief,
It was the epoch of incredulity,
It was the season of light,
It was the season of darkness,
It was the spring of hope,
It was the winter of despair,
We had everything before us,
We had nothing before us,
We were all going direct to heaven,
We were all going direct the other way . . .

—Charles Dickens (1812–1870), *A Tale of Two Cities*

Chapter 1 How to Find Hope

It is a strange world we find ourselves in, these days. Old rules are being rewritten. Things are changing that we never thought would change. Events are happening that we thought we would never see. Things we used to take for granted, now are vanishing. Things don't work the way they used to. And here we are, trying to plot a new course for our life, still needing help with the essential question of our existence:

Where do I go from *here* with my life?

Maybe things are going well in our lives, right now. Or maybe they're not. We may have a life that is unfolding just as we'd hoped. Or our lives may have turned into a nightmare, and we have no idea how we're going to get out of our present predicament. Never mind. So long as we have hope, we'll be all right. The one thing we must not be is hopeless. So, it must be hope that we seek, above and before all else; the only question is, how do we find it? Well, there are four keys.

The First Key to Finding Hope

Experts have discovered, over the years, what is the absolute minimum for finding Hope. And it is just this: *Hope depends upon taking care that we have at least two alternatives, in every situation we find ourselves, and with every task confronting us.*

Not just one way to describe ourselves, *but two ways, at least.*

Not deciding upon just one career, *but two careers, at least.*

Not getting trained or retrained for just one kind of job, *but two different kinds of jobs, at least.*

Not just one way to hunt for a job, *but two ways, at least.*

Not hunting just for one job, *but two jobs, at least.*

Not going after just one size company, *but two sizes, at least, small or large.*

Not just choosing one place where we really would like to find work, *but two places, at least.*

Not finding just one way to approach a place that interests us, *but two different ways, at least.*

Not securing just one job offer, *but two job offers, at least.*

And so on. And so forth.

To have only one plan, one option, in any situation, is a sure recipe for despair. I'll give you a simple example. In a study of 100 job-hunters who were using only one method to hunt for a job, typically 51 abandoned their search by the second month. That's more than half of them. They lost Hope. On the other hand, of 100 job-hunters who were using *two or more* different ways of hunting for a job, typically only 31 of them abandoned their search by the second month. That's less than one-third of them. The latter kept going because they had Hope.

And so this truth should always be on your mind: In order to never become hopeless, *you want to be sure that in every situation you find yourself, you're not putting all your eggs in just one basket.* You must determine to always have at least two alternatives, in every challenge you are facing, that you may overcome—and live what the ancients called "a victorious life."

The Second Key to Finding Hope

In any situation, no matter how much we may feel we are at the mercy of vast forces *out there*, that are totally beyond our control, we can always find something that is within our control, however small, and work on *that*.

To illustrate my point, some years ago, when I was doing a lot of counseling, not just about careers, a friend of mine asked me if I would be willing to see someone he knew. Her name was Mary. She had been diagnosed with multiple sclerosis, or MS. She had been to a wide range of medical specialists: neurologist, psychologist, internist, you name it.

They all had declared there was nothing they could do to help her with the disease. My friend said, "Would you see her?" "Sure," I said, "but I'm not sure there's anything I can do."

The next day my friend brought her over. She walked very stiffly up the front sidewalk, came in, sat down, and after exchanging a few pleasantries, I got down to business. "Mary," I said, "what is multiple sclerosis?" "I don't know," she said, in a dull, emotionless voice. "Well then," I said, "that makes us even; because I don't know, either. But here's what I propose. I'm sure that a huge proportion of whatever MS is, is out of your control. There's nothing you can do about it. But that proportion can't be 100 percent. There's got to be some proportion—let's say it's even just 2 percent, or 5 percent—that is within your control. We could work on that. Do you want to begin that journey?" She said yes. Over the next few weeks she improved, and finally was free of all symptoms (typical of the disease for a spell, but this lasted for a very long time), and now—free of all stiffness—she became a model on 57th Street in New York City.

So it is, that in any situation you find yourself, no matter how overwhelmed you may feel, no matter how much you may feel you're at the mercy of things that are just beyond your control, some part of it *is* within your control: 2 percent, 5 percent, who knows? There is always *something* you can work on. And often, changing that little bit results in changing a whole lot. Maybe not as dramatic a change as with Mary; but change nonetheless.

Above all else, it gives you Hope. *I am not as powerless as I thought.*

This certainly applies to any time we are out of work, particularly if it drags on and on. To paraphrase what I said to Mary, but now I'm talking to those of you who are job-hunters or career-changers: *I'm sure that a huge proportion of the situation you are facing, is out of your control. There's nothing you can do about it. But that proportion can't be 100 percent. There's got to be some proportion—let's say it's even just 2 percent—that is within your control. Determine to find what that is. Then throw all your energies into working on it. Who knows what a difference that may make!*

[Oh, by the way, some examples of what is within your control: getting more sleep; drinking more water (we usually need more water than we think we do); walking more; reading the book *14,000 Things to Be Happy About*[1]; doing the Flower Exercise (chapter 5, here), learning

---

1. By Barbara Ann Kipfer, Workman Publishing, 2007, revised and updated.

to become more observant of the world around you; listening harder
to other people; getting into a supportive community with other job-
hunters; reading this book twice; rethinking your job-hunt; talking
more to successful job-hunters, asking them what they did, step by
step, to find work. And, like that.]

The Third Key to Finding Hope

Assume that nothing that happens to us is just senseless and meaningless, including being out of work for a long time. In the context of
our total life, it will eventually turn out to have meaning.

I recall a talk I heard many years ago, that made a deep and lasting
impression on me. It was a doctor speaking; a doctor turned researcher,
as it happened. He was reporting on a study that some colleagues had
made of Healing, at the hospital where he worked in New York City.
They had long known that some people healed faster than others, but
now they wanted to find out *why*. I cannot cite the study; I lost track of
it, over the years. But I can tell you what I remember.

As I recall, they searched through their records of discharged
patients to find matched pairs: essentially two people of the same age,
with the same background, the same basic health record, who had
undergone the same procedure or operation in that hospital. They
chose the pairs where one member of the pair healed faster than the
other, often by a wide margin. The doctors then contacted each pair
and questioned each one of them at length, to find out what was different about the person who healed faster.

The common explanations that would occur to any thoughtful person proved to have no correlation with the rate of healing. Was the one
who healed faster more physically fit than the other? No. More optimistic than the other? No. Well, then, was it their habits: eating, sleeping, exercising? No. Was it their family history? No. Was it their status
as single or married? No. Was it whether they believed in God, or not?
No. Well then, what was it?

To the researchers' great surprise, it turned out that *those who healed
faster believed that everything that happened to them had meaning, even if*

they didn't know what that meaning was, at the time. The ones who healed slowly did not believe this.

And so, our learning: what you think, can influence your body. It follows that it can influence also our ability to heal as we go through a crisis.

I was most struck by that part of his report which said ". . . even if they didn't know *what* the meaning was." Apparently, just to believe that nothing about our life is meaningless is sufficient.

Naturally, to believe that, always gives you Hope.

So, when we are out of work, for example, we can avoid hopelessness if we believe that nothing that happens to us is senseless and meaningless. We may not see that meaning right now. But in the context of our total life, this experience will eventually turn out to have meaning.

But what do we mean when anyone says, "This time in my life has meaning, even if I don't know what that meaning is, right now." *Why* don't we know it right now?

Well, who knows? If we want to speculate, I think one reason may be that the time we are in, is like an Act I in a two-act play.

I came to this realization in my own life. One time when I was fired without warning, I had an appointment that very afternoon with my dentist. He was an old man and upon hearing my news, he pointed his finger at me, and said, "You won't believe a word of what I'm saying right now, but this will turn out to be the best thing that ever happened to you. I've seen it happen too many times to doubt it."

Well, he was right; that was only Act I. Act II was that which led me eventually to writing this yearly "journal" (*for that is how I think of this book*) which by the grace of God has helped change the life of millions over the past forty annual editions.

The first Act, being fired, seemed meaningless to me, until the second Act, the writing of this book, came along to give the first Act meaning.

So, if you're in—say—a dreary time of unemployment, and it all seems pointless and meaningless to you, remember it may be only Act I. If it seems meaningless now, you would do well to watch for Act II, that follows it. You may yet discover that everything that happens to you does have meaning.

The Fourth Key to Finding Hope

Pay no attention to statistics if they discourage you. Alternatives do give you hope, but statistics can take that hope away, if you give them undue weight.

Much of it depends on what statistics you pay attention to. The media, the Internet, blogs, tweets, twenty-four-hour news channels on TV, newspapers, and magazines, all love statistics. *But they generally are in love with a very particular kind of statistics, namely those that convey bad news.* Discouraging news. Doom and gloom.

Why is this so? I dunno. But it is. Example? Let's take the month of February 2009, the height of the recent Recession. As reported on a website called JOLT (*Job Openings & Labor Turnover*)[2] 4,360,000 people in the U.S. found jobs that month. Yes, you read that correctly. And at the end of that month, 3,006,000 additional vacancies remained unfilled and available. Good news, right? 7,366,000 vacancies were available or filled, that month alone. At the height of the Recession.

Ah, but every month there is a second set of statistics, reported on the first Friday of each month by the Bureau of Labor Statistics, called the Current Population Survey.[3] It is typically called *The Unemployment Statistic*, though it is more accurate to think of it as *"the monthly measure of the size of the working work force in America."* Anyway, the CPS said that during that same month, February 2009, the size of the total labor force in the U.S. shrank by 726,000 jobs. And so, the unemployment rate rose from 7.6 percent to 8.1. Bad news, to be sure.

Okay, there you have it: two sets of statistics, one good news, one bad news. Now, which of these two sets do you think the media pounced on? Yep, you guessed it: *the bad news* set. "726,000 workers lose their jobs," commentators and news analysts shrieked. "Unemployment rises to 8.1 percent." Along with that, they threw in "There are six unemployed workers now for every vacancy." All in all, it was enough to take the heart out of even the most optimistic job-hunter that month. Or any month.

---

2. www.bls.gov/jlt
3. www.bls.gov/cps

We have to always watch *which* statistics we are paying the most attention to. For, surely, statistics can sometimes help us, and not merely depress us.

Let's post a few guideposts here about how statistics can help you:

1. *Statistics can save you from wasting your energy.* For example, when considering job-hunting methods, it can be helpful to know what the odds are that a particular method will richly repay you for the time spent on it, or what the odds are that a particular method will likely be a complete waste of your time. We will see this, when we discuss the five *best* ways to hunt for work, and the five *worst* ways (comparatively speaking).

2. *Statistics can guide you toward particular targets.* They can tell you when a particular company is having the kind of challenges you would love to help solve, and when a company has more problems than you would ever want to deal with, because they're about to tank.

3. *Statistics can encourage you,* if you know how to read them. Know their limits. For example, job-hunting statistics typically summarize the experience of job-hunters who choose only one method of job-search. You, however, know about alternatives: when you are out of work, you know enough to choose two or more methods, and thus increase the odds that you will indeed find meaningful work. So, those statistics don't apply to you.

Just remember, you only need one job. It doesn't matter how many other people are out of work, or how few vacancies there may be. You only need one of them. That's the statistic that matters the most.

Conclusion

The subtitle of this book is *A Practical Manual for Job-Hunters and Career-Changers.* Many readers assume, therefore, that in the first chapter I will jump right into discussing job-hunting strategies and techniques. I used to do that. But eventually I learned that I can teach the most clever, unorthodox, and effective techniques, in the world—but a job-hunter can undo it all if they have the wrong attitude.

Show me two job-hunters. Let's say they are both men. Both are essentially the same age. Both have the same background. Both have the same intelligence and history. Both have been out of work for the same amount of time. It's been many months, now. Both are struggling, financially. They both get by on what little they've saved, what occasionally they can sell, the occasional brief odd job, plus help from family and friends—that sort of thing. But there the similarities end.

The one is quietly smoldering with anger, barely suppressed. He is mad at the universe, and in no particular order, his former employer, his former co-workers, the government, politicians, his profession, his college, friends, and God. He is very quiet, doesn't talk much, and when he does talk, it is to complain about how his life has turned out. He is sullen, gloomy about his future, feels he has been declared disposable, and that his life as he knew it is over.

The other is just as depressed about how his life has turned out, thus far, but he wakes up each morning glad to see the sun, puts on beautiful music, walks a great deal, counts his blessings, is in a job-support group, focuses on other people's troubles, not just his own, is a great listener, spends each new day trying to be a better person than he was the day before, remains active in his job-hunt, tries to learn or study something new each day, essentially sees life as an adventure, and is willing to wait patiently for the next Act to unfold.

Which one of those two do you think is more likely to find a job? You know the answer. Job-hunting almost always involves competing with others for the job, sad to say, and it is our attitude that can give us the advantage. If you are out of work, and having a difficult time of it, my heart goes out to you. But don't just look for better job-hunting techniques. Work, first of all, on your attitude. Then the techniques have an infinitely better chance of working.

So here's the sum of it all. Before we can decide *where do I go from here with my life*, we have to have Hope. We have to believe that what we do will make a difference, that we are not up against huge immutable forces that leave us completely powerless. We will never address the challenges we face in life unless we see, at the end of the tunnel, light and Hope. Hope is the condition for our survival. Lose Hope, and the whole game is lost. Find Hope, hold on to Hope, and all things are possible.

Discussion

Career-counselor: How else would you describe yourself besides "construction worker"?

Job-hunter: I've always been a construction worker.

Career-counselor: Well, that's a "job-title." There are other ways to describe yourself besides a job-title.

Job-hunter: Like what, for example?

Career-counselor: Like: "I am a person . . . who . . . "

Job-hunter: Who what?

Career-counselor: "I am a person . . . who has **these** skills, and **these** knowledges, and **this** experience." Take the job-title off yourself; find a more fundamental way to describe yourself to yourself. And to others. Once you have at least **two** alternative ways of describing yourself, you increase the range of jobs you can apply for, and thus keep Hope alive.

Do not let us speak of darker days;
Let us speak rather of sterner days.
These are not dark days; these are great days—
The greatest days our country has ever lived;
And we must all thank God that we have been allowed . . .
To play a part in making these days memorable
In the history of our race.

—Winston Churchill (1874–1965)

Chapter 2 The Seven Secrets About the Job-Market Today

The term "job-market" is a myth. There is no such thing. For, it implies that there is *one* place to which every employer with a vacancy, and everyone who wants a job, comes. And there they find each other. Wouldn't that be loverly? But it doesn't exist.

Instead, we have millions of markets out there, and a job-hunter or career-changer must decide which of these markets they want to approach.

But let's use the term "job-market" anyway, as at least a metaphor to describe the whole scene.

The job-market keeps changing, evolving, with new characteristics every year. (Make that "every month.") If you're looking for a job, one of the first things you *must* do is *upgrade* your knowledge of the whole job-market. *It sure ain't what it used to be.*

If you're going to go out there, whether to job-hunt or to change careers, there are seven *secrets* about the job-market that you need to know. I use the word *secrets* here because of its traditional meaning as "information that is not known to some people but is known to others."

Some people know one or two of the so-called *secrets* that follow, but not generally speaking all seven. That's true of the public at large, Congress, the media, blogs, websites, and those of us who are job-hunting or changing careers. And yet, it is especially important for us—in particular—to know it. Otherwise, we just won't understand what game we're playing in. So, here we go.

First Secret: Even in the best of times, there are *always* millions of unemployed people who can't find a job—every month. For example, in January 2006 when we weren't in a recession, the number of people who were out of work was 7,067,000. That's a lot of people. *And by the*

11

way, that figure in tough times, say February 2012, stood at 12,500,000, or an increase of 5,433,000—(not 12,500,000)—since "the best of times."[1] Moral: even in the best of times, our so-called "U.S. job-hunting system" sucks. (Not just the U.S.; see Spain, Greece, the U.K., Ireland, and so on.)

Second Secret: Even in the worst of times, there are *always* millions of unemployed people in the U.S. who do find work, every month.[2] Just because you can't *find* job vacancies doesn't mean they don't *exist.* As some 140 million workers currently do have jobs (in the U.S. alone), some jobs are always falling vacant, due to, oh, sickness, retirements, moving, company mergers, career change, new technologies, the birth of new companies or organizations, etc. There are *always* job vacancies out there. For example, in March 2012 the number of people in the U.S. who found work that month was 4,356,000, with 3,737,000 vacancies still waiting to be filled, at the end of that month. That's a total of 8,093,000, *in one month.* Moral: if I am looking for a job or for a new career right now, the basic questions are: Why aren't I among those 8,093,000 each month? And what do I have to do, to change that?

Third Secret: The media do not distinguish between societal problems and job-hunters' problems, when discussing the job-market. You will see the media publicize such statistics as: *currently, 75 million people ages 15 to 24 are out of work globally.*[3] That's a societal problem. A severe societal problem. With that many young people unable to find jobs, you will inevitably find rioting and demonstrations as we have seen these past twelve months in Spain, Greece, plus the U.K. and— even more dramatically, the overthrowing or ousting of governments, as in France, Greece, the Middle East, and Africa. Massive numbers of the unemployed, particularly the young unemployed, are a threat to the stability of any society. Heightening our awareness of that, is an essential mission of the media.

---

1. This figure is recorded monthly at the Bureau of Labor Statistics Employment Situation Summary, found on the Internet at http://tinyurl.com/t68g.
2. This figure is recorded monthly on the Internet at *Job Openings and Labor Turnover*: www.bls.gov/news.release/jolts.nr0.htm.
3. Lisa Abend et al., "Quotes of the Day," *Time*, April 16, 2012, 46.

But the societal problem—the number of people out of work—says nothing about the job-hunter's problem: which is, how do I find a job? If we are out of work, our challenges are not related to how many others are also looking besides us. Rather, since there are always *millions of* vacancies, our finding work depends on three other factors, not often discussed:

The first is that those of us out of work often have only the most elementary job-hunting skills; and I mean *elementary*. We know *resumes* and *interviews*, but little more than that. We are totally unprepared for the twenty-first-century job-hunt. Oh, and Federal money for training us in better job-hunting skills has fallen 13 percent, since 2006.

Austerity

In fact, Federal funding for many things that job-hunters used to be able to count on—unemployment insurance, job support groups, and hiring—is bound to be reduced. Not just here. Everywhere. Politicians in nation after nation are arguing that even though we are just now recovering slowly from a major recession, they must cut the national deficit *now*, delay taxes, reduce spending, cut social programs, and enact *severe austerity measures*. Unfortunately, "austerity measures" is just code for "firing." Cut the budget, and what do you cut? Not just money. Jobs. It is estimated that two million government jobs have disappeared in the past three or four years in the U.S., mostly on the state and local level.[4]

The second factor we face when we are out of work is that it is getting harder and harder to get trained or retrained for other occupations, using government grants. The government, in the name of austerity, is increasingly cutting funds that used to be set aside for training or retraining. "Federal Funds to Train the Jobless are Drying Up," says the headline on page 1 of the April 9, 2012, edition of the *New York Times*. That says it all. They report an 18 percent drop in Federal funding for retraining since 2006. This has resulted in such dramatic consequences as one region (Seattle) being approached by 120,000 people seeking training, but the centers there were *unable* to help 95 percent of them,

---

4. Kevin Drum, "Where the Government Jobs Are," *Mother Jones*, July 8, 2011, http://tinyurl.com/85qqz7x.

due to lack of funds. And in another region (Dallas) where 23,500 people lost jobs in the previous ten weeks, they were able to train only 43 of them. That's 43 people, not 4,300.

The third factor we face when we are out of work is that the longer any of us is out of work, the less willing *some* employers are to hire us. In *an abundance of caution,* they figure we've become rusty, lost our work ethic, and are out of date. And so, we give up hope. Our attitude becomes the problem.

And there you have the problem. Minorities of course have been experiencing these three factors for decades, in country after country around the world. Now it's everybody's turn.

In the face of such societal upheaval, the maxim of this twenty-first century for those of us out of work is: when you're out of work, it's up to you; you can no longer count on being rescued by someone else. You've got to rescue yourself: You've got to hold on to hope. You've got to figure out what retraining you specifically want, and need, and then how to get it, even if there is no government help. And you've got to become better—much better, much, much better—at hunting for a job, which is what this book is all about. Job-hunting is increasingly becoming an essential survival skill.

Fourth Secret: Generally speaking, employers and job-hunters search for each other in entirely different ways. Actually, it's worse than that. Employers and job-hunters typically search for each other in almost *exactly opposite ways.* A chart of employers' preferences vs. job-hunters' preferences would come out looking something like the one on the next page (read down from the top on the left-hand side for employers; read up from the bottom on the right-hand side, for job-hunters or career-changers). Why so opposite? Because of the differing goals of employer vs. job-hunter.

The job-hunter or career-changer's main goal is **conservation of energy**, which means wide coverage. Typically, we want to cover as much territory, reach as many employers as we possibly can, with the least expenditure of time and energy on our part. Hence, we tend to love resumes, and Internet job-postings, and "job-boards" such as Monster or CareerBuilder or even Craigslist. They enable us to do precisely that.

Many If Not Most Employers Hunt for Job-Hunters in the Exact Opposite Way from How Most Job-Hunters Hunt for Them

The Way a Typical Employer Prefers to Fill a Vacancy

1 **6**

From Within: Promotion of a full-time employee, or promotion of a present part-time employee, or hiring a former consultant for in-house or contract work, or hiring a former "temp" full-time. Employer's thoughts: *"I want to hire someone whose work I have already seen."* (A low-risk strategy for the employer.)

Implication for Job-Hunters: See if you can get hired at an organization you have chosen—as a temp, contract worker, or consultant—aiming at a full-time position only later (or not at all).

2 **5**

Using Proof: Hiring an unknown job-hunter who brings proof of what he or she can do, with regards to the skills needed.

Implication for Job-Hunters: If you are a programmer, bring a program you have done—with its code; if you are a photographer, bring photos; if you are a counselor, bring a case study with you; etc.

3 **4**

Using a Best Friend or Business Colleague: Hiring someone whose work a trusted friend of yours has seen (perhaps they worked for him or her).

Implication for Job-Hunters: Find someone who knows the person-who-has-the-power-to-hire at your target organization, who also knows your work and will introduce you two.

4 **3**

Using an Agency They Trust: This may be a recruiter or search firm the employer has hired; or a private employment agency—both of which have checked you out, on behalf of the employer.

5 **2**

Using an Ad They Have Placed (online or in newspapers, etc.).

6 **1**

Using a Resume: Even if the resume was unsolicited (if the employer is desperate).

The Way a Typical Job-Hunter Prefers to Fill a Vacancy

The *main* goal of the typical employer is quite different: *low risk* in hiring. We're talking time and money, here. To see what I mean, if you use the Internet, put into your favorite search engine the phrase "cost of a bad hire." You will see that the answers run between one to five times the bad hire's *annual* salary. Yes, hiring someone who is a mistake, and then having to fire that person and start their search all over again, costs an employer dearly. So, they prefer that they—or someone they know and respect—has actually *seen* the work and the work habits of the prospective employee (that would be You).

Promotion within their own organization is employers' absolute preference. But referrals, particularly recommendations by other trusted employees, are a gold standard. So is recommendation by some fellow employer or colleague whose opinions they trust.

Because of their fear of risk, *some* employers tend to prefer to hire someone who is currently employed. (Not *every* employer, thank heavens!) They also tend to prefer someone with past experience in their field or related, rather than a career-changer who is new to the field and to the job. (There is, however, a way around this, as we shall see in later chapters.)

Keep these differing goals in mind—*low risk* for the employer, vs. *wide-coverage* for the job-hunter or career-changer—and you will completely understand the details in the preceding chart.

Fifth Secret: Job-hunters tend to hunt in the same way regardless of whether the times are good or bad, but employers don't. These days, employers often change their hunting behavior dramatically when times are tough. The reason for this is that when times are good, employers often have difficulty filling their vacancies, so *they will typically cater to the job-hunter's preferences.* We like resumes, so they will take the trouble to solicit, look at, and read, our resumes. We like job-postings, so they will post their vacancies where we can find them: on their own site or on job-boards, typically.

What we are not prepared for, is that during tough times, when employers are finding it much easier to fill a vacancy, many of them will change their behavior. There are a million exceptions to this, but as a generalization they will typically revert to their default position (the top of the chart), and stop reading our resumes and stop posting their vacancies. But we do not change our job-hunting behavior, so we go looking for work the same way we did last year, or four years ago, or ten years ago, or thirty, and suddenly find that nothing is working.

We can search until we're blue in the face. We can work like a dog, send out resumes week after week, search all the Internet job boards day after day, turn to our Facebook, and LinkedIn, and Twitter pages for help, network like crazy, attend job-hunters' support groups week after week, but . . . *nothing!* Everything that used to work, doesn't work anymore. And we are baffled. It is like turning the key in our faithful car, but for the first time in ten years the motor won't start.

We decide, of course, that there is a reason why nothing is working. We conclude that reason is, there are no jobs. It never occurs to us that there are, but the reason nothing is working that used to work, is that employers have changed *their* behavior.

"There Are No Jobs." **Wrong!**

The common belief among job-hunters is that if an employer has a vacancy, *they will always post it* on the Internet—on their own site, or on a job-board or elsewhere. *Not true.* Generally speaking, employers will only post their vacancies if they are having trouble filling a position. Otherwise, they fall back to their preferred strategy: filling it without ever advertising it. This creates what has historically been called "the hidden job market," estimated by experts to include as much as 80 percent of all vacancies. Job-hunters think that if there are no postings, there are no jobs. *No, no, no.* The vacancies have simply gone underground.

There is a remedy, fortunately. When we are out of work we can, in such times as these, start thinking like an employer, learn how employers prefer to look for employees, and figure out how to change our own job-hunting strategies so as to conform to *theirs.* In other words, *adapt to the employer's preferences.*

Sixth Secret: There is no such thing as "employers." Job-hunters after getting turned down in as few as three interviews, will typically conclude, *"Employers* don't want someone with my background, or my age, or my handicap." *Not so fast!* All we can legitimately say at that point, is "Those three employers didn't want me."

There is no such thing as "employers." All generalizations about "employers" *(including those in this book)* are just mental *conveniences.* "Employers" are as different from one another as night and day. "Employers" span a wide range of attitudes, wildly different ideas about how to hire, a wide range of ways to conduct hiring interviews, and as many different attitudes toward handicaps as you can possibly think of. You cannot possibly predict the attitude of one employer from the attitude of another. There are millions of separate, distinct, unrelated employers out there. Unless you look dirty, wild, and disreputable, and smell really bad, if you know what your *talent* is, I guarantee some employer is looking for *you.* Even if you're crazy, there's some employer crazier than you. You have to keep going. Some employers *do* want you. Your job is to find *them.* Keep these two things in mind, as to where they're likely to be found:

1. There is a big difference between **large employers** (those with hundreds or thousands of employees) and **small employers** (alternately defined as those with 25 or fewer employees, those with 50 or fewer employees, or—the most common definition— those with 100 or fewer employees). The chief difference is that large employers are harder to reach, especially if the-person- who-has-the-power-to-hire-you (for the job you want) is in some deep inner chamber of that company, and the company's phone has a voice menu with eighteen impenetrable layers.

2. There is a big difference between **new companies** or enterprises, and those that have been around **for some time**, so far as hiring is concerned. A study reported in *TIME* magazine found that newer small companies (100 or fewer employees) that were less than six years old, created 4.7 million jobs in the year studied (2005), while older small firms created only 3.2 million jobs.[5] So when hiring is tight, you will want to concentrate on small firms, and *newer* small firms, at that.

---

5. "Briefing on the Economy," *Time*, April 11, 2011.

Seventh Secret: Assume that the employers' world is like a foreign country; you must learn their language, and their customs, before you visit.

This is an idea from the authors of a book called *No One Is Unemployable.*[6] They suggested that when you approach the world of business for the first time, you should think of it as going to visit a foreign country; you know you're going to have to learn a whole new language, culture, and customs, there. Same with the job-market. So, let's take a look at that world of the employer.

Employers have a tremendous amount of power in this hiring game; and this explains why parts of the whole job-hunting system in this country will drive you nuts. It wasn't built for you or me. It was built by and for *them.* And they live in a world different from yours and mine, in their head. (That's why I said *foreign* country!) This results in the following six contrasts:

1. You want the job-market to be *a hiring game.* But the employer regards it as *an elimination game*—until the very last phase. Larger companies or organizations are looking at that huge stack of resumes on their desk, with a view—first of all—to finding out who they can eliminate. Eventually they want to get it down to the "last person standing."

2. You want the employer to be taking lots of initiative toward finding you, and when they are desperate they will. Some HR departments will spend hours and days combing the Internet looking for the right person. But generally speaking the employer prefers that it be you who takes the initiative, toward finding *them.*

3. In being considered for a job, you want your solid past performance— summarized on your written resume—to be all that gets weighed, but the employer weighs your whole behavior as they glimpse it from their first interaction with you, to the last. Employers operate intuitively on the principle of *microcosm equals macrocosm.* They believe that what you do in some small "universe" reveals how you will act in a larger "universe." Small "universes," in

---

6. Debra Angel MacDougall and Elisabeth Harney Sanders-Park. The book was published by Worknet Training Services in 1997. A more recent book of theirs is titled *The 6 Reasons You'll Get the Job: What Employers Look for—Whether They Know It or Not,* published in 2010 by Prentice Hall.

the hiring interview, are such things as: Are you late for the appointment? Do you let the interviewer talk half the time, or not? Do you treat everyone with respect and courtesy there, or not? Do you write a thank-you note after the interview—not only to them, but to the receptionist, secretary, and whoever else you interacted with, there—by name—or not? They watch you carefully in these particulars, during and after the interview, because they assume that each of these reveals, in microcosm, how you would act in a larger "universe," like: the job you are applying for! They scrutinize your past, as in your resume, for the same reason: *microcosm* (behavior in the past) *reveals macrocosm* (likely behavior in the future).

4. You want the employer to acknowledge receipt of your resume— particularly if you post it *right on their website*, but the employer generally feels too swamped with other things, to have time to do that, so only 45 percent do. A majority of employers, 55 percent, do not. Don't take it personally.

5. You want to go into the interview with the employer curious to know more about *you*, but the employer is first of all curious about what you know about *them*. Do some research on them before you go in. Employers don't like blind dates.

6. You want employers to save your job-hunt by increasing their hiring, and you want the government to give them incentives to do so. Unhappily, employers tend to wait to hire until they see an increased demand for their products or services. In the meantime, most do not much care for government incentives to hire, because they know such incentives always have a time limit, and once they expire, that employer will be on the hook to continue the subsidy out of their own pocket. What all this adds up to is that you can't count on somebody else coming to save you. The success of your job-hunt depends on you—with a little help from your friends. You must be in charge of it. You must plan it. You must direct it. You must know what works and what doesn't work. Your job-hunt is by its very nature a "self-directed search."

Conclusion

If you're out of work, and are looking for a job, you have every reason in the world to think you are up against overwhelming forces and the situation you face is rather hopeless. **But it's not.**

If you are tired of what you have been doing with your life, and you are dying to make a career-change, you have every reason to think that this is an absolutely lousy time for you to be going about a career-change. **But it's not.**

If you are just graduating from college, and have been thrown on to the labor market at last, you have every reason to think you are up against terrible odds of finding anything decent, and this is the worst time you could possibly have entered the labor market. **But it's not.**

If you are thinking that there's probably nothing a book can do to rescue you during a difficult job-market, it is absolutely understandable that you would think that. **But you'd be wrong.**

Hang in there. Keep on reading. The life you save will be your own.

It is common sense
To take a method and try it.
If it fails, admit it frankly and try another.
But above all, try something.

—Franklin D. Roosevelt (1882–1945)

Chapter 3 The Best and Worst Ways to Look for Jobs

The previous chapter—in case you skipped over it because this chapter sounded more intriguing—was about the nature of "the job-market." This chapter is about *our behavior* in that market, when we are trying to find work or change careers.

We'll begin with a parable. Imagine we find ourselves in some large city that we haven't been to, in ten years. We used to have a friend there, and we wonder if he's still there; or has he moved, or maybe died. We decide to look him up in the phone book. We come up empty. No phone number for anyone by that name. We decide, therefore, that he doesn't live there anymore.

But, we're wrong. It turns out he does still live there. It's just that, like 32 percent of all American homes, he's switched completely from a landline to a cell phone,[1] and cell phones aren't listed in the local phone book there.

So, what was our error?

We picked the wrong method to try and find him. And we thought that because we couldn't find him with our method, this meant that he didn't exist. Didn't exist *there,* at any rate.

It's stretching logic beyond the breaking point to suppose that "can't find" = "doesn't exist." Think about the lifelong battle between ourselves and our car keys.

So here's our lesson: Our job-hunt may be described as *trying to find if something exists.* The "something" in this case are job vacancies, or jobs yet to be created, or needs that are going unmet. In the field that we choose. In the geographical area that we choose. In the size

---

1. Joe McKendrick, "One-Third of US Households Chuck Landlines; Now Use Mobile Only," *SmartPlanet*, December 21, 2011, http://tinyurl.com/8a4ozrv.

company or organization that we choose. As in our search for a friend, *everything depends on the method we use, to try to find them.*

As I've said in the previous chapter, if our method doesn't find them, that doesn't mean the vacancies don't exist. Rather, it means we have to find a new method (or methods) of looking.

This idea doesn't even occur to the vast majority of the unemployed. That's because no one ever told them.

Job-Hunting Methods Were Not Created Equal

There are lots of ways to look for work or for a new career—sixteen, in fact. But unfortunately, these alternatives were *not* all created equal. Some methods of hunting for jobs have a pretty good track record, and therefore will repay you well for time spent pursuing them. But other methods have a really terrible track record, and you can waste a lot of time, and energy, on them, with no results. So, to discuss job-hunting methods is to discuss *conservation of energy. Your* energy.

We're going to talk, then, about the worst ways to look for a job, and then the best and most effective ways. But first a word about my methodology here, such as it is.

"Success rate" here means what percentage of job-hunters who use a particular method actually succeed thereby in finding a job *using just that method.*

You will notice that some of our favorite job-hunting strategies, taught in job-hunting class after job-hunting class, and on websites and in books, are on this *first* list here. (Ouch!)

Estimates (= Guesses)

There is absolutely nothing scientific about the lists that follow. The statistics, the percentages, are often guesses. My guesses.

Why "guesses"? Well, there just isn't much research comparing these methods to one another. Oh, there are vocational researchers out there; but they tend to study *employers'* behavior and preferences, not job-hunters'. Studies about job-hunters' behavior are few and far between, and not worth leaning on too heavily.

On the other hand, if you are in this field for over forty years, as I have been, and you keep your eyes open, you do run into reports of a small study here, a small study there, that gives you a pretty good idea, over time, of what works, what doesn't, and to what degree. I watch for these all the time, and though I don't keep a list of these studies, I do store the basic statistics or impressions in my head, so when it comes time to make guesses, they are *educated* guesses, based on forty years of experience. And sometimes I do have actual statistics.

Overall, I'm pretty confident that I'm in the ballpark here of what actually are the best and the worst ways to look for a job, and to what degree, in the year 2012 and immediately following.

The Five Worst Ways to Look For a Job

Only a 4 to 10% Success Rate

1. **Looking for employers' job-postings on the Internet.** Yeah, I know, you're somewhere between *surprised* and *shocked* at this finding. I was too.

According to a much-quoted 2010 study, 30 percent of all U.S. households have no access to the Internet; that, however, means that 70 percent do.[2] If you're among them, and your goal is to work for someone else, you use the Internet to post your resume and/or to look for employers' "job-postings" (vacancies) on the employer's own website or elsewhere, with "omnibus job-search sites" such as Indeed or SimplyHired, and

---

2. NITA, U.S. Department of Commerce, "Exploring the Digital Nation," November 9, 2011, http://tinyurl.com/7m8j25r.

of course specific "job-boards" such as CareerBuilder, Yahoo/Hot Jobs, Monster, LinkUp, Hound, not to mention "niche sites" for particular industries, and non-job sites such as LinkedIn, Facebook, Twitter, or the immensely popular Craigslist. The question is, how helpful is *this* search on the Internet for jobs?

The answer is: *well, that depends.*

You will hear stories of job-hunters who have successfully used the Internet to find a job. The stories are sometimes very impressive. Here are some examples.

A job-seeker, a systems administrator in Taos, New Mexico, who wanted to move to San Francisco posted his resume at 10 p.m. on a Monday night, on a San Francisco online bulletin board (**Craigslist.org**). By Wednesday morning he had over seventy responses from employers.

Again, a marketing professional developed her resume following guidance she found on the Internet, posted it to two advertised positions she found there, and within seventy-two hours of posting her electronic resume, both firms contacted her, and she is now working for one of them.

I get letters about such successes. For example: *"In May I was very unexpectedly laid off from a company I was with for five years. I did 100 percent of my job search and research via the Internet. I found all my leads online, sent all my resumes via e-mail, and had about a 25 percent response rate that actually led to a phone interview or a face-to-face interview. It was a software company that laid me off, and I am [now] going to work for a publishing company, a position I found online."*

And again: *"Thanks to the Internet, I found what I believe to be the ideal job in [just] eight weeks—a great job with a great company and great opportunities."*

So obviously the Internet *can* do a marvelous job of making it possible for an employer and a job-hunter to get together, in a way that was rarely possible even seventeen years ago. Internet sites devoted to job-hunting—some experts claim there are over 100,000 "job-boards" now—make it possible for job-hunter and employer to get together *faster* than ever before in history. (If you want to try any of these, look particularly at so-called *niche sites* for particular fields; there is an excellent directory of them at Internetinc: **www.internetinc.com/ job-search-websites**).

The question is, *how often* does this use of the Internet actually work? Are these stories just flukes; or is this a universal experience?

Sadly it turns out, despite all the hype, that this job-search method actually *doesn't* work for a huge percentage of those who try it. Researchers have turned up the fact that out of every 100 job-hunters who use the Internet as their search method for finding jobs, 4 of them will get lucky and find a job thereby, while 96 job-hunters out of the 100 will not—if they only use the Internet to look for work.

Exception to the above: If you are seeking a technical or computer-related job, an IT job, or a job in engineering, finances, or health care, the success rate rises, to somewhere around 10 percent. But for the other 12,741 job-titles that are out there in the job-market, the success rate reportedly remains at around 4 percent.

Only a 7% Success Rate

2. **Posting or mailing out your resume to employers.** You mail out resumes blindly to anyone and everyone, blanketing the area. Or you target particular places that interest you, and send them both digital and snail-mail copies of your resume, targeted specifically to them. Ah, but you already knew about this method, didn't you?

What you probably don't know is that this job-search method only has about a 7 percent success rate. That is, out of every 100 job-hunters who use only this search method, 7 will get lucky, and find a job thereby; 93 job-hunters out of 100 will not—if they use only resumes to search for those vacancies that are out there. This comes as a shock to most job-hunters.

Everyone and his brother or sister tells us: a good resume will get you a job. It's virtually an article of faith among the unemployed. Why does everyone keep telling us this, if it's not true? Oh, why did everyone entrust their money to Bernie Madoff? Or why did so many people buy those incredibly risky financial instruments or mortgages that led to the Recession? You tell me.

Resumes make you feel like you're really doing something about your job-hunt. They're out there, working for you. Or so it seems. But in fact they may be moribund or comatose. That is, they may not be getting read, at all, even when posted on an employer's own website. Some employers, in fact, *hate* resumes (I kid you not). So many lies, exaggerations, and distortion of job-hunters' actual experience and knowledge, on their resumes. As much as 82 percent of the time, according to experts whose job it is to verify resumes. When the lies are discovered *after* hiring, well, people lose their jobs. (Remember the recently ousted Yahoo! CEO?)

Anyway, the success rate of resumes is sad. And actually I'm being generous with my estimate of 7 percent. One study suggested that only 1 out of 1,470 resumes actually resulted in a job. Another study said the figure was even worse: 1 job offer for every 1,700 resumes floating around out there.

By the way, about those lies or exaggerations you're tempted to put in your resume: once you post your resume on the Internet, it gets copied quickly by "spiders" from other sites, and you can never remove it completely from the Internet. There are reportedly now at least 40,000,000 resumes floating around out there in the ether, like lost ships on the Sargasso Sea. Yours, among them, can come back to haunt you if a would-be employer "Googles" you.

Only a 7% Success Rate

3. **Answering ads in professional or trade journals, appropriate to your field.** You look at professional journals in your profession or field, and answer any ads there that intrigue you (a directory of them is at the website "the New Magazine City": **http://tinyurl.com/7jzn5zx**).

This search method, like the one above, apparently has about a 7 percent success rate. That is, out of every 100 job-hunters who use only this search method, 7 will get lucky and find a job thereby; 93 job-hunters out of 100 will not—if they use only this method to search for the vacancies that are out there.

Only a 5 to 24% Success Rate

4. **Answering local newspaper ads.** You answer local "want-ads" (in newspapers, assuming your city or town still has a newspaper, online or in print, or both). The Sunday editions usually prove most useful. See the website Job Search Steps at **http://tinyurl.com/d58l8z** for how to use them; as for a directory of their online versions, see Newslink, at **www.newslink.org** (click on "Newspapers" in the top Navbar).

This search method apparently has between a 5 to 24 percent success rate. That is, out of every 100 job-hunters who use only this search method, between 5 and 24 will get lucky and find a job thereby; 76 to 95 job-hunters out of 100 will not—if they use only this method to search for the vacancies that are out there.

The fluctuation between 5 percent and 24 percent is due to the level of salary that is being sought; the higher the salary being sought, the fewer job-hunters who are able to find a job using only this search method. Lower level = 24 percent find this works. High level = only 5 percent find this works.

Only a 5 to 28% Success Rate

5. **Going to private employment agencies or search firms for help.** You go to the private analog to the federal/state agencies (directory of private agencies can be found at **www.yellowpages.com**; put in "Employment agencies" and your local town or city, to get the list).

This method apparently has about a 5 to 28 percent success rate—again depending on the level of salary that is being sought. Which is to say, out of every 100 job-hunters who use only this method, between 5 and 28 will get lucky and find a job thereby; 72 to 95 job-hunters out of 100 will not—if they use only this method to search for those vacancies that are out there.

(The range is for the same reason as noted in #4. It is of interest that the success rate of this method apparently has risen slightly in recent years, in the case of women but not of men: just prior to the recession, 27.8 percent of female job-hunters found a job within two months, by going to the appropriate private employment agency, whether an agency that placed office people, or lawyers, or doctors, or whatever.)

Other Job-Hunting Methods floating in that never-never land between **Least Effective** and **Most Effective**: For the sake of completeness we should note that there are at least six other methods for trying to find jobs, that technically fall somewhere between worst and best ways. So before we get to our list of Best Ways to Look for a Job, let's look at those six; they are:

Asking a former teacher or professor at some school for job-leads. School means high school, trade schools, online schools, community colleges, four-year colleges, or universities. You ask a former professor or teacher or your career/alumni office at schools that you attended if they know of any job-leads.

This also has about a 12 percent success rate.

Taking a civil service examination. You take a civil service exam to compete for a government job. A list of available exams can be found at Federal Jobs Network: **http://federaljobs.net/exams.htm**. This apparently has about a 12 percent success rate.

Going to the state or federal employment services office. These can be found at **www.usa.gov/Agencies/State_and_Territories.shtml**). You go to your local federal/state unemployment service office, or to their OneStop or One-Stop career centers (directory at **www.careeronestop .org**) to get instructions on how to better job-hunt, and also to find job-leads. (They have a special section for returning veterans.) This apparently has about a 14 percent success rate.

Temp agencies. You go to temp agencies (agencies that get you short-term jobs in places that need your time and skills temporarily) and see if the agency/agencies can place you, in one place after another, until some place that you really like says, "Could you stay on, permanently?" At the very least you'll pick up experience that you can later cite on your resume. A directory of such agencies, and people's ratings of them, can be found at the website Rate-A-Temp: **www.rateatemp.com/temp-agency-list**).

This method's usefulness varies widely. In a tough market, *if* you've done your homework on yourself, and *if* you've carefully targeted the companies or organizations you'd like to work for, and *if* you've then carefully chosen a temp agency that serves such companies, the success rate can be impressive. But without such homework and preparation, it's kind of hit or miss.

Going to places where employers pick up workers. *Union Members:* Union members who have access to a union hiring hall, particularly construction workers, have a 22 percent success rate. What is not stated, however, is how long it takes to get a job at the hall, and how short-lived such a job may be; in the trades, it's often just a few days.

Only 11.8 percent of U.S. workers are union members, and most of these are in the public sector; only 6.9 percent of private sector employees are union members.[3] *Day Laborers:* You go to places where employers pick up day workers: well-known street corners in your town (ask around), in order for you to get short-term work, for now, which may lead to more permanent work, eventually. It may initially be yard work, or work that requires you to use your hands; but no job should be "beneath you" when you're completely running out of money. The success rate varies greatly. The jobs usually don't last long, though occasionally they do.

Volunteering. If you're okay financially for a while, but can't find work, you volunteer to work for nothing, short-term, at a place which has a "cause" or mission that interests you. You can find a directory of places that are known to do this, in what are called *"internships"* (www.internships.com) or *"volunteer opportunies"* (listed at **www.globalvolunteernetwork.org** or **www.volunteermatch.org**). Also, you can put into your search engine the name of the city or town where you live, together with the phrase "volunteer opportunities," and see what that turns up. Or you can just walk in to an organization or company of your choice, and ask if they would let you volunteer your time, there.

Your goal is to feel useful, but your distant hope is that maybe somewhere down the line they'll actually want to hire you to stay on, for pay. The odds of that happening in these hard times aren't great, so don't count on it and don't push it; but *sometimes* they may *ask you* to stay. The success rate of this as a method for finding jobs isn't terrific; it largely depends on luck and circumstance. And a handful of other factors: your work ethic, how well you get along with others, etc. But it does happen.

Okay, that's the six in never-never land. Neither worst nor best. Long shots, but worth considering in tough times.

Now to the list we've all been waiting for:

---

3. BLS, US Department of Labor, "Union Members Summary," January 27, 2012, http://tinyurl.com/27c4z5.

The Five Best Ways to Hunt for a Job

Generally speaking, the effectiveness of job-hunting methods is directly related to how much time and effort they demand of you. Tell me a more effective method, and I can guess beforehand that it requires more time and effort than other methods. I know you may have already guessed this. Still, we all keep hoping for that "magic bullet," don't we—the method that works like a charm and doesn't require much of us! *Lots of luck!*

Anyway, here are the five methods that I have observed work the best in finding jobs, during a tough job market particularly.

33% Success Rate

1. **Asking for job-leads from: family members, friends, people you know, in the community.** You ask them one simple question: do you know of any job vacancies at the place where you work—or elsewhere? This search method apparently has about a 33 percent success rate. That is, out of every 100 people who use this search method, 33 will get lucky, and find a job thereby; 67 job-hunters will not—if they use only this method to search for those vacancies that are out there.

You may be surprised that this is one of the five best ways to look for a job, but it only has a 33 percent success rate? Yes; but in the job-market, everything is relative. For example, this method's success rate is almost five times higher than the success rate for resumes. *In other words, by asking for job-leads from your family and friends, you have an almost five times better chance of finding a job, than if you had just sent out your resume.*

47% Success Rate

2. **Knocking on the door of any employer, factory, or office that interests you, whether they are known to have a vacancy or not.** This works best, as you might have guessed, with smaller employers (those having 25 or fewer employees; then, if nothing turns up there, those places that have 50 or fewer employees; or, if nothing turns up there, then those with 100 or fewer employees, etc.). Its success rate varies greatly.

Incidentally, the Personnel Manager or Human Resources office there—*if* they have one—is the employer's friend, not yours. Their basic function is to screen you out, so avoid them if possible. Sometimes, to be sure, you will stumble across an HR person who likes you and is willing to become your advocate, there. If so, you're one lucky woman (or man).

This search method apparently has about a 47 percent success rate. That is, out of every 100 people who use only this search method, 47 will get lucky, and find a job thereby; 53 job-hunters out of 100 will not—if they use only this one method to search for work. But again, for perspective, note that *by thus going face-to-face* you have an almost seven times better chance of finding a job, than if you had just sent out your resume.

65% Success Rate

3. **By yourself, using the index to your phone book's Yellow Pages to identify subjects or fields of interest to you in the town or city where you want to work, and then calling up or visiting the employers listed in that field, to ask if they are hiring for the type of position you can do, and do well.** This method apparently has about a 65 percent success rate. That is, out of every 100 job-hunters or career-changers who use only this search method, 65 will get lucky and find a job thereby; 35 job-hunters out of 100 will not—if they use only this one method to search for them. For perspective, however, note that by doing *targeted phone calls by yourself*, you have a nine times better chance of finding a job, than if you had just sent out your resume.

70% Success Rate

4. **In "a job-club" with other job-hunters, using the phone book's Yellow Pages to identify subjects or fields of interest to you in the town or city where you are, and then calling up or visiting the employers listed in that field, to ask if they are hiring for the type of position you can do, and do well.** This method is the same as the previous method, except here you work in a group and you choose a partner to work with in identifying job-leads. Moreover, you share with the rest of the group what kind of job you are looking for. This method apparently has enjoyed around a 70 percent success rate. That is, out of every 100 job-hunters or career-changers who use only this search method, 70 will get lucky and find a job thereby; 30 job-hunters out of 100 will not—if they use only this one method to search for them. For perspective, however, note that by doing *targeted phone calls with a*

group to support you, you have an almost ten times better chance of finding a job, than if you had just sent out your resume. Why? Well, let's say you're in a job-club that has 48 other members. Once you tell them what you're looking for, you get an extra 48 pair of eyes looking on your behalf, and an extra 48 pair of ears listening on your behalf—all the time that they are out there looking for job-leads themselves.

Note: The success rate for this approach has declined precipitously in the last twenty years. Many experts suppose the reason for this, is that the telephone has become automated in all too many places, and now the job-hunter often can't get past that barrier. Nathan Azrin invented this idea of "the job-club" back in 1973, when phones worked entirely differently.

But barriers to reaching employers on the phone have always been there. The deeper reason for the drop in effectiveness is that there are virtually no "job-clubs" today that follow his model, and there's the problem. Azrin's job-club was all about action. The model called for the job-club to meet every single weekday, all day, doing phoning with partners in the morning, and going out and calling upon employers every afternoon.[4] Most groups that claim they are "job-clubs" today are only shadows of the Azrin model, and may more accurately be described as "job support groups." These tend to meet just once a week at best, for just two or three hours at a time, and devote their meetings to inspiration, pep talks, and exchanging job-leads; but the actual job-hunt occurs outside the group meeting. As a result, the success rate currently may run as low as 10 percent. Azrin's model had an 84 percent success rate.

Even "dumbed down" however, job support groups still have one sterling virtue, and that is, they provide community to the otherwise lonely job-hunter. This is very, very valuable. No one should ever have to job-hunt all by themselves, if they can possibly avoid it. We all need encouragement and support, along the way.

A directory of such job support groups can be found on Susan Joyce's excellent website, job-hunt.org (**http://tinyurl.com/7a9xbb**).

---

4. His detailed manual describing exactly how to do this has been out of print for years; but the desperate (and well-off) can find it for about $100 on the Alibris website. It's called *The Job Club Counselor's Manual: A Behavioral Approach to Vocational Counseling.* Nathan Azrin is of course the author.

86% Success Rate

5. Doing extensive homework on yourself. This doesn't sound like a job-hunting method, but it is. It was originally invented in 1936 by A. W. Rahn, an engineer at Western Electric. He reported an 80 percent success rate with his method. It involves doing extensive homework on yourself before you go out there pounding the pavement. The goal is to better understand who you are, what you have to offer to the job-market, what kind of job would match *that*, and what it is you want your life to count for.

This method has been refined and improved since Rahn's time,[5] and now has an apparent 86 percent success rate, the highest by far of any job-hunting method. You know by now that this means out of every 100 job-hunters or career-changers who use this method, 86 will get lucky and find a job thereby; 14 job-hunters out of 100 will not—if they use only this method to search for vacancies.

Such an effectiveness rate is astronomically higher than virtually every other job-hunting method there is. For example, doing-homework-on-yourself works twelve times better than resumes, when you're looking for work. This means, that by doing the hard thinking this method requires, you have a 1,200 percent better chance of finding a job than if you just send out resumes!

Interested? I can guide you through the necessary steps, in chapter 5.

But first, why does this self-inventory work so well *as a job-hunting method*? There are five reasons that I have observed:

1. By doing this homework on yourself first, you learn to describe yourself in alternative ways, and therefore you can approach multiple job-markets. Retraining, as it is commonly practiced in Western culture, prepares you for only one market. Thus construction workers are retrained, let us say, to be computer repair people. One market. No jobs to be found in that market? Retraining wasted. But with *this* kind of homework, you are embarking on a whole different concept of retraining. You are essentially training or retraining yourself for several markets. This, because

---

5. A detailed history of how this method evolved may be found in *The Career Counselor's Handbook*, Second Edition, by Howard Figler and myself, 2007, Ten Speed Press, pages 48–79. It chronicles how such historic figures as the late Bernard Haldane, Sidney and Mary Edlund, John Crystal, Daniel Porot, and others, improved the method greatly.

you stop identifying yourself by only one job-title. In a tough economy, job-titles like, say, "accountant," just aren't detailed enough. New thinking is called for: you are no longer just "an accountant" or "a construction worker" or whatever. You are a person who has *these* skills and *these* experiences. If teaching and writing and growing things are your favorite skills, then you can approach the job-market of teaching, or that of writing, or that of gardening. Multiple job-markets are open to you; not just one.

2. By doing this homework on yourself, you can describe in great detail exactly what you are looking for. This greatly enables your friends, LinkedIn contacts, and family to better help you. Not just, *"Uh, I'm out of work; let me know if you hear of anything,"* but exactly what kind of "thing," and in what work setting. This greatly increases their helpfulness to you, and therefore your ability to find jobs you would otherwise never find.

3. By ending up, after doing the homework on yourself, with a description of a job that would really excite you, you pour much more energy into your job-search. Before, your job-hunt may have felt more like a duty than anything else. Now, with your vision, you are dying to find *that*. So, you redouble your efforts, your dedication, and your determination when otherwise you might tire and give up. Persistence becomes your middle name, for a prize worth fighting for.

4. By doing this homework, you no longer have to wait for companies to identify themselves as having vacancies, before you decide which ones to approach. In your homework, you choose places you would like to work, and then approach them (*through a "bridge person" who knows both you and them*) regardless of whether or not they have a known vacancy. Often, a job falls vacant just before you walk in the door, and you have no other competition for it.

5. Lastly, when you are facing, let us say, nineteen other competitors for a job you want—who superficially look equal to you in skills and experience—if you did this self-inventory, then you can accurately describe to employers exactly what is unique about you, and what you bring to the table that the others don't.

These will usually turn out to involve adjectives or adverbs, what we normally call traits.

All of this explains why this is the most effective job-hunting method in the world. Though it's not magic. It will still fail to work for 14 out of every 100 people who try only this method alone.

Conclusion

Well, there are your lists. The best and the worst. Now you know which methods are most effective—on two counts: they conserve your energy, and are most likely to produce results in your job-search. But keep in mind, when all is said and done:

1. **Job-hunting is an activity that repeats itself over and over again,** in most people's lives. Lucky you, if that is not the case; but the odds are overwhelming that it will be. According to experts, the average worker, under thirty-five years of age, will go job-hunting every one to three years. And the average worker over thirty-five will go job-hunting every five to eight years! And, in this process, so the experts say, we will each of us probably change *careers* (not just *jobs*) three to five times, during our lifetime.

2. **Job-hunting is not a science; it is an art.** Some job-hunters know instinctively how to do it; in some cases, they were born knowing how to do it. Others of us sometimes have a harder time with it, but fortunately for us in the U.S. and elsewhere in the world, there is help, coaching, counseling, and advice—online and off.

3. **Job-hunting is always mysterious.** Sometimes mind-bogglingly mysterious. You may never understand why things sometimes work, and sometimes do not.

4. **There is no always wrong way to hunt for a job or to change careers.** Anything may work under certain circumstances, or at certain times, or with certain employers. There are only degrees of likelihood of certain job-hunting techniques working or not working. But it is crucial to know that likelihood, as we have just seen.

5. **There is no always right way to hunt for a job or to change careers.** Anything may fail to work under certain circumstances, or at certain times, or with certain employers. There are only degrees of likelihood of certain job-hunting techniques working or not working. But it is crucial to know that likelihood, as we just saw.

6. **Job-hunting always depends on some amount of luck.** Luck, pure luck. Having advanced job-hunting skills doesn't mean absolutely, positively, you will always be able to find a job. It does mean that you can get good at reducing the amount that depends on luck, to as small a proportion as possible.

7. **When we are out of work these days, we need to assume that nothing that worked before will necessarily work now.** There is a book out there with a clever title: *What Got You Here Won't Get You There.*[6] We need to reexamine every job-hunting method there is and reconsider whether there is a better way that we could be going about this.

Some people think that any suggestion that there may be something that a job-hunter is doing wrong, is essentially "blaming the victim" for the situation they are in. This is nuts. Self-examination is the way to improve any company, any marriage, any nation. And any job-hunt. Asking, "Is there something *I* could be doing better" is often the pathway to saving that company, marriage, nation . . . and job-hunt!

When unemployment is dragging on and on, everything should be on the table for examination. We need to question all our assumptions. Assume we are in a new world. Rethink all our strategies. Revisit everything we think we know for sure, and ask if in fact things have changed since the recession. Think whether there is something new we need to learn (remembering, always, that before we can learn we sometimes need to unlearn some things).

Above all, keep in mind the most important truth in this book: **different job-hunting behaviors lead to different results.** The keener the competition, the more important is the manner in which a job-hunter looks for a job in that field or occupation.

---

6. By Marshall Goldsmith, with Mark Reiter. Hyperion, 2007.

Discussion

Job-hunter: Since the information in this chapter is so crucial for our survival in today's world, why do you think this stuff isn't taught in high schools and colleges?

Career-counselor. Well it certainly should be! The reasons why it's not, make up a very long list. You can choose between: because the teachers don't know these facts; because the teachers haven't had to job-hunt recently themselves; because they think the function of a school is to teach ideas, not practical skills, like how to fix a car, or how to run a job-hunt successfully, or how to find an appropriate friend or (eventually) a mate, and so on.

Job-hunter: I think inertia enters in, too. "This is the way we've always done it, and we don't see any reason to change."

Career-counselor: Yes, and don't forget budgets. Education is the victim of a lot of belt-tightening these days, and of course the first staff to be let go are the ones who are experts on how to relate education to the world of work. That's often regarded as "nice but not necessary" information.

Job-hunter: What's the remedy for this missing part of our education?

Career-counselor: Learn it on your own; and then go share it with at least one other person.

Two roads diverged in a yellow wood,
And sorry I could not travel both
And be one traveler, long I stood
And looked down one as far as I could
To where it bent in the undergrowth;

Then took the other, as just as fair,
And having perhaps the better claim,
Because it was grassy and wanted wear;
Though as for that the passing there
Had worn them really about the same,

And both that morning equally lay
In leaves no step had trodden black.
Oh, I kept the first for another day!
Yet knowing how way leads on to way,
I doubted if I should ever come back.

I shall be telling this with a sigh
Somewhere ages and ages hence:
Two roads diverged in a wood, and I—
I took the one less traveled by,
And that has made all the difference.

—Robert Frost (1874–1963)[1]

1. The title of this poem is "The Road Not Taken," from *The Poetry of Robert Frost*, edited by Edward Connery Lathem, published by Holt, Rinehart & Winston, 1916, 1969. Incidentally, the late M. Scott Peck's classic, *The Road Less Traveled*, took its title from this poem.

Chapter 4 Life/Work Planning: Designing a Plan of Attack

When we are out of work, we don't just need to know what our options are—what different methods of job-hunting are available to us. We need to have a plan. An Overall Plan of Attack. Not on *people*. But on *the problem* of how to not only find work, but meaningful work.

All plans of attack basically break down to just two broad categories. Here is both the explanation, and the contrast between them:

	The Traditional Approach	The Creative Approach
What you are looking for	A job.	A "dream job": one which uses your favorite skills and favorite fields or knowledges.
How you see yourself	As a "job beggar." You will be lucky to get them.	As a "resource." They will be lucky to get you.
Your basic plan	Figure out how to "sell" yourself, before you go out hunting.	Figure out what kind of job you'd die to do, before you go out hunting.
Your preparation	Do research to find out what the job-market wants. *"Fitting in" will carry the day!*	Do homework on yourself, to figure out what you do best, AND most love to do. *Enthusiasm will carry the day!*

	The Traditional Approach	**The Creative Approach**
How you figure out which employers to approach	You wait for them to identify they have a vacancy.	Doing "informational interviews," you figure out which organizations most interest you—in light of your homework—even if they do not have a known vacancy at the time.
How you contact them	Through your resume.	Through a "bridge person" (someone who knows you and also knows them). Use LinkedIn to find them.
What the purpose of your resume is	To sell them on why you should be hired there.	To get an interview with them.
What your main goal is if you get an interview	To sell them on why you should be hired there.	To get another interview there.
What do you talk about in the interview	Yourself, your assets, your experience.	50% of the time you let them ask the questions. 50% of the time you ask them the things *you* want to know about the place, and the job there.
What you're trying to find out	Do they want me?	Do I want them? (as well as "Do they want me?")
How you end the final interview there	You ask them: "When may I hope to hear from you?" *(You are leaving things hanging.)*	If you decide you do want to work there, you ask them: "I believe I could be a real asset to you. Given all that we've talked about, can you offer me this job?" *(You are seeking closure.)*
What to do after getting the job, but before you start	Rest.	Keep on job-hunting. (The offer may still fall through before you start, due to unforeseen circumstances there.)

So, which plan of attack should you adopt if you're out of work? Well, that's up to you. Job-hunters typically begin with the so-called *Traditional Approach*. Most of us know how to do it, or can quickly learn.

It doesn't demand much time. Slap together a resume. Post it. Wait to see if you get any responses. Do the interviews. Get the job.

If it works, great! Problem: increasingly, it doesn't work. So, when we are unemployed we stay unemployed. For weeks. For months. Or sometimes for years. The traditional approach doesn't work, but it is the only approach we know. We have no *Plan b.*

Every Job-Hunter Needs a Plan b

When we set out we need a plan. But, to keep hope alive we need *an alternative* plan as well, in case the first one just doesn't work, this time. Fortunately, there is a *Plan b,* if you try *The Traditional Approach,* and it just doesn't work for you. Of course it's the *Creative Approach,* outlined in the right-hand column of the previous chart. It's harder than *The Traditional Approach.* It's more work. It takes longer. It asks you to do more thinking. But that is precisely its value. It forces you to think about your whole life, and what you want out of life. You get to deal with Life's major issues, namely:

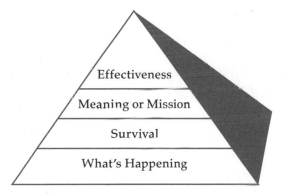

Now, you probably don't care, but just in case you do: this path is actually a field. That field is called: Life/work Planning. That field has textbooks; I've written one of them myself.[1] Life/work planning deals with the four issues you see above: *how do I figure out what's happening?*

---

1. *The Three Boxes of Life and How to Get Out of Them: An Introduction to Life/Work Planning,* by Richard N. Bolles, Ten Speed Press, 1978; now out of print, but available online, *used,* for as little as $4.00 U.S., on Amazon.com, and for $1.00 on Alibris.com.

Then: *how do I ensure that I will survive?* Then: *once I know how to survive, how do I make my life have meaning or some sense of mission?* And, finally: *once I've decided what my mission in life is, how can I be more effective at achieving the goals I've set for myself?*

If you're going to use the interruptions in life to do some hard thinking, *those* are issues really worth thinking about. So, let us begin.

Who Are You?

You begin by doing homework on yourself. Why *on yourself?* Well, think of life as a journey. And recall what travel experts teach about taking a journey (unless it's on a shoestring): they say—before you go—lay out on your bed two piles. In one pile, put all the **clothes** (plus toiletries, and stuff) that you think you'll need to take. In the other pile, put all the **money** you think you'll need to take.

Then, they say, pack only half the clothes, but twice the money.

A parallel ratio occurs in the journey we are all taking, called *Life.* For this part of that journey, you are gonna need only half the information you initially thought you would need about **the job-market**, but twice the amount of information you initially thought you would need about **yourself**.

I know you're probably going to protest that you've lived with yourself all your life, so far, and you don't need any deeper knowledge. Well, maybe. But my experience over the past forty years, with literally millions of job-hunters, is that usually we just don't understand who we are, and what we have to offer the world. Not the fullness of it. Not the richness of it. Solution: a fresh inventory of what you have to offer the world, before you go back out there. And I mean *all* that you have to offer, not just *part* of it. You already know part of it. The problem is that is only *part.* You need to know it all.

Homework for a Career Change

And if you are contemplating a career-change, maybe—after you inventory yourself—you will decide to go train for a new career or direction for your life. Maybe. But first, please, please, inventory what you already have. It's broader, deeper, richer, than you think. And by the way, often you can put together a new career just using what you already know and what you already can do—with just a bit of training or retraining. I'm not talking about changing from salesperson to doctor: for that, you will need to start over again. But most career changes are not that dramatic, as I will show you, in chapter 7.

And so it may turn out that the knowledge you need to pick up can be found in a vocational/technical school, or in a (one- or) two-year college. But it may also be found by "informational interviewing."[2] A job-hunter named Bill had worked for a number of years in retail; now he was debating a career-change—working in the oil industry. But he knew virtually nothing about that industry. However, he went from person to person who worked at companies in that industry, just seeking information about the industry. The more of these "informational interviews" he conducted, the more he knew. In fact, coming down the home stretch, just before he got hired in the place of his dreams, he found he now knew more than the people he was visiting, about their competitors and some aspects of the industry. Sometimes, there is more than one way to pick up the knowledge you need.

I'm Not Sure I Really Need to Do This Homework

Well, maybe not. But let's test that.

1. Take ten sheets of blank paper. Write, at the top of each one, just these three words: **Who Am I?**

2. Then write, on each sheet in turn, just one answer to that question. And only one. Incidentally, don't put down negative stuff, like "I am a procrastinator," or "I am a messy person." If this were a psychological exercise, putting down negative as well

---

2. This term, which I coined, is described in detail in chapter 6.

as positive self-identifications might make sense; but this is a vocational exercise, and the only question of course is, "What is there about me that would attract an employer . . . down the line?" That's why people always put down just positive stuff, as you can see in the example on the next page. It is really "roles" we are looking for, a matter of what different hats you wear. For example . . . for a man it might be: husband, father, advisor, writer, teacher, counselor, friend, etc. For a woman, it might be . . . well, see the next page. In my own case, I am . . . husband, father, advisor, writer, teacher, counselor, friend, etc.

3. When you're done, go back over all ten sheets and expand now upon what you have written on each sheet. Looking at each answer, write below it, *why* you said that, and say *what turns you on* about that answer.

4. When finished with all ten sheets, go back over them and arrange them in order of priority. That is, which identity is the most important to you? That page goes on top. Then, which is next? That goes immediately underneath the top one. Continue arranging the rest of the sheets in order, until what you think is your least important identity is at the bottom of the pile.

5. Finally, go back over the ten sheets, in order, and look particularly at your answer you wrote on each sheet, concerning *What*

"I WANT TO EXPERIENCE A WARM CLIMATE, FLY THROUGH THE AIR, SEE SOME COLOR, EAT A PEACH — I WANT TO LIVE!"

Turns Me On About This? See if there are any common denominators, or themes, among the ten answers you gave. If so, jot them down on a separate piece of paper. Voilà! You have begun to put your finger on Who You Are, with some things you need to keep in mind if you are to feel truly excited, fulfilled, useful, and effective, and operating at the height of your powers.

Here is how one woman did this exercise:

Who Am I?

1. A woman	6. A traveler
2. Esoteric	7. Worldly wise
3. Nature dweller	8. Inquisitive/investigative
4. People person	9. Troubleshooter
5. Creative	10. Manager/leader

What turns you on about the above?

1. Ever-changing, emotion, caring, warm, loving and giving. Strong stock, independent, sexy, magnetic. Mother and teacher. Survivor, activist, unique, and creative.
2. For the love of the mystical, healing of self and the spirit, human sciences and Mother Nature.
3. Where I am happiest for the peace and wondrous beauty of the world and miracles created each and every day. Seasons change, colors, and aromas. Joy of knowing the healing powers of a peaceful and idyllic universe, pure and unsolved.
4. The love of humor and socializing. Being a friend, sharing wisdoms, and helping when in need. Where we can teach and be teached as reflections of each other. To be carried and carry on our journey as we are all one.
5. The appreciation of art, music, literature. To play with your imagination, relaxing and shutting off. To create with different mediums that are fun, exciting, and produce an unknown outcome.
6. Comfortable in facing the unknown with acceptance before I arrive.
7. Knowledge of own wisdom through tragedy, love, travel.
8. Gaining knowledge and understanding through intense questioning and action.
9. To be able to assess a situation, take the bull by the horns, and turn it around. Self-satisfaction and passion seeing the momentum turn to the positive. Mother Theresa.

> 10. Being an example to others in whatever you do. When good is
> not good enough and pushing forward. Individual and creative.
>
> **Any common denominators?** Various creative situations that
> are new to gain knowledge of the unknown through travel, esoteric/
> nature, arts, people.
>
> **What must my career use (and include) for me to be truly happy,
> useful, and effective?** Investigation using creativity in an esoteric or
> environment field with people of like-mindedness. Human sciences/
> Environmental studies/Journalist/Presenter/Traveling/People

---

Now, if this exercise was easy for you, then you have a very good
start in defining who you are. But if it was harder than you thought it
would be, then you can see there is work to be done.

You need to know more about You.

Conclusion

The detailed homework about You begins in the next chapter. The
only requirement is that you must be willing to stick with it, do some
hard thinking, and above all, approach this as *fun*. Well, why shouldn't
it be? It's You you're doing the homework on. What more fascinating
subject do you know? (*Low self-esteem aside, of course! This homework
should help fix* that!)

You've got talent, no doubt about that. You have special gifts, and
skills. You must be sure you own up to what those gifts are. Unemployment is a perfect time. True, it seems to come as an interruption in most
of our lives. But Martin Luther King Jr. had something to say about
that: "*The major problem of life is learning how to handle the costly interruptions. The door that slams shut, the plan that got sidetracked, the marriage that
failed. Or that lovely poem that didn't get written because someone knocked
on the door.*"

Interruptions are opportunities. To pause. To think. To assess where
we really want to go from here with our lives. *The Creative Approach*,
with its demand that you do homework on yourself *before* you set out
on your search for (meaningful) work, helps you take advantage of the
opportunity that this interruption—being out of work—offers.

Use the opportunity. Make this time of your life not only a hunt for a job, but a hunt for a life. A deeper life. A life you're prouder of. A victorious life. The world currently is filled with workers whose weeklong question is, "When is the weekend going to be here?" And, then, "Thank God it's Friday!" Their work puts bread on the table but . . . they are bored out of their minds. They've never taken the time to think out what they uniquely can do, and what they uniquely have to offer to the world. The world doesn't need any more bored workers.

So, do the homework. Dream a little. Dream a lot. One of the saddest lines in the world is, "Oh come now—be realistic." The best parts of this world were not fashioned by those who were realistic. They were fashioned by those who dared to look hard at their wishes and then gave them horses to ride.

Discussion

Job-hunter: It doesn't feel to me like we're in a survival mode in this country. Plenty of people have jobs. I think this country is still very prosperous.

Career-counselor: Well, you're right. To be exact, 142 million people have jobs in this country, at this moment. But any of us can be thrown out of work any time, without warning. And we aren't spending time thinking about that possibility ahead of time, are we?

Job-hunter: No, we aren't. I mean, I can't speak for others, but it never occurred to me that I might be unemployed. And unemployed for this long.

Career-counselor: Well, that's why we call this a survival mode, in this country; and in other countries around the world. Let me give you an analogy. You see a swimmer in danger of drowning. Can't swim very well. Has no life-jacket. Is about to go under the water for the third time. His arms are flailing the water desperately. Get the picture?

Job-hunter: Sure. He's in trouble.

Career-counselor: Yes, but he's in trouble because he didn't put on a life-jacket before he ever went out into the water. If he knew he might have trouble surviving out there, he would have put on that life-jacket.

Job-hunter: So, you're saying . . .

Career-counselor: I'm saying, prepare now, if you want to survive later. Do some Life/work Planning or Designing. Now.

Frequently the real health care problem arises from failure to discover one's life mission. . .

> —Professor Brian Costello, famous Australian
>   clinical psychologist

Know then thyself,
Do not the Market scan
Until you've surveyed all You are—
Then you will have your plan.

> —with apologies to Alexander Pope, 1688–1744

Chapter 5 You Need to Understand More Fully Who You Are

Commonly called Dick Bolles's Flower Exercise

Our previous chapters dealt with hope, the nature of the job-market, your options in that market, and how to design an overall plan of attack on the problem of finding a job. *(I mention this in case you're skipping around.)* Now it's *rethinking* time.

Unemployment becomes life transition, when you can't find a job doing the same work you've always done. Since you have to rethink one thing, many of us elect to rethink *everything*. Something awakens within us. Call it yearning. Call it hope. We come to realize the dream we once dreamed has never died. So now, we decide to go back to get it, regardless of the state of the economy. We want to burn with new fire in our heart.

I Am a Person Who . . .

This begins by stripping yourself of your job-title. You have to stop answering, *"Who are you?"* with, "Oh, I'm a construction worker, or salesperson, or designer, or writer, or whatever." That locks you into the past. You launch yourself into the future by instead answering, *"Who are you?"* with: *"I am a person who . . ."*

"I am a person who . . . has had these experiences." *"I am a person who . . .* is skilled at doing this or that." *"I am a person who . . .* knows a lot about this or that." *"I am a person who . . .* is unusual in this way or that."

Before you answer this question with others, you have to first answer it in your own head.

I Am a Person Who . . .
Is an Artist

Begin by thinking about the general subject of *work*. How would you describe *work*? A way to make money, sure. But *if* it's more than that, then your work is how you express yourself and who you are. And *if given a choice*, whatever work you choose ends up being the expression of your own personality, working through some *medium*.[1] That's obvious in the case of an artist. But it's true of every man and every woman who chooses their work. You are an artist in some sense or another, so a career choice is essentially the choice of what *medium* you prefer, to express who you are.

For the artist, the medium may be oils on canvas, or drama, or poetry, or marble, or the stage. For the rest of us, there are other mediums through which we express our personality and uniqueness.

The Card Sort

On the next page are 21 of them. The mediums are presented as "a card sort." That means, cut them out (there is nothing on the back of them); separate them with scissors so you have 21 cards; and then on a level table or space, lay them out in your own personal order of preference, in a neat vertical column, one below the other.

The question for you to ask yourself as you look at the cards is: *Which of these do I most like to work with?* Put that at the top. *Which next? Which next?* And so on, one under the other, until you have all 21 in a vertical column. Keep rearranging, and changing the order, until you are satisfied with the order you have.

Then note which are your top five to seven, in particular. No matter what job you have, you are an artist at work. These five to seven are your favorite mediums through which you like to express yourself. That's at least a tentative guess, for the moment. You can always change or improve it, as you go.

By way of example, my seven came out to be: *ideas, people, words, graphics, music, electronics,* and *paper,* in that order. No surprises there!

---

1. I always like to give credit for ideas. This idea was first formulated almost a century ago, by an engineer named John Mills at a company called Western Electric, 1918.

WORK MEDIUMS[2]

IDEAS	PEOPLE	OBJECTS, MACHINES
MONEY	SYMBOLS, EQUATIONS	ELECTRONICS, GAMES
GRAPHICS	WORDS	MUSIC
COLOR	LIGHT	SOUND
SPACES, SPACE	WATER	PAPER
WOOD	PLANTS, TREES	FOOD, CROPS, GRAINS
EARTH, MATERIALS, MINERALS	ANIMALS	CLOTHES

2. Copyright © 2012 by Richard N. Bolles. Not to be reproduced without written permission.

I Am a Person Who . . .
Is Like a Flower

Before you put the cards back in a stack, you want to jot down those top favorites, of course. But where? Researchers[3] tell us that if you are trying to make a decision about yourself and your future, there are Three Rules about *where* you jot stuff down:

1. GATHER. Put everything you know about yourself **on one piece of paper.**

2. ORGANIZE. Put **some kind of graphic** on that piece of paper, in order to organize the information about yourself. A graphic— any graphic—keeps that One Piece of Paper interesting, and not just a flood of words and spaces. It also activates the right side of your brain, the intuitive side, that looks at a whole bunch of unrelated data and says, "Aha! I see what it all means."

3. PRIORITIZE. **Prioritize** all this information, when you have finished organizing it. Don't just leave the data *lying there*; put it in its order of importance *to you*. Always. And every time.

So here you have it, on the next page: an outline of the graphic you are going to fill in on the larger version on pages 120–21.

We call the graphic *The Flower Diagram,* or *The Flower Exercise.*

I Am a Person Who . . .
Has Seven Sides to Me

This flower representation of *You* has *seven* petals (including the center) because there are seven sides to You, or seven ways of thinking about yourself.

---

3. For example, (the late) Barbara B. Brown, who was the first to coin the term *biofeedback* and to bring it to the public's awareness back in 1974, with her groundbreaking book (at the time) *New Mind, New Body.* She made these points in a public lecture in 1976. See her bio in www.wikipedia.com.

The Flower
"That One Piece of Paper"[4]

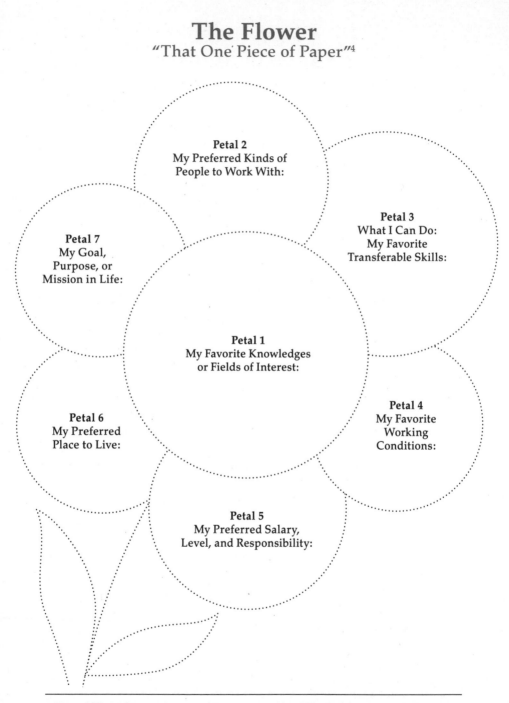

Petal 2
My Preferred Kinds of
People to Work With:

Petal 3
What I Can Do:
My Favorite
Transferable Skills:

Petal 7
My Goal,
Purpose, or
Mission in Life:

Petal 1
My Favorite Knowledges
or Fields of Interest:

Petal 4
My Favorite
Working
Conditions:

Petal 6
My Preferred
Place to Live:

Petal 5
My Preferred Salary,
Level, and Responsibility:

4. The real Flower Diagram for you to fill out as you go through each petal's exercise in this chapter is on pages 120–21.

7 Ways of Describing Who You Are

1. You can describe *who you are* in terms of **what you know**—and what your *favorite* knowledges or fields of interest are, that you have stored in your head (or heart).

2. Or you can describe *who you are* in terms of **the kinds of people** you most prefer to *work with*, and/or the kinds of people—age span, problems, handicaps, geographical location, etc.—you would most like to *help* or serve.

3. Or you can describe *who you are* in terms of **what you can do**, and what your *favorite* functional/transferable skills are.

4. Or you can describe *who you are* in terms of your favorite **working conditions**—indoors/outdoors, small company/large company, tight ship/loose ship,[5] windows/no windows, etc.—because they enable you to work at your top form, and greatest effectiveness.

5. Or you can describe *who you are* in terms of **your preferred salary, level, and responsibility**—working by yourself, or as a member of a team, or supervising others, or running the show—that you feel most fitted for, by experience, temperament, and appetite.

6. Or you can describe *who you are* in terms of **your preferred geographical location**—here or abroad, warm/cold, north/south, east/west, mountains/coast, urban/suburban/rural/rustic—where you'd be happiest, do your best work, and would most love to live.

7. Or you can describe *who you are* in terms of **your goals or sense of mission and purpose** for your life. Alternatively, or in addition, you can get more particular and describe the goals or mission you want *the organization* to have, where you decide to work.

---

5. "Tight ship": you clock in and clock out, work under strict conditions; "loose ship": you have greater leeway about when you come in, or go home, they want your creativity above all else, and there is no time clock or tight supervision of your day.

I Am a Person Who . . .
Is All These Things

You could choose just one, two, or three of these sides of yourself—let us say, "what you know," "what you can do," and "preferred salary"—as your guide to defining what kind of work would match *You*.

But what the Flower Diagram does is describe who you are in *all seven* ways, joined together on one page, in one graphic. After all, you are not just one of these things; you are *all* of these things. The Flower Diagram is a complete, not partial, picture of *You*.

Believe me, you want the complete picture. I'll tell you why. Let's say there is some job out there that matches only one petal, one side to yourself, one way of defining who you are: for example, let's say this job lets you use your favorite knowledges. Period.

It doesn't let you use your favorite skills, nor does it have you working with the kinds of people you most enjoy, nor does it give you the surroundings where you can do your best work.

What would you call such a job? I think *boring*. You would barely be able to wait for Friday to come around. *Thank God it's Friday!* Some of you have already sung that song. A lot.

But now let us suppose you could instead find another kind of work that matches all seven sides of you. All seven petals. What would you call *that* job? You would call it *your dream job*.

So, your total flower is a picture of who You most fully are. But at the same time it's a picture of a job that would give voice to all that you are. Your dream job. Where you would shine, because it uses the best of Who You Are.

So please fill in your Flower. *And try to keep it a joy rather than a duty.*

For the following exercises you will need several blank sheets of notebook paper ($8^1/_2$ x 11 inches) as your worksheets.

I Am a Person Who . . .
Knows These Particular Things

And *loves* using that knowledge. Or knowledges. Or "know hows." (Call it what you will.)

First Petal
My Favorite Knowledges or Fields of Interest

My Favorite Knowledges Petal

Goal in Filling Out This Petal: To summarize all that you stored in your brain. *Required:* From your past, subjects you already know a lot about, and enjoy talking about. *Optional:* For your future, what you would like to learn.

What You Are Looking For: Some guidance as to what field you would most enjoy working in.

Form of the Entries on Your Petal: Basically, they will all turn out to be nouns, but see below.

Example of a Good Petal: *"Graphic design, data analysis, mathematics, how to repair a car, videogames, cooking, music, principles of mechanical engineering, how to run an organization, Chinese, CATIA (Computer Aided Three-dimensional Interactive Application),"* etc.

Example of a Bad Petal: *"Prompt, thorough, analyzing, persistent, communicating."*

Why Bad: Knowledges are always nouns. The words in the bad example above are not. In case you're curious, they are, in order: a trait (adjective), a trait (adjective), a transferable skill (verb), a trait (adjective), and a transferable skill (verb). All in all, that is one mixed bag! You want only knowledges on this particular petal.

There are three things traditionally called skills: *functions, also known as transferable skills; knowledges;* and *traits.* As a general rule throughout this homework, *knowledges are nouns, traits are adjectives or adverbs, and transferable skills are verbs.* If it helps knowing that, great; if not, forget it. Our overarching principle always is: if a generalization or bunch of categories help you, use them. But if they just confuse you, then ignore them!!! Please!

On this Knowledges "petal" *(actually the central part of the Flower)* you will eventually write your final results: your Favorite Knowledges/ Fields of Interest, prioritized in the order of importance to you, on pages 120–21. The *final* results.

Prior to that, you need here, as you will with each petal, a worksheet. Get blank pieces of notebook paper to do this on.

WORKSHEET

Notes About My Favorite Knowledges
1. What You Know About Your Favorite Mediums That Enable You to Work More Confidently in That Medium
2. What You Know from Your Previous Jobs
3. What You Know About, Outside of Work
4. What Fields, Careers, or Industries Sound Interesting to You
Any Other Hunches, Bright Ideas, Great Ideas, etc.

A worksheet is a gathering place, for the results of the exercises you do, but also for every bright idea, every hunch, every remembered dream, every intuition that occurs to you as you are working on that petal. Jot down *everything*. A worksheet is like a fisherman's net, where you want to cast it into the sea in order to capture the largest haul possible, and then sort out the best of your catch, later.

This worksheet can look sloppy, unorganized, and messy. That's okay. Who cares? Only the final petal is supposed to look organized.

This is an important petal—very important—so to unearth your favorite knowledges or fields of interest, four exercises are usually needed. We begin with:

1. What You Know About Your Favorite Mediums That Enables You to Work Better in That Medium

Here, at last, you have the place to jot down your favorite mediums that you like to work with or in—from the Card Sort, remember? My seven, you will recall, were, in order: *ideas, people, words, graphics, music, electronics, and paper*. Put yours down, now (not mine), at the top of the worksheet, in order of your personal favorites. (You may also write your top five on the Favorite Knowledges petal on pages 120–21.) Then, in that same space on the worksheet, jot down anything you *know* about any medium of yours, that enables you to work better in that medium. Think of *what you know* that someone brand new to that medium wouldn't know.

If, for example, a favorite medium for you is computers, then the question is: what do you know, that someone brand new to the medium wouldn't know? Maybe you know the Mac operating system really well. Put down: *Mac OS X 10.7.* Maybe you know how to repair a computer. Put down: *computer repair.* Maybe you know how to use the computer to do graphic design. Put down: *digital graphic design.* Maybe you know how to write source code. Put down: *source code.* Maybe you know the way to write mobile apps for iTunes (or Android). Put down: *how to write mobile apps.* Any things you know that enable you to work better in the medium called *computers*, are Knowledges.

Again, if a preferred medium of yours here is games, then jot down any knowledge you have about games, or a particular game, *that enables you to work better in that medium*. For example, it could be: *how to win at Mass Effect 3*, or perhaps *how to play multiplayer videogames*, or maybe, *the*

Minimax Theorem, or perhaps *theory of zero-sum games,* or the *Xbox 360,* or even *how to play MMORPGs like World of Warcraft, etc.* Any knowledge or "know how" you have about that medium, or anything in that medium, that enables you to work more confidently in that medium, that someone new to the medium wouldn't know, should be put down here.

As you look at a favorite medium, maybe you will come up empty. Can't think of a single thing that helps you work better in that medium. Well, you're probably kidding yourself; but let's let that go, for the time being. Just give this exercise your best shot. It takes time, of course, because it requires *thinking.* You may be sitting there, staring at the walls for a spell, as the sweat stands out upon your brow. But eventually, an idea will break free.

Thinking in terms of whatever *pictures* come to your mind, rather than just searching for *words,* sometimes helps a lot.

There is no penalty for coming up empty. Only for not trying at all.

© ScienceCartoonsPlus.com

"I CAN REMEMBER WHEN ALL WE NEEDED WAS SOMEONE WHO COULD CARVE AND SOMEONE WHO COULD SEW."

2. What You Know from Your Previous Jobs

If you've been out there in the world of work for any time already, you've probably learned a lot of things that you now just take for granted. *"Of course I know that!"* But such knowledges may be important, down the line. So, list them!

Things like: *bookkeeping, handling applications, credit collection of over-due accounts, hiring, international business, management, marketing, sales, merchandizing, packaging, policy development, problem solving, troubleshooting, public speaking, recruiting, conference planning, systems analysis, the culture of other countries, other languages, government contract procedures,* and so on.

To be thorough here, jot down on another piece of paper a list of all the jobs you have ever held, and then *for each job* jot down anything you learned there. For example: "Worked in a warehouse; learned *how to use a forklift and crane, inventory control, logistics automation software, Warehouse Management systems, JIT (just in time) techniques, teamwork principles,* and *how to supervise employees.*"

Or, again, "Worked at McDonald's: learned *how to prepare and serve food, how to wait on customers, how to make change, how to deal with complaints, how to train new employees, etc.*"

Do this with all the jobs you have ever held: where you worked, what you learned there. Then look over everything you've written in *this* exercise, and decide which are your favorite knowledges or interests, that you're glad you picked up. Jot them down on your worksheet, in the space provided for this exercise.

3. What You Know About, Outside of Work

Jot down knowledges you've picked up outside of work, such as: *antiques, gardening, cooking, budgeting, decorating, photography, crafts, spirituality, sports, camping, travel, repairing things, flea markets, scrapbooking, sewing, art appreciation at museums, how to run or work in a volunteer organization,* and so on.

a. Also think of anything you learned in high school (or college) that you prize knowing today: *keyboarding? Chinese? accounting? geography?* What? Jot it all down.

b. Think of anything you learned at training seminars, workshops, conferences, and so on, possibly in connection with a job you had at the time. Jot it all down.

c. Think of anything you studied at home, via online courses, mobile apps, tape programs (likely played in your car while commuting), PBS television programs, etc. Jot it all down.

d. Think of anything you learned out there in the world, such as
*how to assemble a flash mob, how to organize a protest, how to fundraise
for a particular cause, how to run a marathon, how to repair a toilet,*
etc. Jot it all down, in the space provided for this exercise on your
worksheet.

4. What Fields, Careers, or Industries Sound Interesting to You

If you want to pick some career or field from a list of them all, it
helps if you start broadly, and then drill down.

Broadly speaking, then, the job-market consists of the following
four arenas: *agriculture, manufacturing, information,* or *services.* Any
ideas about which of these four is most attractive to you? If so, jot it
down, in the space provided for this exercise on your worksheet.

In order to drill down further than that, your best bet is the government's O*Net Online, assuming you have a computer (**www.onetonline
.org**). *Note that is .org, not .com.*

To begin with, this site has various lists of **career clusters** or **industries** or **job families.** Below is a mashup of these. Please read this list
over, and check off any of these that you want to explore further (*multiple choice preferred, here, in order to have alternatives and therefore Hope*):

❑ Accommodation and Food Services
❑ Administrative and Support Services
❑ Agriculture, Food, and Natural Resources
❑ Architecture, Engineering, and Construction
❑ Arts, Audio/Video Technology, and Communications
❑ Business, Operations, Management, and Administration
❑ Community and Social Service
❑ Computer and Mathematical
❑ Design, Entertainment, Sports, and Media
❑ Distribution and Logistics
❑ Education, Training, and Library
❑ Entertainment and Recreation
❑ Farming, Forestry, Fishing, and Hunting
❑ Finance and Insurance

- ❏ Food Preparation and Serving
- ❏ Government and Public Administration
- ❏ Green Industries or Jobs
- ❏ Health Care, Health Science, and Social Assistance
- ❏ Hospitality and Tourism
- ❏ Human Services
- ❏ Information and Information Technology
- ❏ Law, Public Safety, Corrections, and Security
- ❏ Life, Physical, and Social Sciences
- ❏ Manufacturing
- ❏ Management of Companies and Enterprises
- ❏ Marketing, Sales, and Service
- ❏ Military Related
- ❏ Mining, Quarrying, and Oil and Gas Extraction
- ❏ Personal Care and Service
- ❏ Production
- ❏ Professional, Scientific, and Technical Services
- ❏ Protective Services
- ❏ Real Estate, Rental, and Leasing
- ❏ Religion, Faith, and Related
- ❏ Retail Trade, Sales, and Related
- ❏ Science, Technology, Engineering, and Mathematics
- ❏ Self-Employment
- ❏ Transportation, Warehousing, and Material Moving
- ❏ Utilities

Now, the nice thing about O*Net Online is that once you have chosen anything on the list above, the site has drop-down menus which allow you to go deeper into each *career cluster, industry,* or *job family* that you have checked off. It drills down to career pathways, and then drills down further to individual occupations, and then drills down still further to tasks, tools, technologies, knowledges, skills, abilities, work activities, education, interests, work styles, work values, related occupations, and salary.

The only limitation here, as you will see in chapter 7, *Five Ways to Choose or Change Careers,* is that O*Net *only does this for about 800* *occupations.* Its predecessor, the D.O.T., had 12,741 occupations.[6] So, this does not offer a complete map of the job-market by any means.

And even for those occupations that are listed in O*Net, remember: jobs, industries, and careers are mortal: they are born, they grow, they flourish, they mature, then decline and ultimately die. Sometimes it takes centuries, sometimes merely decades, sometimes even sooner than that. But, eventually, most jobs, industries, and careers are mortal. So, always have a Plan b.

Okay, now you're done with the worksheet for this petal. What next? Well, sort them. Copy the diagram below, on to a piece of notebook paper, and then sort everything—everything—you have on that worksheet into one of these four bins (well, you can forget bin #4, if you'd rather):

YOUR FAVORITE SUBJECTS MATRIX
HIGH

E X P E R T I S E	3. Subjects for Which You Have Little Enthusiasm but in Which You Have Lots of Expertise	1. Subjects for Which You Have Lots of Enthusiasm and in Which You Have Lots of Expertise BINGO!
	4. Subjects for Which You Have Little Enthusiasm and in Which You Have Little Expertise	2. Subjects for Which You Have Lots of Enthusiasm but in Which You Have Little Expertise

LOW   ENTHUSIASM   **HIGH**

Copy the top four or five results from bin #1 and maybe, maybe, an item from bin #2, on to your Favorite Knowledges or Fields of Interest petal, found on page 120–21.

Now you're ready to move on, to consider another side of Who You Are.

---

6. By the way, if you want to use or visit the D.O.T. it's now online at www.occupationalinfo.org, and can be downloaded to your computer.

I Am a Person Who . . .
Has These Favorite Kinds of People

Second Petal
My Preferred Kinds of People to Work With

Why do *the people you prefer* matter at all in the larger scheme of things? Because, the people we work with are either energy drainers or energy creators. They either drag us down, and keep us from being our most effective, or they lift us up and help us to be at our best, and perform at our greatest effectiveness. We'll get into that, in a minute.

My Favorite People Petal

Goal in Filling Out This Petal: To avoid past bad experiences with people at work, since who (*whom?*) you work with can either make the job delightful, or ruin your day, your week, your year.

What You Are Looking For: (1) A better picture in your mind of what kind of people surrounding you at work will enable you to operate at your highest and most effective level. (2) If a medium you chose during the card sort was *people*, then this helps to describe what people you would most like to serve or help: defined by age, problems, geography, and so forth.

Form of the Entries on Your Petal: They can be adjectives describing different kinds of people ("kind," "patient") or it can be types of people, as in the "Holland Code" or "Myers-Briggs" typologies (see page 74).

Example of a Good Petal: (1) *Kind, generous, understanding, fun, smart.* (2) *The unemployed, people struggling with their faith, worldwide, all ages. Holland code: IAS.*

Example of a Bad Petal: *People in trouble, young, smart, in urban settings.* RCI.

Why Bad: It doesn't distinguish between (1) people surrounding me at work and (2) people I want to help or serve. It lumps both together. Not much help. Too vague.

Also, "people-environments" are another way of describing jobs or careers. So, we'll cover that here, too. Now, let us begin.

You'll probably need to copy this chart to a larger piece of paper—$8^1/_2$ x 11 inches—before you start filling it in. And, by the way, you can fill it out alone, or in company with up to five other job-hunters (recommended, because it's a lot more fun to see how other people are bugged by the same kinds of people that you are).

MY FAVORITE PEOPLE CHART

First Column	Second Column	Third Column	Fourth Column
Places I Have Worked Thus Far in My Life	Kinds of People There Who Drove Me Nuts (from the first column) (No names, but describe *what* about them drove you nuts; e.g., *bossy, always pestering me with their personal problems, always left early before job was done, etc.* List these in any order; it doesn't matter—at least in *this* column . . .)	Kinds of People I'd Prefer Not to Have to Work With, In Order of Preference (This is now a ranking of the items in the second column, in exact order of: which is worse? next? etc. Use the Prioritizing Grid, opposite page, to do this.) 1a. 2a. 3a. 4a. 5a.	Kinds of People I'd Most Like to Work With, in Order of Preference (The opposite of those qualities in the third column, in the same order) 1b. 2b. 3b. 4b. 5b.

OUR PRIORITIZING GRID FOR 10 ITEMS OR LESS

PRIORITIZING GRID FOR 10 ITEMS OR LESS

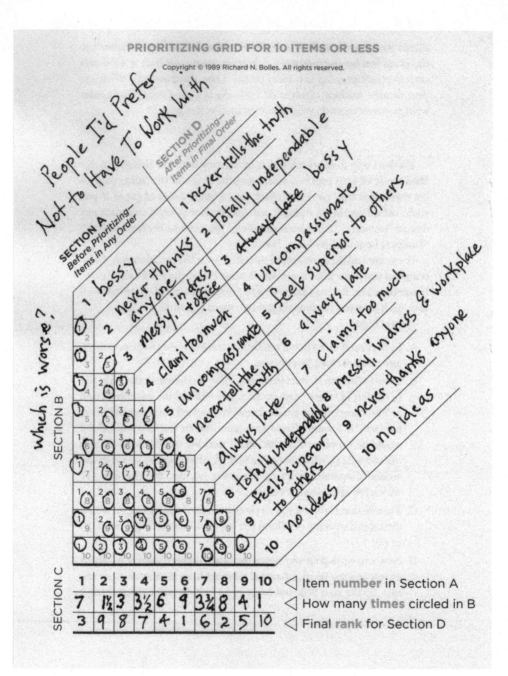

People I'd Prefer Not to Have To Work With

SECTION A — Before Prioritizing—Items in Any Order

SECTION D — After Prioritizing—Items in Final Order

Which is worse?

SECTION B

1 bossy
2 never thanks anyone
3 messy, in dress + office
4 claim too much
5 uncompassionate
6 never tell the truth
7 always late
8 totally undependable
9 feels superior to others
10 no ideas

1 never tells the truth
2 totally undependable
3 always late
4 uncompassionate
5 feels superior to others
6 always late
7 claims too much
8 messy, in dress & workplace
9 never thanks anyone
10 no ideas

SECTION C	1	2	3	4	5	6	7	8	9	10	
	7	1½	3	3½	6	9	3¾	8	4	1	◁ Item **number** in Section A / How many **times** circled in B
	3	9	8	7	4	1	6	2	5	10	◁ Final **rank** for Section D

◁ Item **number** in Section A
◁ How many **times** circled in B
◁ Final **rank** for Section D

Start, of course, by filling in the first column in the chart, and then the second. This will bring you to the third column, and here you're gonna need some help. How do you look back at that stuff in the second column, and prioritize it? Well, you use:

The Prioritizing Grid

I give you my Prioritizing Grid. It asks you to decide between just two items at a time.

Instructions for Using the Prioritizing Grid:

Section A. Write down, in any order, the factors you listed in the second column of the Chart. This grid will accommodate up to ten factors. If you originally listed more than ten, take a guess at which ten factors you disliked the most, and list *those ten*.

Section B. Compare just two items at a time. Begin with that little tiny box to the left of factor #1 and factor #2, in which you will see the tiny numbers 1 and 2. The numbers are clearly shorthand for those factors written out in Section A. The question you would frame for yourself, here, would be as follows: Which of these two factors do I dislike the most? Then, in that little tiny box you circle either the tiny number 1 or 2, depending on which factor you dislike the most.

In similar manner you work your way down the little boxes *nearest* Section A, which as you can see lie in a diagonal running from northwest to southeast. The next little tiny box has the tiny numbers 2 and 3 in it. Same question, except now it's between factor #2 versus factor #3. Circle the appropriate number in that tiny box. Why *diagonal*, rather than just straight across horizontally or straight down, vertically? Because you can get into a knee-jerk reaction if you do it that way (*"Well, I checked factor #5 each time so far, so I guess I should check factor #5 this next time, too."*) Diagonal defeats knee-jerk reactions.

So, work your way on down that diagonal direction. When you've reached the little box at the bottom of that first diagonal (containing the little numbers 9 and 10), go back up to the top and work down the next diagonal (beginning with the little box containing 1 and 3; then the little box containing 2 and 4; then the one containing 3 and 5, etc.

When you've reached the box at the bottom of *that* diagonal direction, go back up to the top, and work down the next diagonal (the little box containing 1 and 4, then the box containing 2 and 5, and so on, down to box containing 7 and 10).

Back up to the top to the next diagonal, the box containing 1 and 5, then the box containing 2 and 6, and so on. Keep this up until you've made a decision about every little box (the final one being 1 versus 10).

Section C. The bottom of the grid has three rows to it, as you can see. The first row is already filled in for you: it's the numbers of the factors in Section A. The second row, just below that, asks how many times each number got circled in *all* of the little tiny boxes. Let's say item 1 got circled 7 times. In the row right beneath #1 in the first row of Section C, you enter the number 7. Next, count how many times item 2 got circled; let's say it was 1 time; put the number 1 right below #2. Continue up through item 10.

Look now at the numbers in that second row. If no number is repeated in that second row of Section C, great! Most likely you'll find a tie. That means two items got circled the same number of times—let's say 2 and 10. How do you resolve the tie? Well, you look back at Section B, to find the little tiny box that had 2 and 10 in it, and see which of those two you circled there; let's say it was 2. Well then, in that second row, give #2 an extra half point. Now its "count" is $1^1/_2$. Leave #10 as it is (count just 1). Do this with each two-way tie.

What do you do if you have a three-way tie—three items each got circled the same number of times? This always means that you contradicted yourself somewhere along the way: one time you said *this* was more important, another time you said, no it wasn't. The only way to resolve the three-way tie is to just guess what is the proper order (for you) as to which of the three you dislike the most, which next, which next. Let's say the tie was that 3, 4, and 7 all got circled the same number of times. You dislike #7 the most, #4 next, and #3 next. Okay, so give an extra $^3/_4$ point *(that's three-quarters of a point)* to #7, an extra $^1/_2$ point to #4, and no extra points to factor #3. Now, no two factors or items have the same count in the second line of Section C.

Go down now to the bottom row there in Section C, and now rank the items, according to their circle count in the second row. The factor that got circled the most, let's say it was item #6, must be given *a final rank* of 1. Therefore, write 1 in the third row, down below item #6. Let's say item #8 got the next most circles; write a 2 down below item #8. Let's say item #1 got the next most circles; write a 3 down below it, on the bottom rank line in Section C. And so on. And so forth.

Section D. Recopy the list that you randomly put down in Section A, but now here in Section D put the list in its exact order of *one you disliked the most, next most,* etc.—according to the ranking in the bottom row of Section C. In terms of our examples above, you would copy item #6 as it was called in Section A, and put it on the very top line in Section D, because it got circled the most. You would copy item #8 as it was called in Section A onto the second line in Section D, because it got circled the next most times. And so on, until you've copied all ten factors in exactly the order of "dis-like-ness" (new word) this Grid revealed.

Now, what do you end up with, there in Section D? A list of your preferences, regarding people environments: *"I would most prefer not to have to work with . . . and I next most prefer not to have to work with. . . ."* etc.

I knew you'd like an example of a finished Prioritizing Grid, which is what you have on page 70. Note that there is a mistake on line 3 in Section D. No matter if you make a mistake. Just cross it out and put the correct information. It's okay not to be perfect.

Now, back to the *Chart* on page 68. Copy the first five factors in Section D of the *grid*, into the third column of *the Chart*. What you've got there, now, is a *negative* list of what you're trying to avoid. What you want is a *positive* list of what you're trying to find.

So, look at the five negative items you just put up there, in the third column of *the Chart*, and write *the opposite*, or something near *the opposite*, directly opposite each item, in the fourth column of the *Chart*. By "opposite" I don't necessarily mean "the exact opposite." If one of your complaints in the third column was: "I was micromanaged, supervised every hour of my day," the opposite, in the fourth column, wouldn't necessarily be "No supervision." It might be "Limited supervision" or something like that. Your call.

Note that by first putting your *negative* list in exact order of what you **most want to avoid** (third column in the Chart), your related *positive* list (fourth column) will have its factors in the exact order of what you **most want to find** in a future job.

Copy now the top 5 on your *positive* list, on to the petal, My Preferred Kinds of People to Work With, on pages 120–21.

Then we move on, to do the rest of the petal.

The *Party Game* Exercise

People-environments aren't just a matter of figuring out who irritates you and who doesn't. Though that is important. But, as mentioned earlier, *people* are also a way of identifying careers.

That's because every career has a characteristic people-environment. Tell us what **career** interests you, and we can tell you, in general terms, what people-environment it will offer—described in terms of six factors.

Or tell us what **people-environment** you want—in terms of those same six factors—and we can tell you what careers will give you *that*. As I always like to give credit where credit is due, you should know that it was the late Dr. John L. Holland who came up with the system for doing this.[7]

Surveying the whole job-market, he said there are basically six people-environments. Let's tick them off:

1. **Realistic** People-Environment: filled with people who prefer activities involving "the explicit, ordered, or systematic manipulation of objects, tools, machines, and animals." "Realistic,"

---

7. There is, incidentally, a relationship between the **people** you like to be surrounded by and your **skills** and your **values**. Most of us don't need to explore that, but if you're curious, you'll need to read John Holland's book, *Making Vocational Choices* (3rd ed., 1997). You can procure it at your local public library or (if you can afford it) by going to the Psychological Assessment Resources (PAR), Inc., website at www3.parinc.com, and entering the word "Holland" in the search engine there; or by calling 1-800-331-8378. The book is $56.00 at this writing. PAR also has John Holland's instrument, called The Self-Directed Search (or SDS, for short), for discovering what your Holland Code is. PAR lets you take the test online for a small fee ($4.95) at www.self-directed-search.com.

incidentally, refers to Plato's conception of "the real" as that which one can apprehend through the senses. ("Knock on wood!")

I summarize this as: **R** = *people who like nature, or plants, or animals, or athletics, or tools and machinery, or being outdoors.*

2. **Investigative** People-Environment: filled with people who prefer activities involving "the observation and symbolic, systematic, creative investigation of physical, biological, or cultural phenomena."

    I summarize this as: **I** = *people who are very curious, liking to investigate or analyze things, or people, or data.*

3. **Artistic** People-Environment: filled with people who prefer activities involving "ambiguous, free, unsystematized activities and competencies to create art forms or products."

    I summarize this as: **A** = *people who are very artistic, imaginative, and innovative, and don't like time clocks.*

4. **Social** People-Environment: filled with people who prefer activities involving "the manipulation of others to inform, train, develop, cure, or enlighten."

    I summarize this as: **S** = *people who are bent on trying to help, teach, or serve people.*

5. **Enterprising** People-Environment: filled with people who prefer activities involving "the manipulation of others to attain organizational or self-interest goals."

    I summarize this as: **E** = *people who like to start up projects or organizations, or sell things, or influence and persuade people.*

6. **Conventional** People-Environment: filled with people who prefer activities involving "the explicit, ordered, systematic manipulation of data, such as keeping records, filing materials, reproducing materials, organizing written and numerical data according to a prescribed plan, operating business and data-processing machines." "Conventional," incidentally, refers to the "values" that people in this environment usually hold—representing the central mainstream of our culture.

    I summarize this as: **C** = *people who like detailed work, and like to complete tasks or projects.*

According to John's theory every one of us has **three** preferred people-environments, from among these six. The letters for your three preferred people-environments gives you what is called your "Holland Code." The question is, Which three?

Back in 1975 I invented a quick and easy way for you to find out, based on John's system. It's turned out it corresponds to the results you would get from the SDS, 92 percent of the time.[8] So if you want a much more certain answer, you should take the SDS. But when you're in a hurry, this is close. I call it "The Party Exercise." Here is how the exercise goes (*do it, please*):

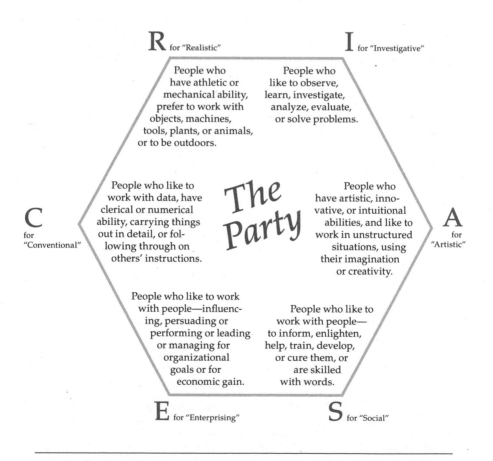

R for "Realistic"   I for "Investigative"

People who have athletic or mechanical ability, prefer to work with objects, machines, tools, plants, or animals, or to be outdoors.

People who like to observe, learn, investigate, analyze, evaluate, or solve problems.

C for "Conventional"

People who like to work with data, have clerical or numerical ability, carrying things out in detail, or following through on others' instructions.

The Party

People who have artistic, innovative, or intuitional abilities, and like to work in unstructured situations, using their imagination or creativity.

A for "Artistic"

People who like to work with people—influencing, persuading or performing or leading or managing for organizational goals or for economic gain.

People who like to work with people—to inform, enlighten, help, train, develop, or cure them, or are skilled with words.

E for "Enterprising"   S for "Social"

8. Amusing anecdote: John was a good friend of mine, and when I first showed him this Party Exercise I had invented, I asked him what he thought of it. With a twinkle in his eye he snorted, "Huh! Probably put me out of business!" Nope, it didn't. His SDS has sold more than thirty million copies, and is the basis for many other career tests or instruments.

Here is an aerial view of a room in which a party is taking place. At this party, people with the same interests have (for some reason) all gathered in the same corner of the room. And that's true for all six corners.

1. Which corner of the room would you instinctively be drawn to, as the group of people you would most enjoy being with for the longest time? (Leave aside any question of shyness, or whether you would have to actually talk to them; you could just listen.)

   Write the letter for that corner here: ☐

2. After fifteen minutes, everyone in the corner you chose leaves for another party crosstown, except you. Of the groups that still remain now, which corner or group would you be drawn to the most, as the people you would most enjoy being with for the longest time?

   Write the letter for that corner here: ☐

3. After fifteen minutes, this group too leaves for another party, except you. Of the corners, and groups, which remain now, which one would you most enjoy being with for the longest time?

   Write the letter for that corner here: ☐

The three letters you just chose are called your "Holland Code."[9]

Put that code here: ☐ ☐ ☐

---

9. Incidentally, John always encouraged people to write down somewhere all six versions (technically called *permutations*) of your code. Thus, if your code were, say, SIA, its permutations would be: SIA, SAI, IAS, ISA, ASI, AIS. This is especially useful if you are ever going to look up careers that correspond to your code. Put "Holland codes for careers" into your favorite search engine, and you will find such sites as www.vista-cards.com/occupations.

Further, he and I worked together on this application of his system to our Daydreams: list all the things you've ever dreamed of doing. Then, to the right of each, try to *guess*—guess!—at what you think the three-letter Holland code would be for each. When done, look at each code and assign a value of 3 to any letter in the first position; assign a value of 2 to any letter in the second position; and assign a value of 1 to any letter in the third position (e.g., in the case of IAS, you'd give 3 points to "I," 2 points to "A," and 1 point to "S"). Do this for every code you've written down, then total up all the points for each letter. How many points did "R" get, how many points did "I" get, etc. Choose the top three with the most points, in order, when you're done, and you have the Holland Code of your daydreams. As John said to me, "This is the most reliable way of determining someone's code, but who would believe it, except you and me?"

Now, copy that code on to the petal, My Preferred Kinds of People to Work With, found on pages 120–21. And we are done (with that petal). Time now to move on to another side of Who You Are.

I Am a Person Who . . .
Can Do These Particular Things

And *loves* having these transferable skills. Or gifts. Or talents. Or abilities. (Or whatever you want to call them.)

Third Petal
What I Can Do (My Favorite Transferable Skills)

My Favorite Transferable Skills Petal

Goal in Filling Out This Petal: To discover what your transferable skills are, that can be used in any field or interest. These are your skills with people, or your skills with data, or your skills with things. They are things you probably were born knowing how to do, or at least you began with a natural gift and have honed and sharpened it since.

What You Are Looking For: Not just what you *can* do, but which of those skills you most *love* to use.

Form of the Entries on Your Petal: Verbs, usually in pure verb form (e.g. *analyze*) though they may sometimes be in *gerund* form (ending in –ing, e.g., *analyzing*).

Example of a Good Petal: (These stories show that I can) *innovate, manipulate, analyze, classify, coach, negotiate;* OR (These stories show that I am good at) *innovating, manipulating, analyzing, classifying, coaching, negotiating.*

Example of a Bad Petal: *Adaptable, charismatic, reliable, perceptive, discreet, dynamic, persistent, versatile.*

Why Bad: These are all *traits*, that is, the *style* with which you do your transferable skills. They are important, but they are not *transferable skills.*

Incidentally, there is a new category floating around in the past ten years, called "soft skills." These are really just another way of speaking of people skills or traits, and involve things like "a good work ethic," "a positive attitude," "acting as a team player," "flexibility," "working well under pressure," and "ability to learn from criticism."

You will also find some people or websites describing *categories* of transferable skills, like "action verbs," or "communication or people skills," "technical skills," "research and analytical skills," "management, supervision, and leadership skills," "clerical and administrative skills," "problem-solving and development skills," "financial skills," etc. It's a hazy science. I still prefer "skills with data, or people, or things." It's simple (so, apparently, am I).

Here, you are looking for what you may think of as the basic building-blocks of your work. So, if you're going to identify your dream job, and/or attempt a thorough career-change, you must, above all else, identify your functional, transferable skills. And while you may think you know what your best and favorite skills are, in most cases your self-knowledge could probably use a little work.

A weekend should do it! In a weekend, you can inventory your *past* sufficiently so that you have a good picture of the *kind* of work you

would love to be doing *in the future.* (*You can, of course, stretch the inventory over a number of weeks, maybe doing an hour or two one night a week, if you prefer. It's up to you as to how fast you do it.*)

A Crash Course on "Transferable Skills"

Many people just "freeze" when they hear the word "skills."

It begins with high school job-hunters: "I haven't really got any skills," they say.

It continues with college students: "I've spent four years in college. I haven't had time to pick up any skills."

And it lasts through the middle years, especially when a person is thinking of changing his or her career: "I'll have to go back to college, and get retrained, because otherwise I won't have any skills in my new field." Or: "Well, if I claim any skills, I'll start at a very entry kind of level."

All of this fright about the word "skills" is very common, and stems from a total misunderstanding of what the word means. A misunderstanding that is shared, we might add, by altogether too many employers, or human resources departments, and other so-called "vocational experts."

By understanding the word, you will automatically put yourself way ahead of most job-hunters. And, especially if you are weighing a change of career, you can save yourself much waste of time on the adult folly called "I must go back to school." I've said it before, and I'll say it again: *maybe* you need some further schooling, but very often it is possible to make a dramatic career-change without any retraining. It all depends. And you won't really *know* whether or not you need further schooling, until you have finished all the exercises in this section of the book.

All right, then, if transferable skills are the heart of your vision and your destiny, let's see just exactly what transferable skills *are.*

Here are the most important truths you need to keep in mind about transferable, functional skills:

1. **Your transferable (functional) skills are the most basic unit—the atoms—of whatever career you may choose.**

    On the next page is a famous diagram of them, invented by the late Sidney A. Fine (reprinted by his permission).

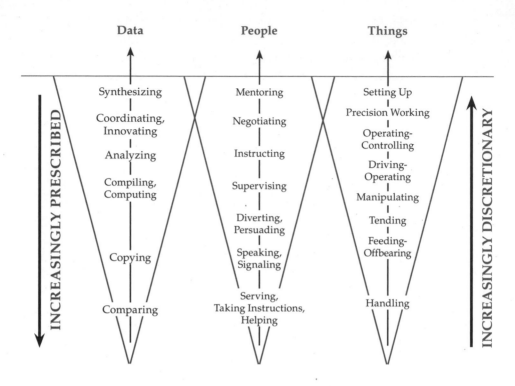

2. **You should always claim the highest skills you legitimately can, on the basis of your past performance.**

As we see in the functional/transferable skills diagram above, your transferable skills break down into three *families*, according to whether you use them with **Data/Information**, **People**, or **Things**. And again, as this diagram makes clear, within each family there are *simple* skills, and there are higher, or *more complex* skills, so that these all can be diagrammed as inverted pyramids, with the simpler skills at the bottom, and the more complex ones in order above it.

Incidentally, as a general rule—to which there are exceptions—each *higher* skill requires you to be able also to do all those skills listed below it. So of course you can claim *those*, as well. But you want to especially claim the highest skill you legitimately can, on each pyramid, based on what you have already proven you can do, in the past.

3. **The higher your transferable skills, the more freedom you will have on the job.**

    Simpler skills can be, and usually are, heavily *prescribed* (by the employer), so if you claim *only* the simpler skills, you will have to *"fit in"*—following the instructions of your supervisor, and doing exactly what you are told to do. The *higher* the skills you can legitimately claim, the more you will be given discretion to carve out the job the way you want to—so that it truly fits *you.*

4. **The higher your transferable skills, the less competition you will face for whatever job you are seeking, because jobs that use such skills will rarely be advertised through normal channels.**

    Not for you the way of classified ads, resumes, and agencies. No, if you can legitimately claim higher skills, then to find such jobs you *must* follow the step-by-step process I am describing here.

    The essence of our approach to job-hunting or career-change is that once you have identified your favorite transferable skills, and your favorite special knowledges, you may then approach *any organization that interests you, whether they have a known vacancy or not.* Naturally, whatever places you visit—and particularly those that have not advertised any vacancy—you will find far fewer job-hunters that you have to compete with.

    In fact, if the employers you visit happen to like you well enough, they may be willing to create for you a job that does not presently exist. *In which case, you will be competing with no one, since you will be the sole applicant for that newly created job.* While this doesn't happen all the time, it is astounding to me how many times it *does* happen. *The reason* it does is that the employers often have been *thinking* about creating a new job within their organization, for quite some time—but with this and that, they just have never gotten around to *doing* it. Until you walked in.

    Then they decided they didn't want to let you get away, since *good employees are as hard to find as good employers.* And they suddenly remember that job they have been thinking about creating for many weeks or months, now. So they dust off their *intention,* create the job on the spot, and offer it to you! And if that new job is not only what *they* need, but is exactly what *you* were looking for, then you have a dream job. Match-match. Win-win.

From our country's perspective, it is also interesting to note this: by this job-hunting initiative of yours, you have helped accelerate the creation of more jobs in your country, which is so much on everybody's mind here in the new millennium. How nice to help your country, as well as yourself!

5. **Don't confuse transferable skills with traits.**

Functional/transferable skills are often confused with **traits**, **temperaments**, or **type**. People think transferable skills are such things as: *has lots of energy, gives attention to details, gets along well with people, shows determination, works well under pressure, is sympathetic, intuitive, persistent, dynamic, dependable,* etc. As mentioned earlier, these are not functional/transferable skills, but traits, or the *style* with which you do your transferable skills. For example, take *"gives attention to details."* If one of your *transferable skills* is *"conducting research"* then *"gives attention to details"* describes the manner or style with which you do the transferable skill called *conducting research.* If you want to know what your traits are, popular tests such as the *Myers-Briggs Type Indicator* measure that sort of thing. [10]

If you have access to the Internet, there are clues, at least, about your traits or "type":

Working Out Your Myers-Briggs Type

www.teamtechnology.co.uk/mb-intro/mb-intro.htm

An informative article about the Myers-Briggs

---

10. The Myers-Briggs Type Indicator, or "MBTI®," measures what is called *psychological type.* For further reading about this, see:

Paul D. Tieger and Barbara Barron-Tieger, *Do What You Are: Discover the Perfect Career for You Through the Secrets of Personality Type* (Revised and Updated), Fourth Edition, Little, Brown & Company, Inc., 2007. For those who cannot obtain the MBTI®, this book includes a method for readers to identify their personality types. This is one of the most popular career books in the world. It's easy to see why. Many have found great help from the concept of personality type, and the Tiegers are masters in explaining this approach to career-choice. Highly recommended.

Donna Dunning, *What's Your Type of Career? Unlock the Secrets of Your Personality to Find Your Perfect Career Path,* Nicholas Brealey Publishing, 2010. This is a dynamite book on personality type. Donna Dunning's knowledge of "Type" is encyclopedic!

David Keirsey and Marilyn Bates, *Please Understand Me: Character & Temperament Types,* B&D Books, 1984. Includes the Keirsey Temperament Sorter—again, for those who cannot obtain the MBTI® (Myers-Briggs Type Indicator)—registered trademark of Consulting Psychologists Press.

The 16 Personality Types

www.personalitypage.com/high-level.html

A helpful site about Myers types

What Is Your Myers-Briggs Personality Type?

www.personalitypathways.com/type_inventory.html

www.personalitypathways.com

Another article about personality types; also, there's a Myers-Briggs Applications page, with links to test resources

Myers-Briggs Foundation home page

www.myersbriggs.org

The official website of the Foundation; lots of testing resources

Human Metrics Test (Jung Typology)

www.humanmetrics.com/cgi-win/JTypes2.asp

Free test, loosely based on the Myers-Briggs

Myers-Briggs Type Indicator Online

www.discoveryourpersonality.com/MBTI.html

On this site you can find the official Myers-Briggs test, $90

The Keirsey Temperament Sorter

http://keirsey.com

Free test, similar to the Myers-Briggs

"I Wouldn't Recognize My Skills If They Came Up and Shook Hands with Me"

Now that you know what transferable skills technically *are*, the problem that awaits you now, is figuring out your own. If you are one of the few lucky people who already know what your transferable skills are, blessed are you. Write them down, and put them in the order of preference, for you, on the Flower Diagram (pages 120–21).

If, however, you don't know what your skills are (and 95 percent of all workers *don't*), then you will need some help. Fortunately, there is an exercise to help.

It involves the following steps:

1. Write a Story (The First of Seven)

Yes, I know, I know. You can't do this exercise because you don't like to write. *Writers are a very rare breed.* That's what thousands of job-hunters have told me, over the years. And for years I kind of believed them—until "texting" came along. Let's face it: we human beings are "a writing people," and we only need a topic we have a real passion for, or interest in, for the writing genie to spring forth from within each of us, pen or keyboard in hand.

So, call the *Seven Stories* you're about to write your personal *offline blog,* if you prefer. But start writing. Please.

Here is a specific example:

> *"A number of years ago, I wanted to be able to take a summer trip with my wife and four children. I had a very limited budget, and could not afford to put my family up in motels. I decided to rig our station wagon as a camper.*
>
> *"First I went to the library to get some books on campers. I read those books. Next I designed a plan of what I had to build, so that I could outfit the inside of the station wagon, as well as topside. Then I went and purchased the necessary wood. On week-ends, over a period of six weeks, I first constructed, in my drive-way, the shell for the 'second story' on my station wagon. Then I cut doors, windows, and placed a six-drawer bureau within that shell. I mounted it on top of the wagon, and pinioned it in place by driving two-by-fours under the station wagon's rack on top. I then outfitted the inside of the station wagon, back in the wheel-well, with a table and a bench on either side, that I made.*
>
> *"The result was a complete homemade camper, which I put together when we were about to start our trip, and then*

*disassembled after we got back home. When we went on our sum-
mer trip, we were able to be on the road for four weeks, yet stayed
within our budget, since we didn't have to stay at motels. I estimate
I saved $1,900 on motel bills, during that summer's vacation."*

Ideally, each story you write should have the following parts, as
illustrated above:

1. **Your goal: what you wanted to accomplish:** *"I wanted to be able to
   take a summer trip with my wife and four children."*
2. **Some kind of hurdle, obstacle, or constraint that you faced**
   (self-imposed or otherwise): *"I had a very limited budget, and could
   not afford to put my family up in motels."*
3. **A description of what you did, step by step** (how you set about
   to ultimately achieve your goal, above, in spite of this hurdle or
   constraint): *"I decided to rig our station wagon as a camper. First I
   went to the library to get some books on campers. I read those books.
   Next I designed a plan of what I had to build, so that I could outfit the
   inside of the station wagon, as well as topside. Then I went and purchased the necessary wood. On weekends, over a period of six weeks,
   I . . ." etc., etc.*

4. **A description of the outcome or result:** *"When we went on our summer trip, we were able to be on the road for four weeks, yet stayed within our budget, since we didn't have to stay at motels."*

5. **Any measurable/quantifiable statement of that outcome, that you can think of:** *"I estimate I saved $1,900 on motel bills, during that summer's vacation."*

Now write *your* story, using the sample as a guide.

Don't pick a story where you achieved something *big*. At least to begin with, write a story about a time when you had fun!

Do not try to be too brief. This isn't Twitter.

If you absolutely can't think of any experiences you've had where you enjoyed yourself, and accomplished something, then try this: describe the seven most enjoyable jobs that you've had; or seven roles you've had so far in your life, such as: wife, mother, cook, homemaker, volunteer in the community, citizen, dressmaker, student, etc. Tell us something you did or accomplished, in each role.

2. Analyze Your Story, to See What Transferable Skills You Used

On the next page, write the title of your first story *above* the number 1. Then work your way down the column *below* that number 1, asking yourself in each case: "Did I use this skill in *this story*?"

If the answer is "Yes," color the little square in, with a red pen or whatever you choose.

Work your way through the entire Parachute Skills Grid that way, with your first story.

Voilà! You are done with Story #1. However, "one swallow doth not a summer make," so the fact that you used certain skills in this first story doesn't tell you much. What you are looking for is **patterns**—transferable skills that keep reappearing in story after story. They keep reappearing because they are your favorites (assuming you chose stories where you were *really* enjoying yourself).

THE PARACHUTE SKILLS GRID[11]

Your Seven Stories

In the space to the left, write above each number, in turn, the name you give to each story. Begin with Story #1. After you have written it, give it a name. Enter that name here (turn page on its side) above #1.

1	2	3	4	5	6	7	Skills with People; as my story shows, I can . . .
							Initiate, lead, be a pioneer
							Supervise, manage
							Follow through, get things done
							Motivate
							Persuade, sell, recruit
							Consult
							Advise
							Coordinate
							Negotiate, resolve conflicts
							Help people link up or connect
							Heal, cure
							Assess, evaluate, treat
							Convey warmth and empathy
							Interview, draw out
							Raise people's self-esteem
							Instruct
							Teach, tutor, or train (individuals, groups, animals)

11. Copyright © 2012 by Richard N. Bolles. Not to be reproduced without written permission.

1	2	3	4	5	6	7	
							Speak
							Listen
							Counsel, guide, mentor
							Communicate well, in person
							Communicate well, in writing
							Divert, amuse, entertain, perform, act
							Play an instrument
							Interpret, speak, or read a foreign language
							Serve, care for, follow instructions faithfully
							Skills with Data, Ideas; as my story shows, I can . . .
							Use my intuition
							Create, innovate, invent
							Design, use artistic abilities, be original
							Visualize, including in three dimensions
							Imagine
							Use my brain
							Synthesize, combine parts into a whole
							Systematize, prioritize
							Organize, classify
							Perceive patterns
							Analyze, break down into its parts
							Work with numbers, compute
							Remember people, or data, to unusual degree
							Develop, improve
							Solve problems

1	2	3	4	5	6	7	
							Plan
							Program
							Research
							Examine, inspect, compare, see similarities and differences
							Pay attention to details
							Use acute senses (hearing, smell, taste, sight)
							Study, observe
							Compile, keep records, file, retrieve
							Copy
							Skills with Things, or My Favorite Medium; as my story shows, I can . . .
							Control, expedite things
							Make, produce, manufacture
							Repair
							Finish, restore, preserve
							Construct
							Shape, model, sculpt
							Cut, carve, chisel
							Set up, assemble
							Handle, tend, feed
							Operate, drive
							Manipulate
							Use my body, hands, fingers, with unusual dexterity or strength

3. Write Six Other Stories, and Analyze Them for Transferable Skills

Now, write Story #2, from any period in your life, analyze it using the grid, etc., etc. And keep this process up, until you have written, and analyzed, seven stories.

If you are finding it difficult to come up with seven stories, it may help you to know how others chose one or more of their stories:[12]

"As I look back, I realize I chose a story that:

- Is somehow abnormal or inconsistent with the rest of my life
- Reveals my skills in a public way
- Is in a field (such as leisure, learning, etc.) far removed from my work
- I remembered through or because of its outcome
- Represented a challenge/gave me pride because it was something:
    - I previously could not do
    - My friends could not do
    - I was not supposed to be able to do
    - Only my father/mother could do it, I thought
    - Only authorized/trained/experts were supposed to be able to do
    - Somebody told me I could not do
    - My peers did not do/could not do
    - The best/brilliant/famous could or could not do
    - I did not have the right degree/training to do
    - People of the opposite sex usually do
- I would like to do again:
    - In a similar/different setting
    - With similar/different people
    - For free for a change/for money for a change

---

12. Copyright © 1994 by Daniel Porot.

- Excited me because:
  - I never did it before
  - It was forbidden
  - I took a physical risk
  - I was taking a financial risk
  - No one had ever done it before
  - It demanded a long and persistent (physical/mental) effort
  - It made me even with someone
- I loved doing it because:
  - I kind of like this sort of thing
  - The people involved were extremely nice
  - It did not cost me anything
- It will support/justify the professional goals I have already chosen"

4. Patterns and Priorities

When you've finished this whole inventory, for all seven of your accomplishments/achievements/jobs/roles or whatever, you want to look for PATTERNS and PRIORITIES.

a. For Patterns, because it isn't a matter of whether you used a skill once only, but rather whether you used it again and again. "Once" proves nothing; "again and again" is very convincing.

b. For Priorities (that is, which skills are most important to you?), because the job you eventually choose may not be able to use all of your skills. You need to know *what you are willing to trade off, and what you are not.* This requires that you know which skills, or family of skills, are most important to you.

So, after finishing your seven stories (or if you're in a hurry, at least five), look through all the pages of the Skills Grid, now, and pick out by guess and instinct, what you think are your top ten favorite skills: not the ones you think the job-market will like the best, but the ones *you* enjoy using the most. Put those ten in Section A of the Prioritizing Grid on the opposite page, and prioritize them.

When you've finished with Section D, copy that list onto the graphic below, as well as onto your Favorite Transferable Skills petal, on pages 120–21.

5. "Flesh Out" Your Favorite Transferable Skills with Your Traits

We discussed traits earlier (page 84). In general, traits describe:

How you deal with time, and promptness.

How you deal with people and emotions.

How you deal with authority, and being told what to do at your job.

How you deal with supervision, and being told how to do your job.

How you deal with impulse vs. self-discipline, within yourself.

How you deal with initiative vs. response, within yourself.

How you deal with crises or problems.

OUR PRIORITIZING GRID FOR 10 ITEMS OR LESS

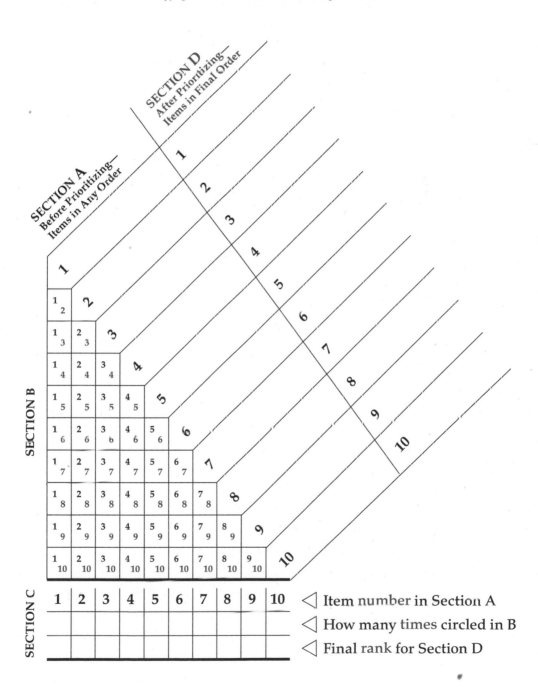

◁ Item number in Section A

◁ How many times circled in B

◁ Final rank for Section D

You need to flesh out your skill-description for each of your six or more favorite skills so that you are able to describe each of your talents or skills with more than just a one-word verb or gerund, like *organizing*.

Let's take *organizing* as our example. You tell us proudly: "I'm good at organizing." That's a fine start at defining your skills, but unfortunately it doesn't yet tell us much. Organizing WHAT? People, as at a party? Nuts and bolts, as on a workbench? Or lots of information, as on a computer? These are three entirely different skills. The one word *organizing* doesn't tell us which one is yours.

A Checklist of My Strongest Traits

I am very . . .

- Accurate
- Achievement-oriented
- Adaptable
- Adept
- Adept at having fun
- Adventuresome
- Alert
- Appreciative
- Assertive
- Astute
- Authoritative
- Calm
- Cautious
- Charismatic
- Competent
- Consistent
- Contagious in my enthusiasm
- Cooperative
- Courageous
- Creative
- Decisive
- Deliberate
- Dependable/have dependability
- Diligent
- Diplomatic
- Discreet
- Driving
- Dynamic
- Effective
- Energetic
- Enthusiastic
- Exceptional
- Exhaustive
- Experienced
- Expert
- Extremely economical
- Firm
- Flexible
- Humanly oriented
- Impulsive
- Independent
- Innovative
- Knowledgeable
- Loyal
- Methodical
- Objective
- Open-minded
- Outgoing
- Outstanding
- Patient
- Penetrating
- Perceptive
- Persevering
- Persistent
- Pioneering
- Practical
- Professional
- Protective
- Punctual
- Quick/work quickly
- Rational
- Realistic
- Reliable
- Resourceful
- Responsible
- Responsive
- Safeguarding
- Self-motivated
- Self-reliant
- Sensitive
- Sophisticated, very sophisticated
- Strong
- Supportive
- Tactful
- Thorough
- Unique
- Unusual
- Versatile
- Vigorous

So, please flesh out each of your favorite transferable skills with an object—some kind of Data/Information, or some kind of People, or some kind of Thing, and then add a Trait (adverb or adjective).

Why adjectives? Well, "I'm good at organizing information painstakingly and logically" and "I'm good at organizing information in a flash, by intuition," are two entirely different skills. The difference between them is spelled out not in the verb, nor in the object, but in the adjectival or adverbial phrase there at the end. So, expand each definition of your six or more favorite skills, in the fashion I have just described.

> When you are face-to-face with a person-who-has-the-power-to-hire-you, you want to be able to explain what makes you different from nineteen other people who can basically do the same thing that you can do. It is often the adjective or adverb that will save your life, during that explanation.

Now, on to another side of Who You Are.

"RUN, SPOT, RUN."

I Am a Person Who . . .
Has Favorite Working Conditions

Fourth Petal
My Favorite Working Conditions

My Favorite Working Conditions Petal

Goal in Filling Out This Petal: To state the working conditions and surroundings, that would make you happiest, and therefore enable you to do your most effective work.

What You Are Looking For: Avoiding past bad experiences.

Form of the Entries on Your Petal: Descriptors of physical surroundings.

Example of a Good Petal: *A workspace with lots of windows, nice view of greenery, relatively quiet, decent lunch period, flexibility about clocking in and clocking out, lots of shops nearby.*

Example of a Bad Petal: *Understanding boss, good colleagues, fun clients, etc.*

Why Bad: These all belong on the petal called Preferred Kinds of People to Work With, not this one, which is—or should be—just about the physical surroundings at your work. Now since this is *your* Flower Diagram, you can put this info on any petal you like. It's just that if you want your *thinking* to be clear, it's useful to preserve the difference between *"what is my physical setting going to be like?"* and *"who will I be working with?"*

Your physical setting where you work can cheer you up or drag your spirits down. It's important to know this before you weigh whether to take a particular job offer, or not. So, let's start with working conditions that made you unhappy in the past, and then flip them over into positives, by filling out the chart on the opposite page.

Plants that grow beautifully at sea level, often perish if they're taken ten thousand feet up the mountain. Likewise, we do our best work under certain conditions, but not under others. Thus, the question: "What are your favorite working conditions?" actually is a question about "Under what circumstances do you do your most effective work?"

As I just mentioned, the best way to approach this is by starting with the things you *disliked* about all your previous jobs, using the chart to list these. Copy this chart onto a piece of notebook paper if you wish, before you begin filling it out. *Column A may begin with such factors as. "too noisy," "too much supervision," "no windows in my workplace," "having to be at work by 6 a.m.," etc.*

If you are baffled as to how to prioritize the Column A list in the space provided for that ranking (Column B), I recommend you use the Prioritizing Grid on the next page. (For a refresher on how to use it,

DISTASTEFUL WORKING CONDITIONS

	Column A — Distasteful Working Conditions	Column B — Distasteful Working Conditions Ranked	Column C **+** The Keys to My Effectiveness at Work
Places I Have Worked Thus Far in My Life	I Have Learned from the Past That My Effectiveness at Work Is Decreased When I Have to Work Under These Conditions	Among the Factors or Qualities Listed in Column A, These Are the Ones I Dislike Absolutely the Most (in Order of Decreasing Dislike)	I Believe My Effectiveness Would Be at an Absolute Maximum, If I Could Work Under These Conditions (The Opposite of These Qualities, in Order):
		1a.	1b.
		2a.	2b.
		3a.	3b.
		4a.	4b.
		5a.	5b.
		6a.	6b.
		7a.	7b.
		8a.	8b.
		9a.	9b.
		10a.	10b.

OUR PRIORITIZING GRID FOR 10 ITEMS OR LESS

◁ Item number in Section A

◁ How many times circled in B

◁ Final rank for Section D

turn to "Instructions for Using the Prioritizing Grid," page 71.) This time, when you compare each two items, the question you must ask yourself is, "If I were offered two jobs, and in the first job offer I would be rid of my first distasteful working condition (1) but not the second (2), while in the second job offer I would be rid of my second distasteful working condition (2), but not the first (1), which job offer would I take?"

After you've finished prioritizing, what have you ended up with, in Section D? The exact list you copy into Column B of your Distasteful Working Conditions chart, page 99.

Now that you have that list in Column B, ranked in terms of most distasteful down to least distasteful working conditions, turn to Column C in that chart and write *the opposite*, or something near *the opposite*, directly opposite each item in Column B.

Copy the top 5 items in Column C, onto the Favorite Working Conditions petal of your Flower Diagram, pages 120–21.

Now, on to another side of Who You Are.

I Am a Person Who . . .
Prefers a Certain Level of Responsibility and Salary

Fifth Petal
My Preferred Salary, Level, and Responsibility

My Preferred Salary Petal

Goal in Filling Out This Petal: To gain a realistic picture of how much money you will need to earn, or want to earn, at whatever job you find.

What You Are Looking For: A range, because most employers are thinking in terms of a range, too. When you negotiate salary, as you will almost certainly have to, you want the bottom of your range to be near the top of theirs.

Form of the Entries on Your Petal: Total dollars needed, weekly, monthly, or annually. Stated in thousands (symbol: K).

Example of a Good Petal: $75K to $85K

Example of a Bad Petal: $120K

Why Bad: Well, it's not a range, which it needs to be; and it's too high unless you put on the petal the reason *why* such a high income is expected, and justified.

Money is important. Or else we've got to barter for our food, clothing, and shelter. So, when we're out of work, unless we have huge amounts of money in our savings account or investments, we are inevitably thinking: "What am I going to do, so that I have enough money to put food on the table, clothes on our backs, and a roof over our heads for myself—and for my family or partner *(if I have one)?*"

Happiness is important, too. So, we may find ourselves thinking: "How much do I really need to be earning, for me to be truly happy with my life?"

Are these two worries—money and happiness—related? Can money buy happiness?

Partly, it turns out. Partly. A study,[13] published in 2010, of the responses of 450,000 people in the U.S. to a daily survey, found that the less money they made, the more unhappy they tended to be, day after day. No surprise, there. And, obviously, the more money they made, measured in terms of percentage improvement, the happier they tended to be, *as measured by the frequency and intensity of moments of smiling, laughter, affection, and joy all day long, vs. moments of sadness, worry, and stress.*

So, money does buy happiness. But only up to a point. That point was found to be around $75,000 annual income (*at the end of 2011, median household income was $51,413[14]*). If people made more money than $75,000, it of course further improved their *satisfaction* with how their life was going, but it did not increase their happiness. Above $75,000, they started to report reduced ability to spend time with people they liked, to enjoy leisure, and to savor small pleasures. Happiness depends on things like that, and on other factors too: good health, a loving relationship, loving friends, a feeling of competence, gaining mastery, respect, praise, or even love, because we are really good at what we do.

So, this petal cannot be filled out all by itself. It is inextricably tied to the other petals—most particularly, to what you love to do, and where you love to do it.

Still, salary is something you must think out ahead of time, when you're contemplating your ideal job or career. Level goes hand in hand with salary, of course.

1. The first question here is at what level would you like to work, in your ideal job?

Level is a matter of how much responsibility you want, in an organization:

---

13. Research by Daniel Kahneman and Angus Deaton, published in the *Proceedings of the National Academy of Sciences,* Early Edition, September 6, 2010.
14. According to Sentier Research, reported by Paul Davidson, "U.S. Median Household Income Up 4% at End of 2011," *USA Today,* February 9, 2012.

❑ Boss or CEO (this may mean you'll have to form your own business)

❑ Manager or someone under the boss who carries out orders

❑ The head of a team

❑ A member of a team of equals

❑ One who works in tandem with one other partner

❑ One who works alone, either as an employee or as a consultant to an organization, or as a one-person business

Enter a two- or three-word summary of your answer, on the Preferred Salary, Level, and Responsibility petal of your Flower Diagram, pages 120–21.

2. The second question here is what salary would you like to be aiming for?

Here you have to think in terms of minimum or maximum. **Minimum** is what you would need to make, if you were just barely "getting by." And you need to know this *before* you go in for a job interview with anyone (*or before you form your own business, and need to know how much profit you must make, just to survive*).

Maximum could be any astronomical figure you can think of, but it is more useful here to put down the salary you realistically think you could make, with your present competency and experience, were you working for a real, *but generous*, boss. (If this maximum figure is still depressingly low, then put down the salary you would like to be making five years from now.)

Make out a detailed outline of your estimated expenses *now*, listing what you need *monthly* in the following categories:[15]

Housing

Rent or mortgage payments . . . . $_____

Electricity/gas. . . . . $_____

Water . . . . $_____

Phone/Internet. . . . . $_____

---

15. If this kind of financial figuring is not your cup of tea, find a buddy, friend, relative, family member, or anyone, who can help you do this. If you don't know anyone who could do this, go to your local church, synagogue, religious center, social club, gym, or wherever you hang out, and ask the leader or manager there, to help you find someone. If there's a bulletin board, put up a notice on the bulletin board.

Garbage removal . . . . $_____

Cleaning, maintenance, repairs[16] . . . . $_____ .

Food

What you spend at the supermarket

and/or farmer's market, etc. . . . . $_____

Eating out . . . . $_____

Clothing

Purchase of new or used clothing . . . . $_____

Cleaning, dry cleaning, laundry . . . . $_____

Automobile/transportation

Car payments . . . . $_____

Gas (who knows?)[17] . . . . $_____

Repairs . . . . $_____

Public transportation (*bus, train, plane*) . . . . $_____

Insurance

Car . . . . $_____

Medical or health care . . . . $_____

House and personal possessions . . . . $_____

Life . . . . $_____

Medical expenses

Doctors' visits . . . . $_____

Prescriptions . . . . $_____

Fitness costs . . . . $_____

Support for other family members

Child-care costs (*if you have children*) . . . . $_____

Child-support (*if you're paying that*) . . . . $_____

Support for your parents (*if you're helping out*) . . . . . $_____

Charity giving/tithe (*to help others*) . . . . $_____

---

16. If you have extra household expenses, such as a security system, be sure to include the quarterly (or whatever) expenses here, divided by three.

17. Your checkbook stubs and/or online banking records will tell you a lot of this stuff. But you may be vague about your cash or credit card expenditures. For example, you may not know how much you spend at the supermarket, or how much you spend on gas, etc. But there is a simple way to find out. Keep notes on your Smartphone or iPad for two weeks (there are apps for that), jotting down everything you pay cash (or use credit cards) for—on the spot, right after you pay it. At the end of those two weeks, you'll be able to take that notepad and make a realistic guess of what should be put down in these categories that now puzzle you. (Multiply the two-week figure by two, and you'll have the monthly figure.)

School/learning
  Children's costs (*if you have children in school*) . . . . . $_____
  Your learning costs (*adult education,*
  job-hunting classes, etc.) . . . . $_____
Pet care (*if you have pets*) . . . . $_____
Bills and debts (*usual monthly payments*)
  Credit cards. . . . . $_____
  Local stores . . . . $_____
  Other obligations you pay off monthly. . . . . $_____
Taxes
  Federal[18] (*next April's due, divided by*
  months remaining until then). . . . . $_____
  State (*likewise*) . . . . $_____
  Local/property (*next amount due, divided by*
  months remaining until then). . . . . $_____
  Tax-help (*if you ever use an accountant,*
  pay a friend to help you with taxes, etc.) . . . . $_____
Savings. . . . . $_____
Retirement (Keogh, IRA, SEP, etc.) . . . . $_____
Amusement/discretionary spending
  Movies, video rentals, etc.. . . . . $_____
  Other kinds of entertainment . . . . $_____
  Reading, newspapers, magazines, books . . . . $_____
  Gifts (birthday, Christmas, etc.). . . . . $_____
  Vacations . . . . $_____

Total Amount You Need Each Month. . . . . $_____

---

18. Incidentally, for U.S. citizens, looking ahead to next April 15, be sure to check with your local IRS office or a reputable accountant to find out if you can deduct the expenses of your job-hunt on your federal (and state) income tax returns. At this writing, some job-hunters can, if—big IF—this is not your first job that you're looking for, if you haven't been unemployed too long, and if you aren't making a career-change. Do go find out what the latest "ifs" are. If the IRS says you are eligible, keep careful receipts of everything related to your job-hunt, as you go along: telephone calls, stationery, printing, postage, travel, etc.

Multiply the total amount you need each month by 12, to get the yearly figure. Divide the yearly figure by 2,000, and you will be reasonably near the *minimum* hourly wage that you need. Thus, if you need $3,333 per month, multiplied by 12 that's $40,000 a year, and then divided by 2,000, that's $20 an hour.

Parenthetically, you may want to prepare two different versions of the above budget: one with the expenses you'd ideally *like* to make, and the other a minimum budget, which will give you what you are looking for, here: the floor, below which you simply cannot afford to go.

Now, enter the salary figure and any notes you want to add, about the level of responsibility you want to take on, to justify this salary, plus any "non-monetary" rewards you seek, on the Preferred Salary, Level, and Responsibility petal, found on pages 120–21.

Optional Exercise

You may wish to put down other rewards, besides money, that you would hope for, from your next job or career. These might be:

❑ Adventure

❑ Challenge

❑ Respect

❑ Influence

❑ Popularity

❑ Fame

❑ Power

❑ Intellectual stimulation from the other workers there

❑ A chance to be creative

❑ A chance to help others

❑ A chance to exercise leadership

❑ A chance to make decisions

❑ A chance to use your expertise

❑ A chance to bring others closer to God

❑ Other:

If you do check off things on this list, arrange your answers in order of importance to you, and then add them to the petal.

Now, we turn to another side of Who You Are.

I Am a Person Who . . .
Prefers Certain Places to Live

Sixth Petal
My Preferred Place to Live

My Preferred Place to Live Petal

Goal in Filling Out This Petal: To define where you would most like to work and live, and be happiest, if you ever have a choice. Or, to resolve a conflict between you and your partner as to where you want to move to, when you retire.

What You Are Looking For: Having a clearer picture about what you hope for, in life. Now or later. Now, if you're able to move and want to make a wise decision as to *where*. Later, If you're currently tied down to a particular place because "I need to be near my kids or my ailing parents, or whatever," in which case this becomes a planning for the future: retirement, or earlier. It's important to think about the future *now*, because an opportunity may come along when you least expect it, and you might pass right by it, unless you've given it some thought, and instantly recognize it.

Form of the Entries on Your Petal: You can stay general *(city, suburbs, rural, up in the mountains, on the coast,* or *overseas);* or you can get very specific if you're really ready to move, naming names and places—as this exercise will teach you to do.

Example of a Good Petal: *First preference: Jackson, Wyoming; Second preference: Honolulu; Third preference: New York City.*

Example of a Bad Petal: *The West; a suburb; snow*

Why Bad: Too broad. Doesn't really offer any help in making a decision. And it isn't prioritized, as the good petal is.

Directions for Doing This Exercise

1. Copy the chart that is on the next two pages, onto a larger (11 x 17-inch) piece of paper or cardboard, which you can obtain from any arts and crafts store or supermarket, in your town or city. If you are doing this exercise with a partner, make a copy for them too, so that each of you is working on a clean copy of your own, and can follow these instructions independently.

2. In *Column 1*, each of you should list all the places where you have ever lived.

3. In *Column 2*, each of you should list all the factors you disliked (and still dislike) about each place. The factors do not have to be put exactly opposite the name in *Column 1*. The names in *Column 1* exist simply to jog your memory.

   If, as you go, you remember some good things about any place, put those factors at the bottom of the next column, *Column 3*.

   If the same factors keep repeating, just put a checkmark after the first listing of that factor, every time it repeats.

   Keep going until you have listed all the factors you disliked or hated about each and every place you named in *Column 1*. Now, in effect, throw away *Column 1*; discard it from your thoughts. The negative factors were what you were after. *Column 1* has served its purpose.

4. Look at *Column 2*, now, your list of negative factors, and in *Column 3* try to list each one's opposite (or near opposite). For example, "the sun never shone, there" would, in *Column 3*, be turned into "mostly sunny, all year 'round." It will not always be *the exact opposite*. For example, the negative factor "rains all the time" does not necessarily translate into the positive "sunny all the time." It might be something like "sunny at least 200 days a year." It's your call. Keep going, until every negative factor in *Column 2* is turned into its opposite, a positive factor, in *Column 3*. At the bottom, note the positive factors you already listed there, when you were working on *Column 2*.

5. In *Column 4*, now, list the positive factors in *Column 3*, in the order of most important (to you), down to least important (to you). For example, if you were looking at, and trying to name a new town,

My Geographical Preferences

Decision Making for Just You

Column 1	Column 2	Column 3	Column 4
Names of Places I Have Lived	From the Past: Negatives	Translating the Negatives into Positives	Ranking of My Positives
	Factors I Disliked and Still Dislike about Any Place		1.
			2.
			3.
			4.
			5.
			6.
			7.
			8.
	Factors I Liked and Still Like About Any Place		9.
			10.

Our Geographical Preferences
Decision Making for You and a Partner

Column 5	Column 6	Column 7	Column 8
Places That Fit These Criteria	Ranking of His/Her Preferences	Combining Our Two Lists (Columns 4 & 6)	Places That Fit These Criteria
	a.	a.	
		1.	
	b.	b.	
		2.	
	c.	c.	
		3.	
	d.	d.	
		4.	
	e.	e.	
		5.	
	f.	f.	
		6.	
	g.	g.	
		7.	
	h.	h.	
		8.	
	i.	i.	
		9.	
	j.	j.	
		10.	

city, or place where you could be happy and flourish, what is the
first thing you would look for? Would it be, good weather? or
lack of crime? or good schools? or access to cultural opportunities, such as music, art, museums, or whatever? or would it be
inexpensive housing? etc., etc. Rank all the factors in *Column 4*.
Use a clean photocopy of the Prioritzing Grid on page 100 if you
need to.

6. If you are doing this by yourself, list on a *scribble sheet* the top ten
   factors, in order of importance to you, and show it to everyone
   you meet for the next ten days, with the ultimate question: "Can
   you think of places that have these ten factors, or at least the top
   five?" Jot down their suggestions on the back of the *scribble sheet*.
   When the ten days are up, look at the back of your sheet and
   circle the three places that seem the most interesting to you. If
   there is only a partial overlap between your dream factors and
   the places your friends and acquaintances suggested, *make sure
   the overlap is in the factors that count the most*. Now you have some
   names that you will want to find out more about, until you are
   sure which is your absolute favorite place to live, and then your
   second, and third, as backups.

   Put the names of the three places, and/or your top five geographical factors, on the Flower Diagram, on the Preferred Place
   to Live petal, pages 120–21.

7. If you are doing this with a partner, skip *Column 5*. Instead, when
   you have finished your *Column 4*, look at your partner's *Column 4*,
   and copy it into *Column 6*. The numbering of *your* list in *Column 4*
   was 1, 2, 3, 4, etc. Number your partner's list, as you copy it into
   Column 6, as a, b, c, d, etc.

8. Now, in *Column 7*, combine your *Column 4 with Column 6* (your
   partner's old *Column 4*, renumbered). Both of you can work now
   from just one person's chart. Combine the two lists as illustrated
   on the chart. First your partner's top favorite geographical factor
   ("a"), then *your* top favorite geographical factor ("1"), then your
   partner's second most important favorite geographical factor ("b"),
   then yours ("2"), etc., until you have twenty favorite geographical
   factors (*yours and your partner's*) listed, in order, in *Column 7*.

9. List on a *scribble sheet* the top ten factors, and both of you should show it to everyone you meet, for the next ten days, with the same question as above: "Can you think of any places that have these ten factors, or at least the top five?" Jot down their suggestions on the back of the *scribble sheet*. When the ten days are up, you and your partner should look at the back of your sheet and circle the three places that look the most interesting to the two of you. If there is only a partial overlap between your dream factors and the places your friends and acquaintances suggested, make sure the overlap is in the factors that matter the most to the two of you, i.e., the ones that are at the top of your list in *Column 7*. Now you have some names of places that you will want to find out more about, until you are sure which is the absolute favorite place to live for both of you, and then your second, and third, as backups.

Put the names of the top three places, and/or your top five geographical factors, on the Flower Diagram, on the Preferred Place to Live petal, pages 120–21.

Conclusion: Was all of this too much work? Then do what one family did: they put a map of the U.S. up on a corkboard, and then they each threw a dart at the map from across the room, and when they were done they asked themselves where the most darts landed. It turned out to be around "Denver." So, *Denver* it was!

And now we turn to the last side of Who You Are.

I Am a Person Who . . .
Has a Certain Goal, Purpose,
or Mission in Life

Seventh Petal
My Goal, Purpose, or Mission in Life

My Purpose in Life Petal

Goal in Filling Out This Petal: To know the moral compass or spiritual values by which you want to guide your life. The most victorious life is one that is dedicated to some larger cause or mission.

What You Are Looking For: Some definition of the purpose and mission of your life. This may help you pick out the kinds of organizations or companies you'd like to work for, if you find ones that are serving the same mission as yours.

Form of the Entries on Your Petal: A description of what kingdom of Life you want to make better, with some attending details.

Example of a Good Petal: *My purpose in life is to help the human spirit. I want there to be more faith, more compassion, more forgiveness, in families, because I have lived.*

Example of a Bad Petal: *More justice in the world.*

Why Bad: An admirable goal, but it is too vague. Doesn't give you any guidance as to what kind of work to look for.

As John L. Holland famously said, "We need to look further down the road than just headlight range at night." The road is the road of Life. You need to dream about the broad outcome of your life, and not just this year's job-search. What kind of footprint do you want to leave on this earth, after your journey here is done? Figure that out, and you're well on your way to defining your life as having purpose and a mission.

The Nine Kingdoms of Mission and Purpose

Generally speaking, mission breaks down into nine kingdoms—corresponding to our nature. As you look these over, the question is, which one appeals to *you* the most? Time for some hard thinking (ouch!). So, read on, *slowly*. Take time to ponder and think.

1. **The Mind.** The question is: *When you have finished your life here on earth, do you want there to be more knowledge, truth, or clarity in the world, because you were here? Knowledge, truth, or clarity concerning what in particular?* If this is You, then your sense of purpose is pointing you toward the kingdom of the mind.

2. **The Body.** The question is: *When you have finished your life here on earth, do you want there to be more wholeness, fitness, or health in the world, more binding up of the body's wounds and strength, more feeding of the hungry, and clothing of the poor, because you were here? What issue in particular?* If this is You, then your sense of purpose is pointing you toward the kingdom of the body.

3. **The Eyes and Other Senses.** The question is: *When you have finished your life here on earth, do you want there to be more beauty in the world, because you were here? If so, what kind of beauty entrances you? Is it art, music, flowers, photography, painting, staging, crafts, clothing, jewelry, or what?* If this is You, then your sense of purpose is pointing you toward the kingdom of the eyes and senses.

4. **The Heart.** The question is: *When you have finished your life here on earth, do you want there to be more love and compassion in the world, because you were here? Love or compassion for whom? Or for what?* If this is You, then your sense of purpose is pointing you toward the kingdom of the heart.

5. **The Will or Conscience.** The question is: *When you have finished your life here on earth, do you want there to be more morality, more justice, more righteousness, more honesty in the world, because you were here? In what areas of human life or history, in particular? And in what geographical area?* If this is You, then your sense of purpose is pointing you toward the kingdom of the conscience.

6. **The Spirit**. The question is: *When you have finished your life here on earth, do you want there to be more spirituality in the world, more faith, more compassion, more forgiveness, more love for God and the human family in all its diversity, because you were here? If so, with what ages, people, or with what parts of human life?* If this is You, then your sense of purpose is pointing you toward the kingdom of the spirit, or (if you prefer) *The Kingdom of God*.

7. **Entertainment**. The question is: *When you have finished your life here on earth, do you want there to be more lightening of people's loads, more giving them perspective, more helping them to forget their cares for a spell, do you want there to be more laughter in the world, and joy, because you were here? If so, what particular kind of entertainment do you want to contribute to the world?* If this is You, then your sense of purpose is pointing you toward the kingdom of entertainment.

8. **Our Possessions**. The question is: *Is your major concern the often false love of possessions in this world? When you have finished your life here on earth, do you want there to be better stewardship of what we possess—as individuals, as a community, as a nation—in the world, because you were here? Do you want to see simplicity, savings, and a broader emphasis on the word "enough," rather than on the word "more, more"? If so, in what areas of human life in particular?* If this is You, then your sense of purpose is pointing you toward the kingdom of possessions.

9. **The Earth**. The question is: *Is the planet on which we stand, your major concern? When you have finished your life here on earth, do you want there to be better protection of this fragile planet, more exploration of the world or the universe—exploration, not exploitation—more dealing with its problems and its energy, because you were here? If so, which problems or challenges in particular, draw your heart and soul?* If this is You, then your sense of purpose is pointing you toward the kingdom of the earth.

In sum, remember that all of these are worthwhile purposes and missions, all of these are necessary and needed, in this world. The question is, which one in particular draws you to it, *the most?* Which one do you most want to lend your brain, your energies, your skills and gifts, your life, to serve, while you are here on this earth?[19]

---

19. And by the way, if you want to have fun, if you have a computer go to the Internet, choose a browser like Google or Bing, and type your kingdom (*the Mind, etc.*) into the search line, and see if anything pops up that intrigues you.

When you are done, enter a summary paragraph of what you have decided your purpose or mission is, on the Goal, Purpose, or Mission in Life petal, on pages 120–21.

P.S. There are two challenges you may want to anticipate, in doing this particular exercise. First Challenge: you just come up empty on this exercise, despite hard thinking. No harm done. If you want an answer, just keep the question on the back-burner of your mind; eventually some insight is going to break through. Tomorrow, next week, next month, or a year from now. Be patient with yourself.

Second Challenge: This subject doesn't grab you at all. Okay. Then instead of writing a statement of purpose or mission for your life, you can write instead a statement outlining what you think about *life*: why are we here, why are *You* here, and so on. This is often called "Your Philosophy of Life":

In writing a philosophy of life, it should be no more than two pages, single spaced, and can be less; it should address whichever of these elements you think are most important; pick and choose. You do not have to write about all of them. In most cases, you will only need two or three sentences about each element you choose to comment on.

Beauty: what kind of beauty stirs us, what the function of beauty is in the world

Behavior: how we should behave in this world

Beliefs: what our strongest beliefs are

Celebration: how we like to play or celebrate, in life

Choice: what its nature and importance is

Community: what our concept is about belonging to each other; what we think our responsibility is to each other

Compassion: what we think about its importance and use

Confusion: how we live with it, and deal with it

Death: what we think about it and what we think happens after it

Events: what we think makes things happen, how we explain why they happen

---

continued

Free will: whether we are "predetermined" or have free will

God: see Supreme Being

Happiness: what makes for the truest human happiness

Heroes and heroines: who ours are, and why

Human: what we think is important about being human, what we think is our function

Love: what we think about its nature and importance, along with all its related words: compassion, forgiveness, grace

Moral issues: which ones we believe are the most important for us to pay attention to, wrestle with, help solve

Paradox: what our attitude is toward its presence in life

Purpose: why we are here, what life is all about

Reality: what we think is its nature, and components

Self: deciding whether physical self is the limit of your being, deciding what trust in self means

Spirituality: what its place is in human life, how we should treat it

Stewardship: what we should do with God's gifts to us

Supreme Being: our concept of, and what we think holds the universe together

Truth: what we think about it, which truths are most important

Uniqueness: what we think makes each of us unique

Values: what we think about ourselves, what we think about the world, prioritized as to what matters most (to us)

When you are done writing, put a summary paragraph on your Goal, Purpose, or Mission in Life petal, on pages 120–21.

I Am a Person Who . . .
Has Completed My Flower

The Flower

"That One Piece of Paper"

PETAL 3
What I Can Do and Love to Do
(My Favorite Transferable Skills):

1   6
2   7
3   8
4   9
5   10

My Favorite Traits (optional)

1
2
3
4
5
6

PETAL 2
My Preferred Kinds of
People to Work With:

1
2
3
4
5

My Holland Code:

☐ ☐
☐ ☐

PETAL 1
My Favorite Knowledges or Fields of Interest:

1
2

PETAL 7
My Goal, Purpose, or
Mission in Life (or my
philosophy about life):

PETAL 4
My Favorite
Working
Conditions:

1

2

3

4

5

Favorite Mediums

1

2

3

4

5

3

4

5

PETAL 6
My Preferred
Place(s) to Live
(sooner or later):

1

2

3

PETAL 5
My Preferred Salary Range:

Level of Responsibility I'd Like:

Other Responsibilities Hoped For:

Readers have asked to see an example of "That One Piece of Paper" all filled out. Rich W. Feller—a student of mine back in 1982, now a world-famous professor and expert in the national career development field—filled out his flower as you see, on the facing page. He said "That One Piece of Paper" has been his lifelong companion ever since, and his guiding star. (The petals then were slightly different.)

Rich Feller, a University Distinguished Teaching Scholar and Professor at Colorado State University, whose own personal "Flower Diagram" is on the facing page, first put his personal "picture" together almost thirty years ago. Here are his comments about its usefulness since, and how "That One Piece of Paper" helped him, how he's used it, and how it's changed.

What the Parachute Flower Has Meant to Me

More than anything I've gained from an academic life, my Flower has given me hope, direction, and a lens to satisfaction. Using it to assess my life direction during crisis, career moves, and stretch assignments, it helps me define and hold to personal commitments. In many ways it's my "guiding light." Data within my Flower became and remain the core of any success and satisfaction I have achieved.

After I first filled out my own Flower Diagram in a two-week workshop with Dick Bolles back in 1982, I decided to teach the Flower to others. My academic position has allowed me to do this, abundantly. Having now taught the Flower to thousands of counselors, career development, and human resource specialists, I continually use it with clients, and in my own transitional retirement planning.

I'm overwhelmed with how little has changed within my Flower, over the years. My Flower is the best of what I am. Its petals are my compass, and using my "favorite skills" are the mirror to a joyful day. I trust the wisdom within "That One Piece of Paper." It has guided my work and my life, ever since 1982, and it has helped my wife and I define our hopes for our son.

The process of filling out and acting on "That One Piece of Paper" taught me a lot. Specifically, it taught me **the importance of the following ten things, often running contrary to what my studies and doctoral work had taught me previously.**

---

continued

Example
(Rich Feller's Flower)

Favorite People-Environment

1. Strong social, perceptual skills 2. Emotionally and physically healthy 3. Enthusiastically include others 4. Heterogeneous in interests and skills 5. Social changers, innovators 6. Politically, economically astute 7. Confident enough to confront/cry and be foolish 8. Sensitive to non-traditional issues 9. I and R (see page 74) 10. Non-materialistic

Favorite Values

1. Improve the human condition 2. Promote interdependence and futuristic principles 3. Maximize productive use of human/material resources 4. Teach people to be self-directed/self-responsible 5. Free people from self-defeating controls (thoughts, rules, barriers) 6. Promote capitalistic principles 7. Reduce exploitation 8. Promote political participation 9. Acknowledge those who give to the community 10. Give away ideas

Favorite Interests

1. Large conference planning 2. Regional geography & culture 3. Traveling on $20/day 4. Career planning seminars 5. Counseling techniques/theories 6. American policies 7. Fundamentals of sports 8. Fighting sexism 9. NASCAR auto racing 10. Interior design

Favorite Skills

1. Observational/learning skills • continually expose self to new experiences • perceptive in identifying and assessing potential of others 2. Leadership skills • continually searches for more resonsibility • sees a problem/acts to solve it 3. Instructing/interpreting/guiding • committed to learning as a life-long process • create atmosphere of acceptance 4. Serving/helping/human relations skills • shapes atmosphere of particular place • relates well in dealing with public 5. Detail/follow-through skills • handle great variety of tasks • resource broker 6. Influencing/persuading skills • recruiting talent/leadership • inspiring trust 7. Performing skills • getting up in front of a group (if I'm in control) • addressing small and large groups 8. Intuitional/innovative skills • continually develop/generate new ideas 9. Develop/plan/organize/execute • designing projects • utilizing skills of others 10. Language/read/write • communicate effectively • can think quickly on my feet

Favorite Working Conditions

1. Receive clinical supervision 2. Mentor relationship 3. Excellent secretary 4. Part of larger, highly respected organization with clear direction 5. Near gourmet and health food specialty shops 6. Heterogeneous colleagues (race, sex, age) 7. Flexible dress code 8. Merit system 9. Can bike/bus/walk to work 10. Private office with window

Geography

1. Close to major city 2. Mild winters/low humidity 3. Change in seasons 4. Clean and green 5. 100,000 people 6. Nice shopping malls 7. Wide range of athletic options 8. Diverse economic base 9. Ample local culture 10. Sense of community (pride)

Salary and Level of Responsibility

1. Can determine 9/12 month contract 2. Can determine own projects 3. Considerable clout in organization's direction without administrative responsibilities 4. Able to select colleagues 5. 3 to 5 assistants 6. $35K to $50K 7. Serve on various important boards 8. Can defer clerical and budget decisions and tasks 9. Speak before large groups 10. Can run for elected office

I learned from my Flower the importance of:

1. Chasing after passions, honoring strengths, and respecting skill identification

2. Challenging societal definitions of balance and success

3. Committing to something bigger than oneself

4. Living authentically and with joy

5. Being good at what matters to oneself and its relationship to opportunity

6. Finding pleasure in all that one does

7. Staying focused on well-being and life satisfaction

8. Personal clarity and responsibility for designing "possible selves"

9. Letting the world know, humbly but clearly, what we want

10. "Coaching" people amidst a world of abundance where individuals yearn for individual meaning and purpose more than they hunger for possessions, abject compliance with society's expectations, or simply fitting in

This technologically enhanced, global workplace we now face in the twenty-first century certainly challenges all we thought we knew about our life roles. Maintaining clarity, learning agility, and identifying development plans have become elevated to new and critical importance, if we are to maintain choice. As a result I've added the following four emphases to "Rich's Flower": *Have, do, learn,* and *give.* That is to say, I try to keep a running list (constantly updated) of ten things that I want to:

1. Have

2. Do

3. Learn

4. Give

Through the practice of answering the four questions listed above, I can measure change in my growth and development.

I feel so fortunate to have the opportunity to share with others how much I gained from the wisdom and hope embedded within "Rich's Flower."

I humbly offer my resume, home location and design, and family commitments on my website at www.mycahs.colostate.edu/Rich .Feller. I'd be honored to share my journey, and encourage others to nurture and shine light on their garden as well. I believe you'll find about 90 percent of the Flower's items influence our daily experience.

Rich Feller
Professor of Counseling and Career Development
University Distinguished Teaching Scholar
Colorado State University
Fort Collins, CO

Okay, you've got your completed Flower. A picture of who you are, in all your glory. Also, a picture of a dream job that you can now go looking for. Nice diagram. What do you do with it? Well, that's the subject of our next chapter.

What is success?
To laugh often and much;
To win the respect of intelligent people
and the affection of children;
To earn the appreciation of honest critics
and endure the betrayal of false friends;
To appreciate beauty;
To find the best in others;
To leave the world a bit better, whether by
a healthy child, a garden
patch or a redeemed social condition;
To know even one life has breathed
easier because you have lived;
This is to have succeeded.

> —Bessie Anderson Stanley, 1904
> Traditionally attributed to Ralph Waldo Emerson
> (1803–1882)

Chapter 6 **Networking and Social Media**

Okay, you've got your completed Flower done. That was the previous chapter. Now what? Your Flower pictorial is beautiful, but what does it mean? What's the next step? These are natural questions. And they bring us to *networking*.

If someone out of work knows only three words about their job-hunt, I'm willing to bet those three words will be: *resumes, interviews,* and *networking*. And if there's one really overworked word in that crowd, it's *networking*.

It's used by more job-hunters, and with the least understanding of it, than any other word that I can think of. Job-hunters will go endlessly to group meetings—job support groups, business presentations, college reunions, even beer parties or cocktail parties—and when you ask them what they're doing, they will say, "I'm unemployed. I'm networking. Isn't that what I'm supposed to do?"

Job-hunters will collect people's business cards day after day, week after week, convinced that this will somehow pay off down the line. At least, that's what they've always heard. They approach networking as something magical, based on the unproved belief: *"He or she who ends up with the most business cards, will be most successful in their job-hunt."*

Job-hunters will "friend" reflexively on Facebook and "link" with everyone they can on LinkedIn, trying to collect as many names as possible. Then there's always Google+.

And if you ask them *why* they are doing this, they will reply, "I dunno. I'm just networking!" And networking, and networking.

Bridge-People (*formerly called Contacts, Links, or Friends*)

Networking is necessary because of a *gap*. When you set out job-hunting there is a gap—between you and a job. That gap may be filled by anything: some needed information, or your resume, or a job posting on the Internet, or—well, you name it.

Most often, however, that gap gets filled by a person. Try asking workers you encounter in your daily life—waiters and waitresses, retail store clerks, supermarket check-out people, computer store salespeople, etc.—"How did you get your job here?" And nine times out of ten, they will say that some *person* told them about it—friend, family, school chum, doctor, a friend on Facebook, a link on LinkedIn, a video-game pal, a link on Instagram, Pinterest, or a total stranger. Either that person worked there, or used to work there, or knew somebody who worked there.

We can think of that person as *a bridge-person*. They know **you**; and they know **them**. They thus bridge the gap between you and a job. Bingo! You learn about the job. You end up getting the job. That is how most jobs get filled. Thanks to that *bridge-person*.

You can't identify a bridge-person until you have a target company or organization in mind. But when that time comes, here's how you go about identifying *bridge-people:*[1]

1. The website, LinkedIn, is your best friend here. Each employer you want to pursue should have a Company Profile page. (Unless the company is just *too small*.) Identify what place you want to approach, and look up its Company Profile page; go there.

2. Start with the company. Ask LinkedIn to tell you the people in your network who work for the company you are targeting. Then sort that list. You can sort it by *employees* there, who share:

   a. A LinkedIn group with You

   b. A former employer with You

   c. A school with You

---

1. I am indebted to my dear friend Susan Joyce for these ideas. She is at job-hunt.org ("put the dash in your job-hunt"). We are working on a book, together.

    d. An industry with You

    e. A language with You

    f. A specific location with You

3. Then go to your school. On that same Company Profile page, look for your school—if you ever attended voc-tech school, community college, college, university, or grad school, ask LinkedIn to tell you who among your fellow alumni work for the company or organization you are targeting.

4. Then go to the company activity. On that same Company Profile page, ask LinkedIn to tell you new hires (who), departures (who), job-title changes, job postings, number of employees who use LinkedIn, where current employees work, where current employees worked before they worked for *this* company, where former employees went after they worked for this company, etc. Insightful statistics!

5. As for connecting with the bridge-people whose names you discover, currently LinkedIn requires you to have one of their *paid* memberships, rather than the *free* one. But if they're still working at the company, you can phone the company and ask for them. Or you can search for their contact information through a larger search engine (Google their name!).

6. If you come up blank (no bridge-person can be found who knows *you* and also knows *them*) you can advertise on LinkedIn, for such connections. They have "ads by LinkedIn Members" available to you, for modest cost (so far!). You can also browse LinkedIn groups, and join those (ten at the most) that seem most likely to be seen by the kinds of companies you are trying to reach. However, don't just join them! Post intelligent questions, respond to intelligent "post-ers" that you think make sense. In other words, attain as high visibility there as you can; maybe *they* will come after *you*.

Bridge-people or not, never forget that people are crucial to your job-hunt—and beyond. We are social animals. Fish swim in water, we swim in a social context.

The Two Ways of Networking

So when you're about to job-hunt or change-careers, what do you need? You need to fill the gap. You need networks. You need intersections between you and other people.

Those intersections may be found—these days—in one of two ways. They may be found **on the Internet** and so-called *social media*; or they may be found out there in the world, by **actually sitting down with the person.**

We will explore, first of all, the tougher of these two: When you need to connect with people by going and actually talking to them face-to-face.

Networking: Part One

Overcoming the Handicap of Shyness: The PIE Method

In this first kind of networking, what's going to torpedo you? What handicap lies in wait? Well, *shyness* is at the top of the list. Call it anything else if you want to—fear, anxiety, nervousness, sweating—but *shyness* it is, and shyness it remains. Often, we, the unemployed, who may be absolute experts at connecting and communicating with people on the Internet—through computer games, apps, Facebook, LinkedIn, Twitter, Instagram, and other social media—suddenly turn to jelly when we have to go face-to-face with people.

Shy. A lot of us would never think to use that word to describe ourselves. But actually, surveys have found as many as 75 percent of us have been painfully shy at some point in our lives. Many of us still are. *(This always comes as a great surprise to my European friends, because they picture Americans as* assertive, aggressive, *and similar words. And sure, some of us are; but that's not who* most *of us are, especially when we're out of work, and have go sit across the desk from employers, face-to-face. I myself have been painfully shy, much of my life. No one would ever guess.)*

So, what to do if we are shy and feel utterly unequipped to tackle all of this? Well, a little bit of history here:

The late John Crystal often had to deal with this problem. So John suggested that the way anyone cures themselves of shyness is through **enthusiasm.** Yes, he said, if you're talking with someone, and you are enthusiastic about the topic under discussion, you will forget that you are shy, in your excitement. Everything depends on what you're talking about, and how you feel about that topic. So, he said, only go after a job you feel really enthusiastic about. Seek information only about a curiosity that you feel enthusiastic about the prospect of learning the answer to. And so on. And so forth.

John followed this up by inventing a practical three-stage plan of action, to cure job-hunters of shyness. Those who have followed John's advice in this regard have had a success rate of 86 percent in overcoming their shyness and fears, and finding a job.

Daniel Porot and I subsequently took John's system, and organized it. We observed that John was really recommending three types of *interviews*: **interviews for employment**, of course; but preceded, necessarily, by **interviewing just for information**, which—among other things—is a warm-up for employment interviews. And this was preceded by **practice interviewing**, which—among other things—is a warm-up for information interviews. Each prepares for the next; a three-stage plan, for overcoming shyness.

Daniel, Europe's premiere job-hunting expert, organized this into an attractive and well-thought-out chart; and gave it its now famous name: *"The PIE Method,"* which has helped thousands of job-hunters and career-changers in Europe, Asia, and the U.S.[2]

Why is it called *"PIE"*?

P is for the *warm-up* phase. John Crystal named this warm-up "The Practice Field Survey."[3] Daniel Porot calls it P for *pleasure.*

I is for "Informational Interviewing."

E is for the employment interview with the-person-who-has-the-power-to-hire-you.

How do you use this P for *practice* to get comfortable about going out and talking to people *one-on-one*?

---

2. Daniel has summarized his system in a book published here in the U.S. in 1996: it is called *The PIE Method for Career Success: A Unique Way to Find Your Ideal Job,* published by JIST Works, Inc. It is now basically out of print. (Almost 40 bucks, used, on Amazon.com, Barnesandnoble.com, or Alibris.com.) Daniel has a wonderful website of "career games," at www.careergames.com.
3. If you want further instructions about this whole process, I refer you to "The Practice Field Survey," pp. 187–196, in *Where Do I Go from Here with My Life?* by John Crystal and me, published by Ten Speed Press.

Initial:	Pleasure **P**	Information **I**	Employment **E**
Kind of Interview	Practice Field Survey	Informational Interviewing or Research	Employment Interview or Hiring Interview
Purpose	To Get Used to Talking with People to Enjoy It; to "Penetrate Networks"	To Find Out If You'd Like a Job, Before You Go Trying to Get It	To Get Hired for the Work You Have Decided You Would Most Like to Do
How You Go to the Interview	You Can Take Somebody with You	By Yourself or You Can Take Somebody with You	By Yourself
Who You Talk To	Anyone Who Shares Your Enthusiasm About a (for You) Non-Job-Related Subject	A Worker Who Is Doing the Actual Work You Are Thinking About Doing	An Employer Who Has the Power to Hire You for the Job You Have Decided You Most Would Like to Do
How Long a Time You Ask For	10 Minutes (and DON'T run over—asking to see them at 11:50 a.m. may help keep you honest, since most employers have lunch appointments at noon)	Ditto	Ditto (or 22 minutes; but notice the time, and keep your word)
What You Ask Them	Any Curiosity You Have about Your Shared Interest or Enthusiasm	Any Questions You Have about This Job or This Kind of Work	You Tell Them What It Is You Like about Their Organization and What Kind of Work You Are Looking For

Initial:	Pleasure **P**	Information **I**	Employment **E**
What You Ask Them (continued)	If Nothing Occurs to You, Ask: **1.** How did you start, with this hobby, interest, etc.? **2.** What excites or interests you the most about it? **3.** What do you find is the thing you like least about it? **4.** Who else do you know who shares this interest, hobby, or enthusiasm, or could tell me more about my curiousity? **a.** Can I go and see them? **b.** May I mention that it was you who suggested I see them? **c.** May I say that you recommended them? Get their name and address.	If Nothing Occurs to You, Ask: **1.** How did you get interested in this work and how did you get hired? **2.** What excites or interests you the most about it? **3.** What do you find is the thing you like the least about it? **4.** What kinds of challenges or problems do you have to deal with in this job? **5.** What skills do you need in order to meet those challenges or problems? **6.** Who else do you know of who does this kind of work, or similar work but with this difference_____? Get their name and address.	You tell them the kinds of challenges you like to deal with. What skills you have to deal with those challenges. What experience you have had in dealing with those challenges in the past.
Afterward: That Same Night	SEND A THANK-YOU NOTE.	SEND A THANK-YOU NOTE.	SEND A THANK-YOU NOTE.

This is achieved by choosing a topic—*any* topic, however silly or trivial—that is a pleasure for you to talk about with your friends, or family. To avoid anxiety, it should not be connected to any present or future careers that you are considering. Rather, the kinds of topics that work best, for this exercise, are:

- **a hobby** you *love*, such as skiing, bridge playing, exercise, computers, etc.
- **any leisure-time enthusiasm of yours**, such as a movie you just saw, that you liked a lot
- **a longtime curiosity**, such as how do they predict the weather, or what policemen do
- **an aspect of the town or city you live in**, such as a new shopping mall that just opened
- **an issue** you feel strongly about, such as the homeless, AIDS sufferers, ecology, peace, health, returning veterans, etc.

There is only one condition about choosing a topic: it should be something you *love* to talk about with other people; a subject you know nothing about, but you feel a great deal of enthusiasm for, is far preferable to something you know an awful lot about, but it puts you to sleep.

Having identified your enthusiasm, you then need to go talk to someone who is as enthusiastic about this thing, as you are. *For best results with your later job-hunt, this should be someone you don't already know.* Use the Yellow Pages, ask around among your friends and family, *who do you know that* loves *to talk about this?* It's relatively easy to find the kind of person you're looking for.

You love to talk about skiing? *Try a ski-clothes store, or a skiing instructor.* You love to talk about writing? *Try a professor on a nearby college campus, who teaches English.* You love to talk about physical exercise? *Try a trainer, or someone who does physical therapy.*

Once you've identified someone you think shares your enthusiasm, you then go talk with them. When you are face-to-face with your *fellow enthusiast*, the first thing you must do is relieve their understandable anxiety. *Everyone* has had someone visit them who has stayed too long, who has worn out their welcome. If your *fellow enthusiast* is worried about you staying too long, they'll be so preoccupied with this fear that they won't hear a word you are saying.

So, when you first meet them, ask for *ten minutes of their time, only.* Period. Stop. Exclamation point. And watch your wristwatch *like a hawk,* to be sure you stay no longer. *Never* stay longer, unless they *beg* you to. And I mean, *beg, beg, beg.*[4]

Then what? Well, a topic may have its own unique set of questions. For example, I love movies, so if I met someone who shared this interest, my first question would be, "What movies have you seen lately?" And so on. If it's a topic you love, and often talk about, you'll *know* what kinds of questions you begin with. But, if no such questions come to mind, no matter how hard you try, the following ones have proved to be good conversation starters for thousands of job-hunters and career-changers before you, no matter what their topic or interest.

So, look these over, memorize them (*or copy them on a little card that fits in the palm of your hand*), and give them a try:

Questions Shy People Can Practice With

Addressed to the person you're doing the Practice Interviewing with:

- How did you get involved with/become interested in this? (*"This"* is the hobby, curiosity, aspect, issue, or enthusiasm, that you are so interested in.)
- What do you like the most about it?
- What do you like the least about it?
- Who else would you suggest I go talk to who shares this interest?
- Can I use your name?
- May I tell them it was you who recommended that I talk with them?
- *Then, choosing one person from the list of several names they may have given you, you say,* "Well, I think I will begin by going to talk to this person. Would you be willing to call ahead for me, so they will know who I am, when I go over there?"

Incidentally, during this Practice Interviewing, it's perfectly okay for you to take someone with you—preferably someone who is more

---

4. A polite, "Oh, do you have to go?" should be understood for what it is: politeness. Your response should be, "Yes, I promised to only take ten minutes of your time, and I want to keep to my word." This will almost always leave a *very* favorable impression behind you.

outgoing than you feel you are. And on the first few interviews, let them take the lead in the conversation, while you watch to see how they do it.

Once it is *your turn* to conduct the interview, it will by that time usually be easy for you to figure out what to talk about.

Alone or with someone, keep at this Practice Interviewing until you feel very much at ease in talking with people and asking them questions about things you are curious about.

In all of this, as you're trying to conquer shyness, *fun* is the key. If you're having fun, you're doing it right. That depends, of course, on how enthusiastic you are, about what you're exploring.

If you're not having fun, you need to keep at it, until you are. It may take seeing four people. It may take ten. Or twenty. You'll know.

The Five Different Kinds
of Informational Interviewing

Now we come back to the problem of your completed but nameless Flower. What we've got here, at this point, is another *gap*. A gap, this time, between your Flower pictorial and your understanding of what job or career it points to. What's going to help you fill that gap? You guessed it: people.

Yes, we come here to the middle letter in **PIE:** Informational Interviewing.

There are five different kinds of information you can find out only or primarily by talking with people. But you want to go through these five kinds of Informational Interviewing—*these five kinds of networking*— in a certain logical order if you just finished your Flower pictorial. So, we'll call these *five steps.* Here they are, in order:

INFORMATIONAL INTERVIEWING STEP ONE:

How to Find Out What Job(s) Your Flower Points To

1. First, look at your completed Flower Diagram, and from the center of the Flower choose the top *three* of your favorite **Knowledges** (or fields of interest, favorite fields, or fields of fascination— whatever you want to call them). All nouns. On one piece of blank paper, say $8^1/_2$ x 11, or on your mobile device, copy these

in the top half of that paper, in their order of importance to you (most important at the top). Beneath them all, midway down the page, draw a line, straight across.

2. Then, look at the Skills petal on your completed Flower Diagram and choose your top *five* favorite **Transferable Skills**. All verbs. Copy them down, in order, below the line.

3. Now, take this page and show it to at least five friends, family members, or professionals whom you know. Ask them what jobs or work this page suggests to them. Tell them you just want them to take some wild guesses, combining as many of the eight factors on that page, as possible. Plan b: If they absolutely draw a blank, tell them interests or special knowledges (in the top half of the page) usually point toward a career field, while transferable skills (in the bottom half) usually point toward a job-title or job-level, in that field. So, ask them, in the case of your favorite special knowledges, "What career fields do these suggest to you?" And in the case of your transferable skills, "What job-title or jobs do these skills suggest to you?"

4. Jot down *everything* these people suggest to you, on your computer, iPad, smartphone, or small pad of paper. Whether you like their suggestions, or not. This is just brainstorming, for the moment.

5. After you have done this for a week or so, with everyone you meet, sit down and look at all these notes. Anything helpful or valuable here? If you see some useful suggestions, circle them and determine to explore them. If nothing looks interesting, go talk to five more of your friends, acquaintances, or people you know in the business world or nonprofit sector. Repeat, as necessary.

6. As you ponder any suggestions that look worth exploring, consider the fact we saw in chapter 5, that all jobs can be described as working primarily with *people* **or** working primarily with *information/data* **or** working primarily with *things*. Most jobs involve all three, but which is your *primary* preference? It is often your *favorite* skill that will give you the clue. If it *doesn't*, then go back and look at the *whole* Transferable Skills petal, on your Flower

Diagram. What do you think? Are your favorite skills weighted more toward working with *people*, or toward working with *information/data*, or toward working with *things*?

7. Just remember what you are trying to do here: find a name for your flower. What you call it—name of Flower, name of a field based on your favorite subjects, the name of your new career, or whatever—doesn't matter. You are trying to find the names of careers or jobs that would give you a chance to use your skills in the most effective way. You want competence, and therefore happiness, in the job-market.

8. If you would be unique, you must combine, as much as you can, two or three fields: that's what can make you unique, with very little competition from others.

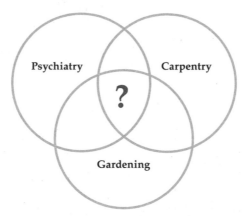

Here is how to go about doing that: let us say your three favorite knowledges are gardening and carpentry and a limited knowledge of psychiatry. What you want to do is use all three expertises, not just one of them—if you possibly can. So, put those three favorite knowledges on a series of overlapping circles, as seen above. Now, to figure out how to combine these three, imagine that each circle is a person; that is, in this case, Psychiatrist, Carpenter, and Gardener. You ask yourself which person took the longest to get trained in their specialty. The answer, here, is the psychiatrist. The reason you ask yourself this question, is that the person with the longest training is most likely to have the broadest overview of things. So, you go to see a psychiatrist, either at a private clinic or at a university or hospital. You ask for fifteen minutes of his or her time, and pay them if necessary. Then you ask the psychiatrist if he or she knows how to combine psychiatry with *one*—just one, initially—of your other two favorite knowledges. Let's say you choose gardening, here. "Doctor, do you know anyone who combines a knowledge of psychiatry with a knowledge of gardening or plants?"

Since I'm talking about a true story here, I can tell you what the psychiatrist said: "Yes, in working with catatonic patients, we often give them a plant to take care of, so they know there is something that is depending on them for its future, and its survival."

"And how would I also employ a knowledge of carpentry?"

"Well, in building the planters, that's a start, isn't it?"[5]

This is the way you explore how to combine your three favorite knowledges, all at once, no matter what those three may be. The Internet can also be useful, sometimes, with this research.

During this stage of your information gathering, don't ever think to yourself: "Well, I see what it is that I would die to be able to do, but I know there is no job in the world like that." Dear friend, you don't know any such thing. You haven't completed your informational interviewing, yet. Now I grant you that after you have completed it, and conducted your job-search, you still may not be able to find all that you want—down to the last detail. But you'd be surprised at how much of your dream you may be able to find.

Sometimes it will be found in stages. One retired man I know, who had been a senior executive with a publishing company, found himself bored to death in retirement, after he turned sixty-five. He decided he didn't care what field he worked in, at that point, so he contacted his favorite business acquaintance, who told him apologetically, "Times are tough. We just don't have anything open that matches or requires your abilities; right now all we need is someone in our mail room." The sixty-five-year-old executive said, "I'll take that job!" He did, and over the ensuing years steadily advanced once again, to just the job he wanted: as a senior executive in that organization, where he utilized all his prized skills, for a number of years. Finally, he retired for the second time, at the age of eighty-five.

---

5. (Parenthetically, healers also use pets as they do plants. See www.sniksnak.com/therapy.html.)

Always keep in mind your dream. Get as close to it as you can. Then be patient. You never know what doors will open up.

INFORMATIONAL INTERVIEWING STEP TWO:

How to Try On Careers Before You Decide Which Ones to Pursue

Maybe you're looking for the same kind of work you've previously done; you know that industry or field, and you know it well. Okay, then *you* can skip this step.

But what if you just can't find any jobs in your old field or industry (think: *record stores*). Suppose you just have to go for a career change. Or maybe you really *want* to do a career change. You've found one, or ones, that sound attractive. But before you go and get all the training or education it requires, or before you go job-hunting for that career, you need to *try it on.*

This is exactly analogous to shopping at a clothing store and trying on different suits (or dresses) that you see in their window or on their racks. Why do you try them on? Well, the suits or dresses that look *terrific* in the window don't always look so hot when you see them on *you.* The clothes don't hang quite right, etc.

It's the same with careers. Ones that *sound* terrific in books or in your imagination don't always look so great when you actually see them up close and personal.

What you want of course is a career that looks terrific—in the window, *and* also on you. So this is where you need to go talk to people who are already doing the kind of job or career that you're thinking about. The website LinkedIn should be invaluable to you, in locating the names of such people.

Once you find them, if they live nearby ask for twenty minutes of their time face to face—Starbucks?—and keep to your word, unless. during the chat they *insist* they want to go on talking. *Some* workers— not all—are desperate to find someone who will actually listen to them; you may come as an answer to their prayers.

Here are some questions that will help when you're talking *with workers who are actually doing the career or job you think you might like to do*:

- "How did you get into this work?"
- "What do you like the most about it?"

- "What do you like the least about it?"
- And, "Where else could I find people who do this kind of work?" (*You should always ask them for more than one name, here, so that if you run into a dead end at any point, you can easily go visit the other name[s] they suggested.*)

If at any point in these informational interviews with workers, it becomes more and more clear to you that this career, occupation, or job you are exploring definitely doesn't fit you, then the last question (above) gets turned into a different kind of inquiry:

- "Do you have any ideas as to who else I could talk to—*about my skills and special knowledges or interests*—who might know what other careers use the same skills and knowledge?" If they come up with names, go visit the people they suggest. If they can't think of anyone, ask them, "If you don't know of anyone, who do you think might know?"

Sooner or later, as you do this informational interviewing with workers, you'll find a career that fits you just fine. It uses your favorite skills. It employs your favorite special knowledges or fields of interest. Okay, now you must ask **how much training, etc., it takes, to get into that field or career.** You ask the same people you have been talking to, previously.

More times than not, you will hear *bad news*. They will tell you something like: "In order to be hired for this job, you have to have a master's degree and ten years' experience at it."

Is that so? Keep in mind that no matter how many people tell you that such-and-such are the rules about getting into a particular occupation, and there are no exceptions—believe me there *are* exceptions to almost *every* rule, except for those few professions that have rigid entrance examinations as, say, medicine or law. Otherwise, *somebody* has figured out a way around the rules. You want to find out who these people are, and go talk to them, to find out *how they did it.*

So, in your informational interviewing, you press deeper; you search for *exceptions*:

"Yes, but do you know of anyone in this field who got into it without that master's degree, and ten years' experience?

"And where might I find him or her?

"And if you don't know of any such person, who do you think might know?"

In the end, maybe—just maybe—you can't find any exceptions. It's not that they aren't out there; it's just that you don't know how to find them. So, what do you do when everyone tells you that such and such a career takes *years* to prepare for, and you can't find *anyone* who took a shortcut? What then?

Good news. Every professional specialty has one or more *shadow* professions, which require much less training. For example, instead of becoming a doctor, you can go into paramedical work; instead of becoming a lawyer, you can go into paralegal work; instead of becoming a licensed career counselor, you can become a career coach. There is always a way to get *close*, at least, to what you dream of.

INFORMATIONAL INTERVIEWING STEP THREE:

How to Find Out What Kinds of Organizations Have Such Jobs

Before you think of individual places where you might like to work, it is helpful to stop and think of all the *kinds* of places where one might get hired, so you can be sure you're casting the widest net possible. *(A fisherman's metaphor, of course.)*

Let's take an example. Suppose in your new career you want to be a teacher. You must then ask yourself: *"What kinds of places hire teachers?"* You might answer, *"Just schools"*—and finding that schools in your geographical area have no openings, you might say, *"Well, there are no jobs for people in this career."*

But wait a minute! There are countless other *kinds* of organizations and agencies out there, besides schools, that employ *teachers*. For example, corporate training and educational departments, workshop sponsors, foundations, private research firms, educational consultants, teachers' associations, professional and trade societies, military bases, state and local councils on higher education, fire and police training academies, and so on and so forth.

"Kinds of places" also means places with different *hiring options*, besides full-time, such as:

- places that would employ you part-time (maybe you'll end up deciding, or having, to hold down two or even three part-time jobs, which together add up to one full time job);
- places that take temporary workers, on assignment for one project at a time;
- places that take consultants, one project at a time; ·
- places that operate primarily with volunteers, etc.;
- places that are nonprofit;
- places that are for-profit;
- and, don't forget, places that you yourself could start up, should you decide to be your own boss (see chapter 12).

During this interviewing for information, you should not only talk to people who can give you a broad overview of the career that you are considering. You should also talk with actual workers in those kinds of organizations, who can tell you in more detail what the tasks are in the kinds of organizations that interest you.

INFORMATIONAL INTERVIEWING STEP FOUR:

How to Find Out the Names of Particular Places That Interest You

As you interview workers about their jobs or careers, somebody will probably innocently mention, somewhere along the way, actual names of organizations that have such kind of workers—plus what's good or bad about the place. This is important information for you. Jot it all down. Keep notes religiously!

But you will want to supplement what they have told you, by seeking out other people to whom you can simply say: "I'm interested in this kind of organization, because I want to do this kind of work; do you know of particular places like that, that I might investigate? And if so, where they are located?" Use face-to-face interviews, use LinkedIn, use the Yellow Pages, use search engines, to try to find the answer(s) to that question. Incidentally, you must not care, at this point, if they have *known* vacancies or not. The only question that should concern you for the moment is whether or not the place looks interesting, or even intriguing to you. *(The only caveat is that if times are still tough, you will probably want to modify your search to the extent that you investigate smaller places—100 or fewer employees—rather than larger; and newer places, rather than older.)* But for a successful job-hunt you should choose places based on *your interest in them*, and not wait to choose places until you've heard they have a vacancy. Vacancies can suddenly open up in a moment, and without warning. One job-hunter I know approached a place at 11:00 in the morning, and got the exact job he wanted; the vacancy had opened up at 9:30, when the previous employee suddenly quit and walked out.

What will you end up with, when this step is done? Well, you'll likely have either *too few names* or *too many* to go investigate. There are ways of dealing with either of these eventualities.

Too Many Names: You will want to cut the territory down, to *a* manageable number of *targets.*

Let's take an example. Suppose you discover that the career that interests you the most is *welding.* You want to be a welder. Well, that's a beginning. You've cut the 23 million U.S. job-markets down to:

• **I want to work in a place that hires welders.**

But the territory is still too large. There might be thousands of places in the country, that use welders. You can't go visit them all. So, you've got to cut down the territory, further. Suppose that on your Preferred Place to Live petal you said that you really want to live and work in the San Jose area of California. That's helpful: that cuts down the territory further. Now your goal is:

• **I want to work in a place that hires welders, within the San Jose area.**

But, the territory is still too large. There could be 100, 200, 300 organizations that fit that description. So you look at your Flower Diagram for further help, and you notice that under *working conditions* you said you wanted to work for an organization with fifty or fewer employees. Good, now your goal is:

- **I want to work in a place that hires welders, within the San Jose area, that has fifty or fewer employees.**

This territory may still be too large. So you look again at your Flower Diagram for further guidance, and you see that you said you wanted to work for an organization that works with, or produces, wheels. So now your statement of what you're looking for, becomes:

- **I want to work in a place that hires welders, within the San Jose area, has fifty or fewer employees, and makes wheels.**

Using your Flower Diagram, you can thus keep cutting down the territory, until the *"targets"* of your job-hunt are no more than ten places. That's a manageable number of places for you to *start with*. You can always expand the list later, if none of these ten turns out to be promising or interesting.

Too Few Names: In this case, you want to expand the territory. Your salvation here is probably not going to be Informational Interviewing face-to-face, but print or digital directories. There is, first of all, the Yellow Pages of your local phone book, either in print or online. Look under every heading that is of any interest to you. Also, see if the local chamber of commerce publishes a business directory; often it will list not only small companies but also local divisions of larger companies, with names of department heads; sometimes they will even include the North American Industry Classification System (NAICS) codes, which is useful if you want to search by the code of your chosen field. Thirdly, see if your town or city publishes a business newsletter, directory, or even a Book of Lists on its own. It will, of course, cost you, but it may be worth it. Some metropolitan areas (San Francisco comes to mind) have particularly helpful ones. Forty of them are listed at **www.bizjournals.com**.

5,708,000 POSSIBLE TARGETS (EMPLOYERS)

57,000 POSSIBLE TARGETS

5,700 POSSIBLE TARGETS

1,000 POSSIBLE TARGETS

500 POSSIBLE TARGETS

300 POSSIBLE TARGETS

60 POSSIBLE TARGETS

If you are diligent here, you won't lack for names, believe me—unless it's a very small town you live in, in which case you'll just have to cast your net a little wider, to include other towns, villages, or cities that are within commuting distance from you.

INFORMATIONAL INTERVIEWING STEP FIVE:

How to Learn All About a Place Before You Walk In

At some point you will be happy. You've found a career that you would die to do. You've interviewed people *actually doing that work*, and you like it even more. You've found names of places that hire people in that career.[6]

Okay, now what? Do you rush right over there? No, you research those places first. This is an absolute *must*. I met an employer once who said, "I'm so tired of people walking in the door and saying, 'Uh, what do you guys do, here?' that the next person who comes in and has researched who we are and what we do, I'm going to hire on the spot." He called me the next week to tell me that's exactly what he did. Remember, companies and organizations love to be loved. You demonstrate you love them when you have taken the trouble to find out all about them, before you walk in. That's called *research*.

What is it you should research about places before you approach them for a hiring-interview? Well, first of all, you want to know something about the organization from the inside: what kind of work they do there. Their style of working. Their so-called *corporate culture*. And what kinds of goals they are trying to achieve, what obstacles or challenges they are running into, and how your skills and knowledges can help them. In the interview you must be prepared to demonstrate that you have something they need. That begins with finding out *what* they need.

Secondly, you want to find out if you would enjoy working there. You want to take the measure of those organizations. Everybody takes the measure of a workplace, but most job-hunters or career-changers only do it *after* they are hired there.

In the U.S., for example, a survey of the federal/state employment service once found that 57 percent of those who found a job through

---

6. Just make sure you don't stop until you have the names of at least two careers, or jobs, that you think you could be happy doing. Never, ever, put all your eggs in one basket. I'll say again what I said in chapter 1: the secret of maintaining hope out there in the jungle is always having alternatives.

that service were not working at that job just thirty days later, and this was *because* they used the first ten or twenty days *on the job* to find out they didn't really like it there at all.

You, by doing this research ahead of time, are choosing a better path by far. Essentially, you are *screening out* places *before* you commit to them. How smart!

That's what you need to know, ahead of time. Now, how do you find it out? There are several ways, some face to face, some not:

- **Friends and Neighbors.** Ask *everyone* you know, if they know anyone who works at the places that interest you. And, if they do, ask them if they could arrange for you and that person to get together, for lunch, coffee, or tea. At that time, tell them why the place interests you, and indicate you'd like to know more about it. (*It helps a lot if your mutual friend is sitting there with the two of you, so the purpose of this little chat won't be misconstrued.*) This is the vastly preferred way to find out about a place. However, obviously you need a couple of additional alternatives up your sleeve, in case you run into a dead end here.

- **People at the Organizations in Question, or at Similar Organizations.** The website LinkedIn has an extensive menu where you can find a company's name. They will tell you who works there, or used to work there. An email will sometimes produce an interesting contact; but in this increasingly busy busy life, even the best-hearted people may sometimes say they just cannot give you any time, due to overload. If so, respect that.

  You can go in person to organizations and ask questions about the place. This is not recommended with large organizations that have security guards and so on. But with small organizations (in this case, 50 employees or fewer) you sometimes can find out a great deal by just showing up. Here, however, I must caution you about several *dangers*.

  First, make sure you're not asking them questions that are in print somewhere, which you could easily have read for yourself instead of bothering *them*. This irritates people.

  Second, make sure that you approach the gateway people— front desk, receptionists, customer service, etc.—*before* you ever approach people higher up in that organization.

Third, make sure that you approach subordinates rather than the top person in the place, if the subordinates would know the answer to your questions. Bothering the boss there with some simple questions that someone else could have answered is committing job-hunting suicide.

Fourth, make sure you're not using this approach simply as a sneaky way to get in to see the boss, and make a pitch for them to hire you. You said this was just information gathering. Don't lie. Don't ever lie. They will remember you, but not in any way you want to be remembered.

- **What's on the Internet.** Many job-hunters or career-changers think that every organization, company, or nonprofit, has its own website, these days. Not true. Sometimes they do, sometimes they don't. It often has to do with the size of the place, its access to a good Web designer, its desperation for customers, etc. Easy way to find out: if you have access to the Internet, type the name of the place into your favorite search engine (*Google, Bing, or whatever*) and see what that turns up. Try more than one search engine. Sometimes one knows things the others don't.

- **What's in Print.** Not books; their time lag is too great. But often the organization has timely stuff—in print, or on its website— about its business, purpose, etc. Also, the CEO or head of the organization may have given talks, and the front desk there may have copies of those talks. In addition, there may be brochures, annual reports, etc., that the organization has put out, about itself. How can you get copies? The person who answers the phone there, if you call, will know the answer, or at least know who to refer you to. Also, if it's a decent-size organization, public libraries in that town or city may have files on that organization—newspaper clippings, articles, etc. You never know; and it never hurts to ask your friendly neighborhood research librarian.

- **Temporary Agencies.** Many job-hunters and career-changers have found that a useful way to explore organizations is to go and work at a temporary agency. To find these, put into Google the name of your town or city and (on the same search line) the words "Temp Agencies" or "Employment Agencies." Employers turn to such agencies in order to find a) job-hunters who can work part-time for a limited number of days; and b) job-hunters who can work full-time for a limited number of days. The advantage to you of temporary work is that if there is an agency that loans out people with your particular skills and expertise, you get a chance to be sent to a number of different employers over a period of several weeks, and see each one from the inside. Maybe the temp agency won't send you to exactly the place you hoped for, but sometimes you can develop contacts in the place you love, even while you're temporarily working somewhere else—if both organizations are in the same field.

Some of you may balk at the idea of enrolling with a temporary agency, because you remember the old days when such agencies were solely for clerical workers and secretarial help. But the field

---

Send a Thank-You Note, Please, *Please*, Pleeze

After *anyone* has done you a favor, during your job-hunt, you must *be sure* to send them a thank-you note by the very next day, at the latest. Such a note goes to *anyone* who helps you, or who talks with you. That means friends, people at the organization in question, temporary agency people, secretaries, receptionists, librarians, workers, or whomever.

Ask them, at the time you are face-to-face with them, for their business card (if they have one), or ask them to write out their name and work address, on a piece of paper, for you. You *don't* want to misspell their name. It is difficult to figure out how to spell people's names, these days, simply from the sound of it. What sounds like "Laura" may actually be "Lara." What sounds like "Smith" may actually be "Smythe," and so on. Get that name and address, *but get it right,* please.

And let me reiterate: thank-you notes must be prompt. E-mail the thank-you note that same night, or the very next day at the latest. Follow it with a lovely copy, handwritten or printed, nicely formatted, and sent through the mail. Most employers these days prefer a printed letter to a handwritten one, but if your handwriting is beautiful, then go for it.

Don't ramble on and on. Your thank-you note can be just two or three sentences. Something like: *"I wanted to thank you for talking with me yesterday. It was very helpful to me. I much appreciated your taking the time out of your busy schedule to do this. Best wishes to you,"* and then sign it. Of course, if there's any additional thought you want to add, then add it. *Do* sign it.

has seen an explosion of services in the last decade, and as I mentioned elsewhere there are temporary agencies these days (*at least in the larger cities*) for many occupations. In your city you may find temporary agencies for: accountants, industrial workers, assemblers, drivers, mechanics, construction people, engineering people, software engineers, programmers, computer technicians, production workers, management/executives, nannies (for young and old), health care/dental/medical people, legal specialists, lawyers, insurance specialists, sales/marketing people, underwriters, professionals, financial services, and the like, as well as for the old categories: data processing, secretarial, and office services. See your local phone book, under "Temporary Agencies."

- **Volunteer Work.** Another useful way to research a place before you ever ask them to hire you there, is to volunteer your services at the place that interests you.

What If I Get Offered a Job Along the Way, While I'm Just Gathering Information?

Not likely. Let me remind you that during this part of your networking, you are talking to *workers*, not employers.

Nonetheless, an occasional employer *may* stray across your path during all this Informational Interviewing. And that employer *may* be so impressed with You, that they want to hire you, on the spot. So, it's *possible* that you'd get offered a job while you're still doing your information gathering. Not very *likely*, but *possible*. And if that happens, what should you say?

Well, if you're desperate, you will probably have to say *yes*. I remember one wintertime when I was in my thirties, with a family of five, when I had just gone through the knee of my last pair of pants, we were burning pieces of old furniture in our fireplace to stay warm, the legs on our bed had just broken, and we were eating spaghetti until it was coming out our ears. In such a situation, you can't afford to be picky. You've got to put food on the table, and stave off the debt-collectors. Now.

But if you're not *desperate*, if you have time to be more careful, then you respond to the job-offer in a way that will buy you some time. You tell them what you're doing: that the average job-hunter tries to screen a job *after* they take it. But you are examining careers, fields, industries, jobs, and particular organizations *before* you decide where you would do your best and most effective work. And you're sure this employer would do the same, if they were in your shoes. (If they're not impressed with your thoroughness and professionalism, at this point, than I assure you this is not a place where you want to work.)

Add that your Informational Interviewing isn't finished yet, so it would be premature for you to accept their job offer, until you're *sure* that this is the place where you could be most effective, and do your best work.

Then, you add: "Of course, I'm tickled pink that you would want me to be working here. And when I've finished my personal survey, I'll be glad to get back to you about this, as my preliminary impression is that this is the kind of place I'd like to work in, and the kind of people I'd like to work for, and the kind of people I'd like to work with."

In other words, *if you're not desperate yet,* you don't walk immediately through any opened doors, but neither should you allow them to shut.

As I said, this scenario is highly unlikely. You're networking with *workers.* But it's nice to be prepared ahead of time, in your mind, just in case it does ever happen.

Networking: Part Two

Networking Through Social Media

Networking isn't just about going face to face. Networking has greatly changed from what it was, oh, even ten years ago. I said earlier that fish swim in water, humans swim in a social context. With the advent of social media on the Web, we are no longer just swimming in a pool; we have moved to an ocean.

Thanks to social media sites like *Facebook, Twitter, LinkedIn, Yelp, YouTube, TripAdvisor, Wikipedia, MakeProjects, GroupMe,* and similar— communities gather,[7] share information, make recommendations, aid decision-making, foster cooperation and invention, plus new ways to

---

7. Many of the social media sites create groups you can join. As a consequence, 82 percent of social network users and 85 percent of Twitter users participate in groups, according to the Pew Internet and American Life Project's 2011 survey.

work,[8] and new ways to get in touch with each other—it is an ocean indeed.

> *Information and Introduction. It's so much easier now to do network-ing as information-gathering, or networking as a search for "bridge-people," than was ever possible before. It used to be an agonizing desperate search for the right people. Now, for anybody with even a modest acquaintance with social media, that search is one hundred times easier. Faster. More accurate. And, less time-consuming.*

Here are a few background thoughts about social media:

1. Mastery of social media is becoming important to employers, with the result that there are actually job-titles for people with this expertise: *online community manager, social media analyst, chief social media officer,* and even *chief listening officer* (responsible for seeing the company actually listens, and responds, to what's being said out there—something that Toyota, for example, failed to do, according to a recent study[9]).

2. There are tools for creating social networks where none existed before, particularly within your own company, like **https://yammer.com**.

3. Each social media site has a different scope, a different emphasis, and a different audience. Look for the things that matter to you. Choose a site appropriately. If you have a particular issue, and you just don't know how to find the appropriate social site, do a search on Google. For example, if ex-military who are hunting for help in getting back into civilian life, Google "ex-military job-hunting" they will turn up a number of sites to help them with that job-hunt, such as: **www.jobswap.com, www.dol.gov/vets, LinkedIn.com, www.hireds.com, http://fedshirevets.gov,** and **www.woundedwarriorproject.org.**

---

8. Social media is beginning to change the way work is done. See www.menloinnovations.com where all work—all work—is done in pairs.
9. A study reported in the May 23, 2011, issue of the *New York Times.*

4. You can stay up-to-date on social media developments, by sub-scribing to the free daily e-mail called *Smartbrief on Social Media*. Sign up at **www.smartbrief.com/socialmedia**.

5. For an extensive list of current social networking websites go to **http://tinyurl.com/k2jhx**. You can click on the little icon imme-diately beneath "Global Alexa Page Ranking" and get them listed in their order of popularity (from "Most Popular" down to "Least Popular").

Now let's look at some of the most popular social media sites, and see how they might be helpful with your *networking*:

LinkedIn

Website url: **www.linkedin.com**

Background: Business-oriented networking website. 161+ million users worldwide, with more than 44 million of them in the U.S.

General Description: 70 to 90 percent of employers, depending on which survey you look at, use LinkedIn for trolling in general, or researching a job-hunter in particular.

Usefulness to Job-Hunters:

1. LinkedIn allows you to post a mini-version of your resume, which they call your Profile. (*Be sure it is as complete as you can possibly make it! LinkedIn says you are 40 times more likely to be approached if your profile is complete, than if it is not.*)

2. LinkedIn allows you to have recommendations from any of your links. So, don't just sit there; encourage those who know you well to post a recommendation of you or your work: 85 percent of employers say a positive online reputa-tion influences their hiring decisions.

3. LinkedIn enables you to click on "Companies," and then elect to "follow" particular companies that interest you.

4. LinkedIn has "Jobs" at the top of its homepage. Click on it, and see what openings LinkedIn knows about, currently.

5. LinkedIn lets you search for particular job vacancies, using the Advanced Search Option, by keyword, location—country,

postal code, miles from a location—experience level, industry, company, job-title, job function, and date posted.

6. LinkedIn allows you to search for people in particular business fields where you are, regardless of whether you know
   them or not.

7. LinkedIn tells you who might be "bridge-people" (they call
   them "inside connections" here) for particular companies.
   How? *JobInsider,* which is part of the Browser Toolbar for
   Firefox, or Internet Explorer. If you have access to either
   of these Web browsers, click on "Tools" at the bottom of
   any LinkedIn page, and choose *JobInsider.* Then when you
   are browsing *Monster, CareerBuilder, HotJobs, Craigslist, Dice,
   Vault, and the like,* if you click on a particular company's
   ad, it will identify people you are linked to, who work at
   that company, or people in your groups, whom you can ask
   to be introduced to. This is explained in a video at **http://
   tinyurl.com/3kt5mv8.**

8. While LinkedIn is free, they have a Premium membership
   (of course), where—for either $30 or $50 a month (choose
   one)—you get extra attention and privileges.

9. For more detailed ideas on LinkedIn and job search, the
   best article IMHO is by Guy Kawasaki, which you can
   find at **http://tinyurl.com/3thvknr.** He has a related blog
   for small businesses on LinkedIn, at **http://tinyurl.com/
   yevgehz.**

LinkUp

Website url: **http://linkup.com**

Background: This is a job-search engine, *not to be confused with
LinkedIn.*

General Description: This site pulls job openings only from
employers' websites (24,378 at current count).

Usefulness to Job-Hunters: If you live in areas covered by
LinkUp, you may find a job opening here.

Facebook

Website url: www.facebook.com

Background: Hugely popular; more than 900 million users worldwide.

General Description: The world's largest social media site (but you probably already knew that).

Usefulness to Job-Hunters:

1. Facebook lets you sign up on pages devoted to Job-hunting and Careers. For example, www.facebook.com/jobhunting.

2. Facebook has an app that enables you to hunt for people who work at a particular company or organization, or who share a particular interest of yours: www.facebook.com/profilesearch.

3. Facebook has an app that enables you to see where your friends work, and helps you build a professional network, plus discover job openings: http://apps.facebook.com/careeramp.

4. Facebook has an app that enables you to do networking, find friends of friends, and search millions of job listings: http://branchout.com.

Twitter

Website url: http://twitter.com

Background: A social networking and micro-blogging site; 8 percent of Internet users are on Twitter.

General Description: Allows you to send micro-messages using 140 characters or fewer.

Usefulness to Job-Hunters:

1. Twitter will take a background. When you are out of work, you can convey your status in that background (tastefully, professionally). For a tutorial on how to do this, go to http://tinyurl.com/5obsoue.

2. Twitter will take a bio. Mention what you're looking for, there. You have 140 characters, so practice the art of succinctness. Put a link to an online resume in your bio.

3. Twitter will take an avatar. Make it professional looking.

4. Twitter has a "follow" option. Follow anyone who is helpful to your job-hunt. If you don't have a clue, follow Susan Joyce of **job-hunt.org**, Internet expert Joel Cheesman of **http://cheesman.typepad.com**, and/or Guy Kawasaki (you can follow his top ten per day from @guykawasaki10).

5. Tweet about your job search. Make *sure* you've done your homework first, and can state *exactly* what kind of work you're looking for.

6. Put a link in some of your tweets to your website, if you have one. *If you don't have one, and you are an expert in some area of knowledge or performance, start your own website. See* **http://bravenet.com** *for free help, or* **www.bluehost.com** *for inexpensive hosting ($6 a month).* Establish yourself as an expert in your field on Twitter.

7. Sign up at **www.twitjobsearch.com** to locate various job-opportunities around the world. Choose what they call "channels" and then receive instant notification of jobs thereafter. Also sign up at **http://tweetmyjobs.com**.

Texting

Website url: None. You choose a phone number on your contacts list, and then select "Send text."

Background: Wildly popular.

General Description: Text messaging between mobile phone users. Allows you to send brief text messages (160 English characters or less) using the Short Message Service (SMS) or more ambitious messages containing image, video, and sound content (known as MMS messages).

Usefulness to Job-Hunters: For the infinite number of occasions where you need instant help, texting is very useful. For example, you're on your way to an interview and you suddenly think of a question you might be asked, that you don't know how to answer. You can text a more experienced friend and get the answer before you even arrive at the door of the employer. Moreover, it's helpful to have that answer spelled out on your mobile screen, as you go up in the elevator (tall building??) so you can practice.

Yelp

Website url: **https://yelp.com** *(https as opposed to http in any site's url, means their information is heavily encrypted [128 bit], which is considered unhackable).*

Background: Has more than 40 million unique visitors per month.

General Description: Community reviews of various businesses.

Usefulness to Job-Hunters: If there is a particular business or organization you are interested in, you may find feedback about it, here.

Stack Exchange

Website url: **http://stackexchange.com**

Background: A network of 51 question and answer sites, with a community contributing, answering, evaluating, and voting; same genre as Quora, Aardvark, Answers.com, etc.

General Description: Useful for finding fast answers to puzzling questions.

Usefulness to Job-Hunters: When you're trying to find something, someone, some business, this is a good place to go to, and see if they know the answer, without your having to do detailed research *forever*. Great time-saver.

Skype

Website url: **www.skype.com**

Background: Over 665 million registered users, bought by eBay in 2005, Microsoft in 2011.

General Description: Telephone calls over the Internet, utilizing both voice and video; free if the hookup is between registered users.

Usefulness to Job-Hunters: You can use video interviewing for informational interviewing with members of your network who live far away. More important, if an employer lives in another country of interest to you, and you or they want to do an interview, this is an inexpensive way to do it. If an employer can only talk to you over the phone, this at least adds video to your phone call, if the employer is also a Skype user. You can find interview tips on the Web at sites such as Alison Doyle's **http://tinyurl.com/nmbt5r.**

YouTube

Website url: **www.youtube.com**

Background: Wildly popular; 375 million unique visitors offered 75 billion video streams in 2011.

General Description: You can find a video on almost any subject, or post a video of your own, thus saving you from using up bandwidth on your own website (if you have one).

Usefulness to Job-Hunters: You can post a video resume, you can demonstrate your skills in a demonstration video you shoot, and post, etc. You can create your own channel through a widget (**www.widgetbox.com/widgets**). Widgets can be embedded on all your other sites, as well. You might even find some videos devoted to job-hunting techniques, such as: **http://tinyurl.com/4ynl42n** *(smile).*

Blogs

Website url: if it's your blog, you know the url. If you're looking for someone else's, do a search through Google, or Technorati (below).

Background: 160 million blogs, averaging 1 million posts a day according to Technorati (**http://technorati.com**)—the central headquarters for all things blog.

General Description: At their best, blogs offer an expert's advice and wisdom.

Usefulness to Job-Hunters: If you can find a blog on your particular field or industry, you may discover openings through that blog. Also consider starting your own blog related to the field in which you are you looking for work, where—if you keep your blog focused—you can develop a reputation as an expert in your specialty, thus attracting the attention of prospective employers— maybe. (*Possible but not likely; still, you never know. It's worth trying!*) Remember, the Web is the modern way to attract attention to yourself. A blog, carefully managed, can ideally serve that purpose. Of course, you are only one out of 160 million blogs, so don't put all your eggs in this basket.

Online Universities

Website url: **www.phoenix.edu**; **www.kaplan.edu**; **www.capella .edu**

Background: According to Global Language Monitor's July 2010 ranking, the three top online universities are the University of Phoenix, Kaplan University, and Capella University.

General Description: Offers both courses and degree programs, either by yourself or interacting with an instructor or other students online.

Usefulness to Job-Hunters: You can go to school online, get trained in new skills, etc., while still pursuing your job-hunt. For example, you can get trained in such skills as using a computer or particular software programs, accounting, marketing, business plans, etc. You can even get a college degree while job-hunting.

The Future Is Coming at Us, Fast

These are some of the principal sites that job-hunters are turning to, today. But what of tomorrow? Tomorrow is populated with clouds, and apps, and QR tags, and new technologies, as yet undreamed. And one thing you can be sure of: with so many people out of work—not only here, but around the world—some bright souls are going to figure out how to make these serve job-hunters and career-changers, whatever else they may do. Maybe one of those bright souls will even turn out to be You.

Dangers of Living in a Social Media World

Social media sites are wonderful. And useful. Amazingly so. But entering social networks is like setting out to explore a mysterious forest. There is much there that is awe-inspiring, and beautiful to behold; you will be so glad you set out on this journey.

But also, there are dangers lurking in that forest: wild beasts, often ravenous ones.

The first beast is called *Identity Theft.* You must take care not to give your Social Security number or credit card information to any site whose url does not begin with *https.* That *s* is important. Just *http* won't do. You want a secure site, one whose url begins with https, which means it's encrypted (128 bit) and virtually unhackable. But be warned: this beast usually tries to lure you into its lair by offering to give you something for practically nothing, or to claim to straighten out something that is wrong with your bank account, or credit card, or financial records. Don't give them the information they ask for. If you think something might genuinely be wrong, disconnect from the site giving you that warning, and once you're free of them, go dial the Internet address of the bank, or whatever, using a lookup through Google. Never use the site *the beast* suggests.

The second wild beast waiting for you in the social media forest is called *Fraud.* This beast takes the initiative in approaching you, and basically offers you money you know you're not entitled to, or asks you to deposit money for them (their check is always bogus) and give them back a portion of it (before their check bounces!). In the U.S. the FBI maintains a helpful list of fraudulent schemes, and what you can do to avoid being suckered (**www.fbi.gov/scams-safety/fraud**).

The third beast is called *Unwarranted Charges on Your Bill.* You get a notice to call them back about *anything*—an "undeliverable package," or whatever. When you call that phone number (area codes 284, 473, 649, 664, 784, 809, or 876) you are calling the Caribbean, and the charges will probably run you $50 or more on your next phone bill. And if you sign up for some service or subscription online, always study your credit card bill monthly, to see if they are continuing to charge you multiple times, when you thought it would only be once.

The fourth beast is called *False Reviews.* You will have to be on your guard against this one if you have your own business and/or your own website. Competitors may (can) pay someone to post rave reviews on their site (but not yours) or negative reviews on your site. Where do they go shopping for such helpful(!) people? Oh, from among their loyal friends, or by going to such otherwise innocent sites as fiverr (http://fiverr.com) and hiring someone to do it for them.

The fifth beast is called *Rumors*. You know, such things as "Steve Jobs is giving away trial iPads for $15"—that sort of thing. Go to www .snopes.com to find out what's true, and what isn't. (Steve: R.I.P.)

The sixth and final beast is *The Social Media Site That Will Not Die.* You go social, you try it out for a while, you want to terminate your account there, but you just can't. You try everything, but nothing works. What now? Well, fortunately, there is a site designed to help you precisely with that problem. It's called http://suicidemachine.org. Its sole mission is to help you get off social media sites you no longer want to be on; it works, too! (A similar site, Seppukoo, died in February of 2011.)

Conclusion

In this post-recessionary world, networking is an essential job-finding skill. But most of us, newly unemployed, don't understand why we should network, and what we should network *about*. And most of us think networking is just confined to social media, and the Internet. Or just a matter of collecting a lot of business cards.

We need at once a broader and a more detailed understanding of networking, if we want to survive in this twenty-first century. This chapter was long, but it was long because networking—rightly understood—has to be described in abundant detail.

I wanted to emphasize in this chapter a forgotten truth: there are two main kinds of networking. And, **even in this social media age, going face to face is still critically important.** Getting good at doing that, is often the secret of job-hunting success. And supplementing that with the social media world makes networking easier and more effective than it ever used to be. So many interesting, helpful websites on our laptops, smartphones, and tablets!

Just remember: all kinds of networking depend, for their effectiveness, on your having first done your homework . . . understanding fully who you are, by completing the Flower exercise back in chapter 5.

But suppose you don't want to do that? Too much trouble! Takes too long! Well, there are faster ways of choosing a career. That's the subject of our next chapter.

Fairy Godmother,
Make that eight mice, one pumpkin, and
Four pairs of glass slippers, would you?
I'm trying to think big, here.

—Cinderella (edited)

Chapter 7 Five Ways to Choose or Change Careers

If you wandered in, in the middle of the *previous* chapter, you could be forgiven for thinking that *it* was the chapter dealing with choosing a career.

After all, it prescribed and described a careful, thorough process for ensuring that you were choosing a career that fit you like a glove: a dream career, or dream job, as it is often called.

The step-by-step process described there, involved:

1. Doing the Flower Exercise, which gave you the basic building blocks of Who You Are, so you could match a career to You.

2. Then getting names of careers that fit those building blocks (*or petals*).

3. Then figuring out how to combine three fields into one career, so as to make yourself unique.

4. Then "trying on" the jobs to see if they fit *You*, by talking to actual workers in that kind of career.

5. Then finding out what *kinds* of organizations have such jobs.

6. Then finding out the *names* of particular places that interest you, where you could do your most effective work.

7. And, finally, learning about particular places before walking in to talk to them about working there, whether or not they have a known vacancy at that moment.

Essentially, what this way of choosing your next career does, is illustrated in the following diagram:

THE SYSTEMATIC BREAKDOWN AND BUILDING UP TO DEFINE A CAREER THAT FITS YOU

But maybe this demands more of you than you're willing to give, and you want to find some other way of choosing or changing careers. Not so much *thinking*. Not so much time. Suppose you know what you'd like to do, but it's a very different career than you presently have. Let's say you are presently *an accountant working for a television network*, and you want to become *a reporter on new medical developments*.

If you go out into the job-market as the first—accountant in the television industry—and you try to find a job as the second—reporter in medicine—well, it can sometimes be done, particularly if while you are still working at your present career, you start up a blog or website devoted to the field of medicine, and new breakthroughs. Once you become well known on the Web in this new role, you *may* develop a reputation for yourself, and thus have some legitimacy in looking for the new career flat out. But what if? What if that doesn't work? Then what do you do? What's your Plan b? Or c?

Choosing or Changing a Career in Two Steps

Here's a plan that has worked very well for many career-changers. Let's start simple: a job is *a job-title* in a *field*. A dramatic career-change involves trying to change both at the same time. It's what's called a Difficult Path in the diagram on page 170. Problem, you can't claim any prior experience. Interviewer: "Were you ever a reporter before?" Your answer: *No.* Interviewer: "Were you ever in the medical field before?" Your answer: *No.*

On the other hand, if you change only one of these *at a time* you can always claim prior experience. Let's say, in the chart on the next page, you make two successive moves, over a period of say three years: A to B to D. Interviewer during the first move: "Were you ever in this kind of work before?" Your answer: *"Yes, I've been an accountant for x number of years."* Interviewer during your second move: "Were you ever in this kind of work before?" Your answer: *"Yes, I've been in medicine for x number of years."*

On the other hand, let's say in the chart on the next page, you make a different set of two moves in a period of say three years: A to C to D. Interviewer during your first move: "Were you ever in this kind of work before?" Your answer: *"Yes, I've been in television for x number of years."* Then, interviewer during your second move: "Have you ever done this kind of work before?" Your answer: *"Yes, I've been a reporter for x number of years."*

Thus, by making the career change in two jumps rather than one, you are always able to claim (legitimately) that you are *experienced*. Your likelihood of getting hired is infinitely greater.

THREE TYPES OF CAREER-CHANGE, VISUALIZED

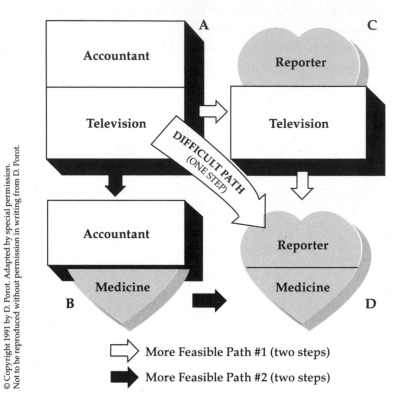

The Third Way of Choosing or Changing a Career

Okay, besides the Flower Exercise and its follow-up, and then the Two-Step Process, what's the third way of choosing or changing a career?

Now aren't you smart! Yes, you guessed it: the third way is Testing.

I'm not sure how well they work, but you will find vocational (and psychological) tests[1] everywhere: in books, on the Internet, in the offices of guidance counselors, or vocational psychologists, career coaches,

---

1. They're technically not "tests." Their real name is instruments, or assessments. But we'll use the popular name for them, here.

etc. And sometimes this turns out to be exactly the kind of guidance, the kind of insight, the kind of direction, that career choosers or changers are looking for.

But why only *sometimes?* Why doesn't this search for *a magic bullet* always work? Aha! Good question!

Six Warnings About Testing

1. You are absolutely unique. There is no person in the world like you. It follows from this that no test can measure YOU; it can only describe the family to which you belong.

   Tests tend to divide the population into what we might call groups, tribes, or families—made up of all those people who answered the test the same way. After you've taken any test, don't ever say to yourself, "This must be who I am." (No, no, this must be who your family am.[2])

   I grew up in the Bolles family (surprise!) and they were all very "left-brained." I was a maverick in that family. I was right-brained. Fortunately, my father was an immensely loving man, who found this endearing. When I told him the convoluted way by which I went about figuring out something, he would respond with a hearty affectionate laugh, and a big hug, as he said: "Dick, I will never understand you." Tests are about families, not individuals. The results of any test are descriptors—not of you, but of your family—i.e., all those who answered the test the same way you did. The SAI family. Or the blue family. Or the INTJ family. Or whatever. The results are an accurate description of that family of people, in general; but are they descriptors also of you? Depends on whether or not you are a maverick in that family, the same way I was in mine. These family characteristics may or may not be true in every respect to you. You may be exactly like that group, or you may be different in important ways.

2. Don't try to figure out ahead of time how you want the test to come out. Stay loose and open to new ideas.

   It's easy to develop an emotional investment that the test should come out a certain way. I remember a job-hunting workshop where I asked

---

2. Yes, I know that is bad grammar. But press on: if you want to explore testing in any more depth, there is an excellent course online, from S. Mark Pancer, at Wilfred Laurier University in Waterloo, Ontario, Canada, at www.wlu.ca/page.php?grp_id=265&p=2941. Pay special attention to Lectures 1 and 19.

*everyone to list the factors they liked about any place where they had
ever lived, and then prioritize those factors, to get the name of a new
place to live. We had this immensely lovable woman from Texas in the
workshop, and when we all got back together after a "break" I asked her
how she was doing. With a glint in her eye she said, "I'm prioritizing,
and I'm gonna keep on prioritizin', until it comes out: Texas!" That was
amusing, as she intended it to be; it's not so amusing when you try to
make the test results come out a certain way. If you're gonna take tests,
you need to be open to new ideas. If you find yourself always trying to
outguess the test, so it will confirm you on a path you've already decided
upon, then testing is not for you.*

3. In taking a test, you should just be looking for clues, hunches, or
   suggestions, rather than for a definitive answer that says "this is
   what you must choose to do with your life."

   *And bear in mind that an online test isn't likely to be as insightful as
   one administered by an experienced psychologist or counselor, who may
   see things that you can't. But keep saying this mantra to yourself, as you
   read or hear the test results: "Clues. Clues, I'm only looking for clues."*

4. Take several tests and not just one. One can easily send you down
   the wrong path.

   *People who do a masters or doctorate program in "Testing and Mea-
   surement" know that tests are notoriously flawed, unscientific, and inac-
   curate. Sometimes tests are more like parlor games than anything else.
   Basing your future on tests' outcomes is like putting your trust in the
   man behind the curtain in* The Wizard of Oz.

5. In good career planning, you're trying, in the first instance,
   to broaden your horizons, and only later narrow your options
   down; you are *not* trying to narrow them down from the outset.

   Bad career planning looks like this:

   *Most computerized tests embody the idea of starting
   with a wide range of options, and narrowing them
   down. So, each time you answer a question, you narrow down the number of options. For example, if you
   say, "I don't like to work outdoors," immediately all
   outdoor jobs are eliminated from your consideration,
   etc., etc.*

A model of good career planning looks like this, instead:

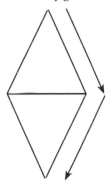

Good career-choice or career planning postpones the "narrowing down," until it has first broadened your horizons, and expanded the number of options you are thinking about. For example, you're in the newspaper business; but have you ever thought of teaching, or drawing, or doing fashion? You first expand your mental horizons, to see all the possibilities, and only then do you start to narrow them down to the particular two or three that interest you the most.

So, what's a good test? All together now: *a test that broadens to show you new possibilities for your life.*

And, what's a bad test? Again, all together: *a test that narrows the possibilities for your life. Often this is the result of a counselor's interpretation of a test, or rather misinterpretation.*

I'll give you an example: I met a man who, many years before, had taken the Strong Inventory.[3] *He was told, by his counselor, that this inventory measured that man's native gifts or aptitudes. And, in his particular case, the counselor said, the inventory revealed he had no mechanical aptitude whatsoever. For years thereafter, this man told me, "I was afraid to even pick up a hammer, for fear of maiming myself. But there finally came a time in my life when my house needed aluminum siding, desperately, and I was too poor to hire anyone else to do it for me. So I decided I had to do it myself, regardless of what the test said. I climbed the ladder, and expected to fail. Instead, it was a glorious experience! I had never enjoyed myself so much in my whole life. I later found out that the counselor was wrong. The inventory didn't measure aptitudes; it only measured current interests. Now, today, if I could find that counselor, I would wring his neck with my own bare hands, as I think of how much of my life he ruined with his misinterpretation of that test."*

6. Testing will always have "mixed reviews." On the one hand, you can run into successful men and women who will tell you they took this or that test twenty years ago, and it made all the difference in their career direction and ultimate success.

---

3. See www.personalitydesk.com and similar websites.

Other men and women, however, will tell you a horror story about their encounter with testing, like the one just mentioned.

So, it's up to you. If you like tests, help yourself. There are lots of them on the Internet. Counselors can also give them to you, for a fee; if you want one, shop around.

If you want to know where to start, you might try these tests, which are the ones I personally like the best:

- *Dr. John Holland's Self-Directed Search*
  We saw this already in chapter 5 with the People petal (page 74) but in case you don't remember, this is at: **www.self-directed-search.com** and costs $4.95

- *Supplemented by the University of Missouri's Career Interests Game,* at **http://tinyurl.com/yeu4zvv**

- *Carolyn Kalil's True Colors Test,* at **www.truecolorscareer.com/quiz.asp**

If you want further suggestions, you can type "career tests" or "person-ality tests" into Google, and see what turns up. Michael Robinson's web-site, **www.careerplanner.com**, for example, has both: a personality test that's free, and a detailed career test with matching careers, that costs 32 bucks.

The Fourth Way of Choosing or Changing a Career

We continue thumbing through our menu of the various ways to choose or change a career. If neither **The Flower Exercise**, nor **The Two-Step Process**, nor **Testing** gives you the answers you want, or the process you want, there is a fourth way: the Internet. More specifically, there is **O*Net Online**, which we mentioned earlier in chapter 5. It has an interesting history, which I won't bore you with. But what it has become is a digital, online treasure house of information, and up-to-date information at that, about careers.

Go browse the site (**www.onetonline.org**) and you will see. Sug-gested careers (or occupations) are grouped or classified by any or all of the following: by industries in great demand, green economies, largest number of openings anticipated, STEM disciplines (that would be Science, Technology, Engineering, and Math), amount of preparation or training required, O*NET-SOC codes, Military Occupation Classification (equivalencies), abilities required, occupational knowledge required, interests, skill sets, work values, work activities required, values you want at work, tasks, duties, tools, technology, machines, equipment, software, and so on. It goes on and on. Then, once you find an occupation you want to know more about, it uses a specially developed Content Model (**www.onetcenter.org/content.html**), which can run ten to twelve pages of print-out for each occupation. Run by the U.S. government's Department of Labor, it is very thorough, but also very limited.[4] Chief among its limitations is the fact that while its predecessor, *The Dictionary of Occupational Titles,* Fourth Edition, covered 12,741 occupations, O*Net covers only 800 or so.

That's a lot of careers, occupations, and jobs left *uncovered and unmentioned.* Economics (cost) was apparently a large part of the reason for this decision. Still, you may find a lot of very helpful stuff, there. Especially for returning veterans (**www.mynextmove.org/vets**).

Oh by the way, in case you were curious: O*Net stands for Occupational Information Network.

The Fifth and Last Way of Choosing or Changing a Career

Well, okay, so if neither **The Flower Exercise,** nor **The Two-Step Process,** nor **Testing,** nor **O*Net Online** pleased you, *of course* there is a fifth way to choose or change a career.

This one is based not primarily on your needs or wishes, but on projections about the coming needs of the job-market itself, during the present decade, 2010–2020. **What the Job-Market Will Need** is found in the government's Occupational Outlook Handbook 2012–2013 at your local library, or better yet, online at **www.bls.gov/ooh.**

---

4. For devoted career counselors, historians, scholars, research students, or anybody who can't sleep or has too much time on their hands, there is an interesting technical discussion of O*Net's limitations in a 2009 research paper by Robert J. Harvey of Virginia Tech, to be found on the Internet by entering "Robert J. Harvey Construct Validity and the O*NET Holistic Rating Scales" into your favorite search engine. *(Phew!)*

Here you can browse careers/occupations by occupational group, number of new jobs projected to be available, faster than average job growth projected, level of education or training required, median pay, etc. Oh, and it has a lovely feature called "similar occupations." That's great if for any reason you don't qualify for some job that otherwise really fascinates you.

Still on the subject of What the Job-Market Needs, if you don't trust government projections, or simply want more timely information, then into your favorite Internet browser put "Hot jobs for [*year*]" and see what articles, blogs, interviews, etc. turn up.

One word of advice: do take what you read with a grain of salt. Make that *a barrel.* "Projections" is just a nice word for "guesses." The way that *some* of these guys and gals decide what constitutes "a hot job" would make your hair stand on end. I know; I've talked with them. *(Think dart boards.)*

Conclusion: Eight Cautions About Career Change

Whenever you have to choose or change a career, here are eight cautions to keep in mind. Many of them you've already seen; this is just a reminder:

#1. Go for *any* career that seems interesting or even fascinating to you. But *first* talk to people who are already doing that work, to find out if the career or job is as great as it seems at first impression. Ask them: *What do you like best about this work? What do you like least about this work? And, how did you get into this work?* This last question, which sounds like mere cheeky curiosity, actually can give you important job-hunting clues about how you could get into this line of work or career.

#2. In going from one career to another, make sure that you preserve constancy in your life as well as change, during the transition. In other words, don't change *everything.* Remember the words of Archimedes[5] about his mythical long lever: *Give me a fulcrum and a place to stand, and with a lever I will move the Earth.* You need a place to stand, when you move your life around, and that place is provided by the things that stay constant about you: your character, your relationships, your faith, your values, your transferable skills.

#3. For long-term job satisfaction, you do better to start with yourself and what *you* want, rather than with the job-market, and what's "hot." The difference is "enthusiasm" or "passion."

#4. The best *work*, the best career, for you, the one that makes you happiest and most fulfilled, is going to be one that uses: your *favorite* transferable skills, in your *favorite* subjects, fields, or special knowledges, in a job that offers you your *preferred* people-environments, your *preferred* working conditions, with your *preferred* salary or other rewards, working toward your *preferred* goals and values. This requires thorough self-inventory. Detailed instructions are to be found back in chapter 5.

#5. The more time and thought you can give to the choosing, the better your choice is going to be. There is a penalty for seeking "quick and dirty" fixes.

#6. If you are young, or relatively young, you don't have to get it right, the first time. It's okay to make a mistake, in your choice. Bucky Fuller used to always say that *Man* was the only creature that learns primarily from making mistakes. You'll have time to correct a bad decision. Most of us have three to five *careers* during our lifetime, and heaven only knows how many jobs.

#7. Choosing and then finding employment in a new career that you really fancy, should be fun, as much fun as possible. The more fun you're having, the more you can be sure you're doing it right. To make it more fun, take a large piece of white paper, and then with some colored pencils or pens draw a picture of your ideal life: where you live, who's with you, what you do, what your dwelling looks like, what your ideal vacation looks like, etc. Don't let *reality* get in the way. Pretend a magic wand has been

---

5. Archimedes (ca. 235 BCE), Greek inventor, mathematician, and physicist. His saying here is loosely paraphrased.

waved over your life, and it gives you everything you think your ideal life would be. Now, *of course* you're going to tell me you can't draw. Okay, then make symbols for things, or create little "doodads," with labels—anything so that you can *see* all together on one page your vision of your ideal life—however haltingly expressed.

The power of this exercise sometimes amazes me. Reason? By avoiding words and using pictures or symbols as much as possible, it bypasses the left side of the brain ("the safekeeping self," as George Prince calls it) and speaks directly to the right side of your brain ("the experimental self"), whose job is to engineer change. Do fun things like this, as you're exploring a new life for yourself.

#8. One final word of caution, here: if you're just graduating from high school, don't go get a college degree in some career field just because you think that will guarantee you a job! It will not.

I wish you could see my emails, filled with bitter letters from people who believed this myth, went and got a degree in a field that looked just great, thought it would be a snap to find a job, but are still unemployed two years later. Good times or bad. They are bitter (often), angry (always), and disappointed in a society that they feel lied to them. Now that they have that worthless degree, and still can't find a job, they find a certain irony in the phrase, *"Our country believes in getting a job by degrees."*

To avoid this costly mistake, what you must do is choose a career, explore it to death, find out if you love it, and *then* go get your degree. Not because it guarantees a job, but because you feel passion, enthusiasm, and energy with this choice. You feel you have found a life about which other people only dream.

Well, yes, you do have
Great big teeth; but, never mind
That. You were great to at least
Grant me this interview.

—Little Red Riding Hood (ageless)

Chapter 8 Do I Really Need a Resume?

Well, you already have one.

In "the old days" before the Internet became popular with job-hunters, the only way an interviewer could learn much about you was from a piece of paper that you yourself wrote—with maybe a little help from your friends—called your resume, or C.V. (an academic term meaning "curriculum vitae"). On that paper was a summary of where you had been and all you had done in the *past*. From that piece of paper, the employer was supposed to guess what kind of person you are in the *present* and what kind of employee you'd be in the *future*.

The good thing about all this, from your point of view, was your *control* over what went on that piece of paper; you could omit anything that was embarrassing, or anything from your past that you have long since regretted. Short of their hiring a private detective, or talking to your previous employers, a prospective employer couldn't find out much else about you. That was nice. But now those days are gone forever.

In This Twenty-First Century: Google Is Your New Resume

There is a new resume in town, and it's called *Google*. All any employer has to do is type your name into a search engine like Google, and bammo! if you've been anywhere near the Internet (and over 78 percent of us in the U.S. have[1])—if you've posted anything on Facebook, Twitter, MySpace, or YouTube, or if you have your own website

---

1. As of December 2011, according to Internet World Stats (www.internetworldstats.com). That means 245 million of us.

or webcasts or photo album or blog, or if you've been on anyone else's Facebook page, every aspect of you may be revealed. So naturally, a vast majority of employers now Google your name—*yes, Google has become both noun and verb*—before they'll consider hiring you.

So, if they do that with your name while you're job-hunting, what will they see? They'll see those impressive achievements you've done, where you far exceeded people's expectations—they're there. But they'll also see those playful photos you've allowed your friends to post on your Facebook page or theirs, that make you look like an idiot. They're there, too. And the indiscreet comments you made when you were upset about this or that. And more.

All these things, together, comprise your new resume, a richer body of data about you than your old resume ever aspired to be. And from this, now, prospective employers can better guess what kind of person you are and what kind of employee you'd be. Or at least they think they can. Heaven help you if you Google yourself and recoil with horror at the distorted picture of yourself that emerges en toto.

There's your new resume, using the word *resume* loosely. *Bye, bye, control.* "The Internet is the first, second and third stop for employers today when considering you for a job," says Michael Fertik, the CEO of Reputation.com.[2] And over 70 percent of employers now report that they have *rejected* applicants on the basis of what they found through Google. It doesn't have to be so blatant as a photo of you at a drunken party; it can be something as simple as your gossip about previous employers.

Is there anything you can do about this new Google resume of yours? Well, yes actually, there are four things you can do. You can *edit, fill in, expand,* and *add.* Let's see what each of these involves.

1. **Edit.** First of all, think of how you would like to come across, when you are being considered for a job. Make a list of adjectives you'd like the employer to think of, when they consider hiring you. For example, how about: professional? experienced? inventive? hard working? disciplined? honest? trustworthy? kind? What else? Make a list.

---

2. Bob Sullivan, "When It Comes to Online Reputation, 'Life's Not Fair, and Companies Aren't Either'," *The Red Tape Chronicles,* MSNBC, September 30, 2011, http://tinyurl.com/cb8xfez.

Then Google yourself and read over everything the search engine pulls up about you. Go over any pages you have put up on social sites like Facebook, MySpace, or YouTube, and remove anything you posted there, or allowed others to post, that contradict the impression you would like to make, anything that might cause a would-be employer to think, "Uh, let's not call them in, after all." Look particularly for unflattering pictures or four-letter text.

If you don't know how to remove an item from a particular site, type or speak the following into a search engine like Google: "How to remove an item from my page on *whatever*." I'd tell you how to do this, but the last time I looked, it took about nineteen steps, for example, to do a thorough "scrub" on Facebook. And I'm sure those instructions are now outdated. You want *current* information; so look at *the date* on any items the search engine pops up. Pick the most recent, before looking at the suggested posts that are further back in time.

Do this "scrub" on any and every site that you know you're on. The site itself may not tell you, but using your favorite search engine, you should have no trouble finding *somebody's* detailed instructions for scrubbing any site. I guarantee you're hardly the first one with this need, so someone clever has already figured out how to do it, and posted the answer.

Now to the second of the four things you can do about your new Google *resume* (so to speak):

2. **Fill In.** On any of these sites, but on LinkedIn or Plaxo in particular, if they allow you to fill out a profile, fill it out completely. I mean *completely;* cross every t, and dot every i. Leave no part of the profile blank unless you have a very good reason. If you're on Twitter, fill out your bio completely, there (69 percent of all users already have). See **http://blazingminds.co.uk/write-twitter-bio-gains-followers** for instructions.

More importantly, *be sure* to keep each profile up to date. Really up to date. There is *nothing* that makes you look less professional than having an obviously outdated profile.

Last thought here: I mentioned LinkedIn; be sure to get on it, if you're not already. More than 150 million other people have, and it became the first social media site to go public. It's the site of first resort when some employer is curious about you. It allows corporate and agency headhunters to avoid advertising an open position, but nonetheless to go "trolling" on LinkedIn for what employers call "passive job-seekers." *You ain't lookin' for them, but they're sure lookin' for you.* Of course you have no control over whether they find you, except for being sure you have a completely filled-out profile. (They search by keywords.)

Now to the third thing you can do about your new Google resume:

3. **Expand.** Expand your presence on the Internet. How to do this? Several ways:

Forums. Professional sites like LinkedIn have forums, or groups, organized by subject matter. Other social networking sites, like Facebook, have pages devoted to particular subjects. Look through the directory of those groups or forums, choose one or two that are related to your industry or interests, and after signing up, speak up regularly *whenever you have something to say that will quietly demonstrate you are an expert in your chosen subject area.* Otherwise, keep quiet. Don't speak up about just anything. You want to be seen as a specialist—knowledgeable, and focused. You want to get noticed by employers when they're searching for expert talent *in your field or specialty.*

Blogs. Start a blog (short for "web log," as you probably know), if you don't already have one.[3] It doesn't matter what your expertise is; if it's related to the job you are looking for, do a blog, and update it regularly. And if you don't know how to blog, there are helpful sites such as Blogger.com, at **http://tinyurl.com/294vgzr**, which can give you detailed instructions.

If you already have a blog, but it roams all over the countryside in terms of subject matter, then start a new

---

3. As of March 2012, there are 160 million blogs in the U.S. (http://tinyurl.com/8x7vrp4).

blog that is more narrowly preoccupied with your particular area of expertise. Post helpful articles there, focused on action steps, not just thoughts. Let's say you are an expert plumber; you can post entries on your blog that deal with such problems as "how to fix a leaky toilet," etc. Generally speaking, employers are looking for blogs that deal with concrete action, rather than lofty philosophical thought. Unless, of course, they represent a think tank.

Twitter. Some experts claim that blogs are so *yesterday.* Communication is moving toward *brief,* and *briefer.* Texting has become wildly popular.[4] So has Twitter. Twitter allegedly has over 100 million users, who post over 300 million tweets a day, though in truth 2.2 percent of Twitter users generate 60 percent of all those "tweets."[5] Twitter's advantage is that it has hashtags,[6] and Google is indexing all those tags and "tweets." Savvy employers know how to do Twitter searches on Google (or on Twitter itself, for that matter). All you have to figure out is which hashtags employers are likely to look for, when they want to find someone with your expertise and experience.

Videos. Presentation is not only getting briefer, but it is moving more and more toward the visual, these days. People like to *see* you, not just read you. Enter the immensely popular website, YouTube. As for shooting the videos, the Flip video camcorder used to be the most popular and inexpensive way to record yourself; but it was allowed to go belly up. Sad! It was displaced, as you might guess, by smartphones, which usually can do video, and sometimes rather surprisingly good video.

As for where to post your video, once you have it, there is the obvious—YouTube—of course; for other possibilities see Friday Traffic Report's list at **http://tinyurl .com/yjnokur.**

---

4. The average American sends 41.5 text messages *per day* (http://tinyurl.com/72rzu3j).
5. Lauren Dugan, "2.2% of Twitter Users Account for 60% of All Activity," *MediaBistro,* December 17, 2010, http://tinyurl.com/4ywf2yf.
6. http://en.wikipedia.org/wiki/Tag_(metadata).

Now to the fourth and final thing you can do about your new Google resume:

4. **Add.** The kind of resume everyone thinks of when they hear the word (the pre-Google resume) still has its uses. It's going to take any employer or HR department some time to sift through all the stuff about you that may appear when they do a Google search. You would help them by summarizing and organizing the pertinent information about yourself. You do this by composing an old type resume.

Here's an outline you may find useful for gathering that information about yourself.

A Starter Kit, for Writing Your Resume

This is adapted, with the written permission of my friend Tom O'Neil, from an original document of his, which was and is copyright protected under the New Zealand Copyright Act (1994) © cv.co.nz 2001. You may contact Tom at **www.cv.co.nz.**

A resume is about your past. Here is a framework for recalling that past.

Think of your working and personal experiences and skills that you believe you possess innately, or have learned. Which ones are you proud of? What things have you done in your life or work experience that no one else has done? Take some blank sheets of paper and fill in any answers that occur to you, please.

It is important to be quantitative when you do this (e.g., mention dates, percents, dollars, brand names, etc.).

Volunteer, Community, and Unpaid Work

1. Have you completed any voluntary or unpaid work for any organization or company? (e.g., church, synagogue, mosque, school, community service, or special needs organization)

Educational

2. Did you work while you were studying? If so, did you receive any promotions or achievements in that role?
3. Did you gain any scholarships?
4. Were you involved in any committees, etc.?
5. Did you win any awards for study?
6. Did you have any high (e.g., A or A+) grades? If so, what were the subjects—and grades?

Sales or Account Management

Have you ever been in sales? If so, what were some of your achievements? For example:

7. Have you ever consistently exceeded your set budget in that role? If so, by what percent or dollar value?
8. Have you exceeded your set budget in a particular month(s)/quarter(s) in a role? If so, by what percent or dollar value?
9. What level were you, compared to other sales professionals in your company? (e.g., *"Number three out of twenty on the sales team."*)
10. Have you ever increased market share for your company? If so, by what percent or dollar value?
11. Have you ever brought in any major clients to your company?
12. What major clients are/were you responsible for managing and selling to?

13. Did you ever manage to generate repeat business or increase current business? If so, by what percent or dollar value?

14. Have you won any internal or external sales awards?

15. Did you develop any new successful promotional or marketing ideas that increased sales?

Administration, Customer Service, and Accounts

Have you ever been in customer service or helped run a business unit? If so:

16. Did you assist in reducing customer complaints, etc.?

17. Did you set up or improve any systems and/or processes?

18. Was there a quantifiable difference in the company or business unit when you first joined the business or project and when you completed the project or left the business?

19. Did you take any old administration or paperwork-based systems and convert them into an IT-based system?

Responsibility

20. Have you ever been responsible for the purchase of any goods or services in some job? (e.g., air travel or PC acquisition)

21. Have you ever had any budget responsibility? If so, to what level? (e.g., *"Responsible for division budget of $200,000 per annum."*)

22. Have you ever been responsible for any staff oversight? If so, in what capacity and/or how many staff members were you responsible for?

23. Were you responsible for any official or unofficial training? If so, what type, for whom, and how many people have you trained? (e.g., *"Responsible for training twelve new staff in customer service as well as in using the in-house computer system."*)

24. Were you responsible for any official or unofficial coaching or mentoring of other staff?

Events or Conference Planning or Logistical Management

25. Have you organized any events or conferences? If so, how large were they (both people attending and total budget if possible) and where and when was the event(s) held?

26. Have you been involved in any major relocation projects?

27. Have you had responsibility with regard to any major suppliers? If so, who?

Computers

28. What systems, software, and hardware experience do you have? Desktop, notebook, mobile, smartphones? Mac OS, Android, or what? And how deep is your expertise with any of these?

29. What software have you utilized? Or what software have you developed? Apps? Systems software?

30. Have you developed any websites? If so, what were they, and did they positively affect any business you were doing? Are you on LinkedIn, Plaxo, Twitter, Facebook, YouTube, etc., and if so how deep an expertise do you have with any of these sites?

31. Were you involved in any special projects that were outside of your job description?

Mechanical

32. Other than computers, have you had experience on any kinds of machines or equipment? Please list them together with the number of years.

33. If you ever worked on transportation devices, what was the airplane, farm equipment, truck, car, machine, or bike brands that you serviced, maintained, or repaired?

Building, Construction, Electrical, and Plumbing

34. If you ever worked in those fields, were there any major projects you have worked on? How much did the project(s) cost? (e.g., *"Reception refurbishment—ABC Bank [Auckland Central Head Office] $1.2m."*)

General

35. How long have you spent within any industry? (e.g., *"Twelve years experience within the fashion industry."*)

36. Were you promoted in any of your roles? If so, in what years and to which roles?

37. Was extra authority awarded to you after a period of time within a role? (e.g., *"Commenced as receptionist; then, after three months, awarded by being given further clerical responsibilities including data entry and accounts payable."*) It is not necessary that these responsibilities awarded to you should have changed your job title and/or salary.

38. Have you been asked to take part in, or lead, any trainee management courses or management development programs?

39. Were you asked to get involved in any special projects outside your job description? Or, did you ever volunteer for such? What was the result?

Positive Feedback

40. Have you ever received any written or verbal client, customer, or managerial commendations or letters of praise?

41. Can you think of any occasions where you gave excellent customer service? If so, how did you know the customer was satisfied? (Also: What was the outcome? How did it benefit the company?)

42. Did you receive any awards within your company or industry? (e.g., *"Acknowledged for support or service of clients or staff, etc."*)

Memberships

43. Have you been a representative on any committees (e.g., health and safety committee)? Any special responsibilities there?

44. Do you belong or have you belonged to any professional clubs such as Toastmasters, Lions, or Rotary?

Published or Presented Work

45. Have you had any articles, papers, or features published in any magazines, journals, or books? If so, what publications and when? Have you written any books?

46. Have you presented any topics at any conferences or completed any public speaking? If so, what subjects have you talked about and how large was the audience? List in detail.

Looking Ahead

- What value do you think you would add to a potential employer's business? How would you be "a resource" or even "a resource-broker" for them, rather than just "a job beggar"? What kind of problems are you good at solving?

- How do you think you would stand out compared to other applicants who have about the same qualifications as you have?

That should give you a good start. Modify the list any way you want to—add items and questions to it, change the wording, whatever.

If you need additional guidance, search Google for the topic "how to write a resume," or "tips on writing a resume" or "keywords on an electronic resume" or "examples of resumes." This will not only turn up free resources and advice on the Internet and for-fee resources, such as professional resume writers, but also the names of books, if you want to get very thorough.[7] You should look particularly for resume books by Yana Parker and Susan Whitcomb.

---

7. Books that I like: *Resume 101* by Quentin J. Schultze, PhD, Ten Speed Press, 2012; and *How to Write the Perfect Resume: A Resume Writing Guide Complete with Resume Templates* by Michael T. Robinson, available at www.CareerPlanner.com, 2010.

E-J Dyer   **Street, City, Zip**   **Telephone No.**

**I SPEAK THE
LANGUAGE OF
MEN, MACHINERY,
AND MANAGEMENT . . .**

OBJECTIVE   Sales of Heavy Equipment

QUALIFICATIONS   • Knowledge of heavy equipment, its use and maintenance.

                       • Ability to communicate with management and with men in the
                       field.

                       • Ability to favorably introduce change in the form of new equip-
                       ment or new ideas . . . the ability to sell.

EXPERIENCE   • Maintained, shipped, budgeted and set allocation priorities for
                       85 pieces of heavy equipment as head of a 500-man organization
                       (1975–1977).

Men and   • Constructed twelve field operation support complexes, employing
Machinery   a 100-man crew and 19 pieces of heavy equipment (1965–1967).

                       • Jack-hammer operator, heavy construction (summers 1956–1957–1958).

Management   • Planned, negotiated and executed large-scale equipment purchases
                       on a nation-to-nation level (1972–1974).

Sales   • Achieved field customer acceptance of two major new computer-
                       based systems:

                       —Equipment inventory control and repair parts expedite system
                       (1968–1971)

                       —Decision makers' training system (1977–1979)

                       • Proven leader . . . repeatedly elected or appointed to senior posts.

EDUCATION   B.A. Benedictine College, 1959 (Class President; Yearbook Editor;
                       "Who's Who in American Colleges")

                       • Naval War College, 1975 (Class President; Graduated "With High-
                       est Distinction")

                       • University of Maryland, 1973–1974 (Chinese Language)

                       • Middle Level Management Training Course, 1967–1968 (Class
                       Standing: 1 of 97)

PERSONAL   Family: Sharon and our sons Jim (11), Andy (8) and Matt (5) desire to
                       locate in a Mountain State by 1982; however, in the interim will con-
                       sider a position elsewhere in or outside the United States . . . Health:
                       Excellent . . . Birthdate: December 9, 1937 . . . Completing Military
                       Service with the rank of Lieutenant Colonel, U.S. Marine Corps.

SUMMARY   A seeker of challenge . . . experienced, proven and confident of clos-
                       ing the sales for profit.

As for what is the proper form for a resume, there are no rules. The only question is: is there a particular place or kind of place where you'd like to work, and if so, will the person there who has the power to hire you for the kind of job you want, be persuaded by your resume to invite you in? If the answer is, Yes, then it matters not what form your resume takes.

To illustrate my point, I used to have a hobby of collecting "winning" resumes—that is, resumes that had actually gotten someone an interview and, ultimately, a job. Being playful by nature, I would show these without comment, to employer friends of mine, over lunch. Many of them didn't like these winning resumes at all. "That resume will never get anyone a job," they would say. Then I would reply, "Sorry, you're wrong. It already has. I think what you mean is that it wouldn't get them a job *with you.*"

The resume reproduced on the previous page is a good example of what I mean; it's dated, but it's still my favorite.

Like the employer who hired him, I loved this resume. Yet some of the employers I showed it to *(over lunch, as I said)* criticized it for using a picture or for being too long, or for being too short, etc. In other words, had Jim sent that resume to *them,* they wouldn't have invited him in for an interview.

Some employers will like your resume, some won't. Trouble is, you don't know which employer likes *what.* That's why many job-hunters, if they use resumes, pray as they mail their resume: *Please, dear God, let them be employers who like resumes in general, and may the form of my resume appeal to those employers I care about, in particular.*

Whatever form you decide on, write it and then post it *everywhere* online: on the omnibus job boards, famous job boards, community bulletin boards, and niche sites. For lists of such sites, go to Quintessential Careers' website at **http://tinyurl.com/3nnqhse**.

There are resume distribution services that can do this blanket posting for you, if you wish, sometimes without a fee, but most often for about fifty bucks (see **www.forwardyourresume.com** for evaluations of the top five such services). Whether this strategy is useful or not, depends a lot on *luck.*

If you're posting your resume yourself, put it on the actual website of companies that interest you, if they have a site, and if their site permits that. (You *have* already chosen companies or organizations that interest you, I hope—whether or not they have any known vacancies.)

If you post your resume on the sites of particular employers, large or small, don't count on any acknowledgment or reply. Just post the thing, cross your fingers, and pray it arrives at the right time, at the right place.

This strategy—planting your resume on the Internet amidst all the other stuff that an employer will find if they Google you—will work better with small companies than with large ones, and with *newer* small companies, especially.

Alternatives to a Classic Resume

Many experts suggest that instead of sending a resume to particular employers who interest you, that you send just a "cover letter" instead, summarizing all that a longer resume might have covered. If you don't know what a cover letter is, or how to write it, the Internet can rescue you handily. Just type "cover letters" into your favorite search engine. You'll be surprised at how many tips, examples, etc., you find. Look particularly for Susan Ireland's Cover Letter Guide at **http://susan ireland.com/coverletterwork.htm**. It's free. Incidentally, recent surveys have revealed that many employers prefer a cover letter to a resume.

Another alternative to a classic resume is a Job or Career Portfolio. A portfolio may be electronic (posted on the Internet) or on paper/in a notebook/in a large display case (as with artists), demonstrating your accomplishments, experience, training, commendations, or awards, from the past. Artists have a portfolio, with samples of their work. You probably knew that. But portfolios are equally apt in other fields.

Instead of "portfolio" we might just call them "Evidence of What I Can Do and Have Done," or "Proof of Performance." For guidance on how to prepare a job-portfolio, and what to include, type "job portfolios" into Google; you'll get a wealth of tips and information. I particularly recommend Martin Kimeldorf's site, **http://amby.com/ kimeldorf/portfolio**.

Some Friendly Reminders

I've covered some of these cautions in other chapters, but it never hurts to repeat them.

1. If you're blanketing the Internet with your resume, be cautious about including any stuff on the resume that would help someone locate you, particularly if you're a female. No, I'm not being sexist. It's just that there are some sick people out there. Sick in the head, that is. Remember the Craigslist killer? I'd be *sure* to leave out my address and home phone number if I were you. Just your email address should more than suffice.

2. If you are targeting particular employers, rather than or in addition to job-sites, then keep in mind that a resume is best not sent solely by email, particularly if it's an attachment, not embedded right in the email. Many employers, leery of viruses, will not even open email attachments (such as your resume). Send it by email if you want, but always send a nicer version of it by the postal service, or UPS, or FedEx, etc. (Remember? *Hope depends on alternatives.*)

3. If you're going to snailmail a resume to a target employer, pay attention to the paper you write or print it on. Picture this scenario: an employer is going through a whole stack of resumes, and on average he or she is giving each resume about eight seconds of their time (true: we checked!). Then that resume goes either into a pile we might call "Forgeddit," or a pile we might call "Bears further investigation." And what determines which pile? The *feel* of the paper. Yes, that employer's first contact with your resume is with their fingers. By the pleasure or displeasure of their fingers, they are prejudiced in your favor before they even start reading, or prejudiced against you. Usually they are not even aware of this. Anyway, this is why you want the paper to feel good. That usually means using paper weighing at least 28 pounds (a paper's *weight* is on the outside of every package). And you want it to be easy to read—so be sure it's nicely laid out or formatted, using a decent-sized font, size 12 or even 14, etc.

4. A resume should have a purpose, at least in your mind. If you're just posting it online, anywhere and everywhere, your intention *might be* just to collect and organize all pertinent information about yourself in one place, in contrast to your Google *resume* (as it were), where the information about you lies scattered all over the land.

5. On the other hand, if you're targeting individual employers, then your resume should have only one purpose, as I've said elsewhere: to get yourself invited in, for an interview. This truth, however, is not widely understood. Most job-hunters (and more than a few resume writers) assume a resume's purpose is to "sell you," or secure you a job. Hey, if the resume gets you invited in, for an interview, *that's* the time to sell yourself. In person. Face to face. Not on paper.

6. So, read over *every single sentence* in your resume and evaluate it by this one standard: "Will this item help to get me invited in? Or will this item seem too puzzling, or off-putting, or a red flag?" If you doubt a particular sentence will help get you invited in for an interview, then omit that sentence. If it's important, make notes to cover it *in the interview*. And if there is something you feel you will ultimately need to explain, or expand upon, save that explanation for the interview, also. Your resume is, above all, no place for "true confessions." (*"I kind of botched up, at the end, in that job; that's why they let me go, as I'm sure they'll tell you when you check my references."*) Save true confessions for the end of the interview, and only if you're confident at that point that they really want you.

7. Ditto for discussing any nonvisible handicap you may have. Generally speaking—there are exceptions—don't mention it in the resume. And when you're in the interview, don't discuss right off the bat what you can't do. Focus all their attention, initially, on what you can do—that you can perform all the tasks required in this job. Save what you can't do for the moment where they say they really want you.

8. If you're coming out of some culture that has its own language (military, clergy, etc.) get help in translating your experience into

the language of employers. "Preached" should be replaced by "taught." "Commanded" should be replaced by "supervised," etc.[8]

9. Finally, don't include references on your resume. Some career counselors and resume writers will disagree with me on this, but I think references are better offered after prospective employers have had a chance to see and talk with you. And please, please, please, never list somebody as a reference, at any time in your job-hunt, without first getting their written permission to do so. Further, if they consent, ask them to give the letter of recommendation to *you*. That way, you can read it over and decide if you really want to use it. Some of your preferred references may turn out to be people who are by nature brutally honest. Don't *assume* they'll give you a raving recommendation. If they've never actually seen you at work, they may say so, and decline to say whether you'd be an asset or not. That kind of "recommendation" is honest, but it won't help you get the job. You want to find that out *before* any prospective employer sees it. Then you can use it or deep-six it, as you please.

10. Some employers hate resumes. Why should that be any surprise? Currently, according to experts, 82 percent of all resumes have to be checked out, concerning the facts stated or the experience claimed. Lies are endemic on resumes. Other employers love resumes, but not for the reasons you think. They love them because they offer an easy way to cut down the time employers have to spend on job-hunters. Remember, for the employer, hiring is essentially an elimination game: in a large organization, they're looking for a reason—any reason—to cut their stack of resumes down to a manageable size. Remember, it only takes a skilled human resources person about eight seconds to scan a resume (thirty seconds, if they're really dawdling), so getting rid of fifty job-hunters—I mean getting rid of fifty *resumes*—takes only half an hour or less. Whereas, interviewing those fifty job-hunters in person would have required a minimum of twenty-five hours. Great time savings—for them!

---

8. Returning vets from Iraq and Afghanistan will find help on such sites as job-hunt (http://tinyurl.com/86a8rkn), Real Warriors (http://tinyurl.com/6u3vawm), and MyNextMove.org, maintained by the government's O*Net Online site.

Wild Life, by John Kovalic, © 1989 Shetland Productions. Reprinted with Permission.

Where You Post Your Resume Makes a Difference

The number of interviews employers need to conduct to find a hire, stays pretty constant—around 5.4—*once they've sifted through all the resumes or applications.* So, to conserve their energy, they ask themselves, *"Where would I have to read or sift through the least number of resumes, before I decide who to do those 5.4 interviews with?"* Fortunately, we know the answer. Somebody did a study.[9] This should guide you in your resume strategy, if you're going to use a resume to supplement Google.

If employers post their vacancy on a job-board such as Career-Builder.com or Monster.com, they have to look through **219** resumes from job-hunters who respond, before they find someone to interview and hire.

If employers consider resumes from job-hunters who come through social media sites, such as LinkedIn or Facebook, they have to look through **116** resumes, before they find someone to interview and hire.

If employers post their vacancy on their own website, they have to look through **33** resumes from job-hunters who respond, before they find someone to interview and hire.

If the job-hunter takes the initiative to find a very specific job, rather than waiting to find a vacancy, and does this, say, by typing the name of that kind of job into a search engine, then sending resumes to any

---

9. From an analysis, released in April 2011, by Jobs2web Inc., of 1,300,000 job applications and 26,000 hires in 2010.

companies whose name turns up, employers only have to look through 32 applications, before they find someone to interview and hire.

And if the job-hunter takes even more initiative, chooses a company where they'd like to work, and gets a referral (i.e., gets some employee within that company to recommend them), employers have to look through only 10 such candidates, before they find someone to interview and hire.

Conclusion

Okay, one more time: do you really need a resume?

Well, no you don't, and yes you do.

You already have a kind of *resume* if you've been posting any stuff on the Internet. That resume is found by a prospective employer using Google, on you.

You've got to clean up *that* resume, edit, fill in, expand, and add to it, before they see it.

But that, alone, is not enough. You need to supplement what's already there, by sitting down and organizing the most pertinent information about you—whether it's on the Internet or not—by writing the old kind of resume.

Once written, you can post it everywhere on the Internet, but if you decide to target particular employers, then you need to edit *that* resume, before sending it to those employers. The criterion by which you weigh every sentence in it is, *will this help get me invited in, for an interview?* If not, yank it!

These ancient truths reign, when all is said and done:

The primary purpose of a resume is to get yourself invited in for an interview (*with a prospective employer, of course*).

The primary purpose of that interview is to get yourself invited back for a second interview. And so on. And so forth.

THE TEN GREATEST MISTAKES
MADE IN JOB INTERVIEWS

Whereby Your Chances of Finding a Job Are Greatly Decreased

I. Going after large organizations only (such as the Fortune 500).

II. Hunting all by yourself for places to visit.

III. Doing no homework on an organization before going there.

IV. Allowing the Human Resources department to interview you (their primary function is to look for reasons to screen you OUT).

V. Setting no time limit when you first begin the interview, and then overstaying your welcome.

VI. Letting your resume be the only agenda discussed during the job-interview.

VII. Talking primarily about yourself throughout the interview, and what benefit the job will be for you.

VIII. Failing to give examples of the skills you claim you have.

IX. Basically approaching the employer as if you were a job-beggar, hoping they will offer you any kind of a job, however humble.

X. Not sending a thank-you note right after the interview.

Chapter 9 Sixteen Tips About Interviewing

There are three types of interviews, as we saw in chapter 6:

Interviews for fun or practice, done with people who are passionate about the same thing you are;

Interviews for information, done with information specialists, experts in the industry that interests you, or employees holding down the same job as you are exploring; and

Interviews for hire, done with employers in general, and the person who has the power to hire you for the job you want, in particular.

This chapter is about this third kind of interview, the one for hire. Here are sixteen tips about that kind of interview.

Tip #1

An interview resembles **dating**, more than it does buying a used car (*you*). An interview is analogous to two people trying to decide if they want "to go steady."

An interview is not to be thought of as **marketing** yourself: i.e., selling yourself to a half-interested employer. Rather, an interview is part of your **research**, i.e., the *data-collecting process* that you have been engaged in, or should have been engaged in, during your whole job-hunt. While you are sitting there, with the employer, the question you are trying to find an answer to is: *"Do I want to work here, or not?"* You use the interview to find out. Only when you have concluded Yes, do you then turn your energy toward *selling* yourself.

An interview is not to be thought of as a test. It's a *data-collecting process* for the employer, too. They are trying to decide if you fit. They are using the interview to find out *"Do I want him or her to work here? Do they have skills, knowledge, or experience that I really need? Do they have an attitude toward work, that I am looking for? And, how will they fit in with my other employees?"*

Tip #2

An interview should be prepared for, *before* you ever go in, by taking these three steps:

1. Research the organization or company, before going in. Go to their website if they have one, and read everything there that is "About Us." If your town has a public library, ask your local librarian for help in finding any news clippings or other information about the place. And, finally, ask all your friends if they know anyone who ever worked there, or works there still, so you can take them to lunch or tea or Starbucks and find out any *inside* stories. All organizations love to be loved. If you've gone to the trouble of finding out as much about them as you can, they will be flattered and impressed, believe me—because most job-hunters never go to this amount of trouble. Most just walk in the door, knowing nothing about the organization. I told you earlier about the guy who ran a large organization in Virginia; he said to me, *"I'm so tired of people coming in here, saying, Uh, what do you do here? that the next person who comes in here and has done some prior research on us, I'm going to offer a job."* He called me a week later to say, *"I kept my word."*

2. When it is you who is taking the initiative in setting up the interview, specify the time you are asking of them—unless they ask you to stay longer. Experts recommend you only ask for twenty minutes, and observe this commitment *religiously.* Watch your watch or timepiece like a hawk! Stay aware of the time, and don't stay one minute longer than the twenty minutes, unless the employer *begs* you to—and I mean, *begs.* Always prepare to end it

at the time you specified, with, "*I said I would only take twenty min-utes of your time, and I like to honor my agreements.*" This will **always** make a big impression on an employer!

3. As you go to the interview, keep in mind that if this is **the person-who-actually-has-the-power-to-hire-you**, then they are just as anxious as you are. Why? Because, the hiring-interview is not a very reliable way to choose an employee. In a survey conducted some years back, among a dozen top United Kingdom employers,[1] it was discovered that the chances of an employer finding a good employee through the hiring-interview was only 3 **percent better** than if they had picked a name out of a hat. In a further ironic finding, it was discovered that if the interview was conducted by someone who would be working directly with the candidate, the success rate dropped to 2 **percent below** that of picking a name out of a hat. And if the interview was conducted by a so-called human resources expert, the success rate dropped to 10 **percent below** that of picking a name out of a hat.

No, I don't know how they came up with these figures, and maybe they are flat wrong, but I don't think so. They are totally consistent with what I have learned about the world of hiring dur-ing the past forty years. I have watched so-called experts make *wretchedly* bad choices about hiring *in their own office*, and when they would morosely confess this to me some months later, over lunch, I would playfully tease them with, "If *you* don't even know how to hire well for your own office, how do you keep a straight face when you're called in as a hiring consultant by another orga-nization?" And they would ruefully reply, "We *act as though* it were a science." Well, let me tell you, dear reader, hiring is *not* a science. It is a very, very hazy art, done ineptly by most of its employer-practitioners, in spite of their own past experience, their very best intentions, and their carloads of good will.

---

1. Reported in the *Financial Times Career Guide* for the United Kingdom.

Tip #3

What this adds up to, is that the hiring-interview is not what it seems to be. It seems to be one individual (*you*) sitting there, scared to death, while the other individual (*the employer*) is sitting there, blasé and confident. But what it really is, is two individuals (*you* and *the employer*) sitting there supremely anxious. It's just that employers have learned to *hide* their fears better than you have, because they've had more practice. But this employer is, after all, a human being just like you. In most cases, they were *not* hired to do *this*. It got thrown in with all their other duties. And they dread making the wrong decision.

The employer's fears include *any* or *all* of the following:

A. That you won't be able to do the job: that you lack the necessary skills or experience, and the hiring-interview won't uncover this.

B. That if hired, you won't put in a full working day, more often than not.

C. That if hired, you'll take frequent sick days, on one pretext or another.

D. That if hired, you'll only stay around for a few weeks or at most a few months, until you find a better job.

E. That it will take you too long to master the job, and thus it will be too long before you're profitable to that organization.

F. That you won't get along with the other workers there, or that you will develop a personality conflict with the boss.

G. That you will only do the minimum that you can get away with, rather than the maximum that the boss is hoping for. Since every boss these days is trying to keep their workforce smaller than it was before the Recession, they are hoping for the maximum productivity from each new hire.

H. That you will always have to be told what to do next, rather than displaying initiative—that you will always be in a responding mode, rather than an initiating mode (and mood).

I. That you will have a disastrous character flaw not evident in the interview, and turn out to be either dishonest, or irresponsible, a spreader of dissension at work, lazy, an embezzler, a gossip, a sexual harasser, a drunk, a drug-user or substance abuser, a liar, incompetent, or—in a word—*an employer's worst nightmare.*

J. *(If this is a large organization, and your would-be boss is not the top person)* that you will bring discredit upon them, and upon their department/section/division, etc., for ever hiring you in the first place—making them lose face, possibly also costing them a raise or a promotion from the boss upstairs.

K. That you will cost a lot of money, if they make a mistake by hiring you.

No wonder the employer interviewing you may be as anxious as you are. In your heart, be as compassionate toward them, as you hope they will be toward you. Forget the title—"employer" or "employee"— both of you are just *persons.*

Tip #4

During the interview, determine to observe "the 50-50 Rule." Studies have revealed that, in general, the people who get hired are those who mix speaking and listening fifty-fifty in the interview. That is, half the time they let the employer do the talking, half the time in the interview they do the talking. People who didn't follow that mix, were the ones who didn't get hired, according to the study.[2] My hunch as to the *reason* why this is so, is that if you talk too much about yourself, you come across as one who would ignore the needs of the organization; if you talk too little, you come across as trying to hide something about your background.

Tip #5

In answering the employer's questions, observe "the twenty-second to two-minute rule." Studies[3] have revealed that when it is your turn to speak or answer a question, you should plan not to speak any longer

---

2. This one was done by a researcher at Massachusetts Institute of Technology, whose name has been lost in the mists of time.
3. This one was conducted by my friend and colleague, Daniel Porot, of Geneva, Swtizerland.

than two minutes at a time, if you want to make the best impression. In fact, a good answer to an employer's question sometimes only takes twenty seconds to give. (But not less than that, else you will be assumed to be "a grunter," lacking any communication skills.)

Tip #6

Determine to be seen as a part of the solution, not as a part of the problem. Every organization has two main preoccupations for its day-by-day work: the **problems—they generally prefer "challenges"**—they are facing, and what **solutions to those challenges** their employees and management are coming up with. Therefore, the main thing the employer is trying to figure out during the hiring-interview with you, is: will you be part of the solution there, or just another part of the *problem.*

In trying to answer this concern, you should figure out prior to the interview how a *bad* employee would "screw up," in the position you are asking for—such things as *come in late, take too much time off, follow his or her own agenda instead of the employer's, etc.* Then plan to emphasize to the employer during the interview how much you are the very opposite: your sole goal "is to increase the organization's effectiveness, service, and bottom line."

Be aware of the skills all employers are looking for, these days, regardless of the position you are seeking. They are looking for employees: *who are punctual, arriving at work on time or better yet, early; who stay until quitting time, or even leave late; who are dependable; who have a good attitude; who have drive, energy, and enthusiasm; who want more than a paycheck; who are self-disciplined, well-organized, highly motivated, and good at managing their time; who can handle people well; who can use language effectively; who can work on a computer; who are committed to teamwork; who are*

flexible, and can respond to novel situations, or adapt when circumstances at work change; who are trainable, and love to learn; who are project-oriented, and goal-oriented; who have creativity and are good at problem solving; who have integrity; who are loyal to the organization; who are able to identify opportunities, markets, and coming trends. **Above all, they want to hire people who can bring in more money than they are paid.** *So, plan on claiming all of these that you* **legitimately** *can, during the hiring-interview, with evidence (short short stories of your past achievements, such as the skills identification stories you wrote in chapter 5).*

Tip #7

Realize that the employer thinks the way you are doing your job-hunt is the way you will do the job. So, make sure that you illustrate throughout the interview what you claim will be true of you, once hired. For example, if you plan on claiming that you are very thorough in all your work, be sure to be thorough in the way you have researched the company or organization ahead of time. The manner in which you do your job-hunt and the manner in which you would do the job you are seeking, are not assumed by most employers to be two unrelated subjects, but one and the same. They can tell when you are doing a slipshod, half-hearted job-hunt (*"Uh, what do you guys do here?"*), and this is taken as a clear warning that you will do a slipshod, half-hearted job, were they foolish enough to hire you. Most people job-hunt the same way they live their lives.

Tip #8

Try to think of some way to bring evidence of your skills, to the hiring-interview. For example, if you are an artist, a craftsperson, or anyone who produces a product, try to bring a sample of what you have made or produced—in scrapbook or portfolio form, with photos, or even videos. (Just in case.) If you are a programmer, bring examples of your code. And so on.

Tip #9

Do not bad-mouth your previous employer(s) during the interview, even if they were terrible bosses. Employers sometimes feel as though they are a fraternity or sorority. During the interview you want to come across as one who displays courtesy toward *all* members of that fraternity or sorority. Bad-mouthing a previous employer only makes this employer who is interviewing you, worry about what you would say about *them*, after they hire you.

(I learned this in my own experience. I once spoke graciously about a previous employer during a job-interview. Unbeknownst to me, the interviewer already knew that my previous employer had badly mistreated me. He therefore thought very highly of me because I didn't bad-mouth the guy. In fact, he never forgot this incident; talked about it for years afterward.)

Plan on saying something nice about any previous employer, or if you are pretty sure that the fact you and they didn't get along will surely come out, then try to nullify this ahead of time, by saying something simple like, "I usually get along with everybody; but for some reason, my past employer and I just didn't get along. Don't know why. It's never happened to me before. Hope it never happens again."

Tip #10

Naturally, the employer is going to ask you questions, as a way of helping them figure out whether or not they want to hire you. Books on *interviewing*, of which there are many, often publish long lists of these questions, with timeworn, semi-clever answers suggested, and the recommendation that you memorize the answers to all those questions. Their lists include such questions as:

- Tell me about yourself.
- What do you know about this company?
- Why are you applying for this job?
- How would you describe yourself?
- What are your major strengths?

- What is your greatest weakness?
- What type of work do you like to do best?
- What are your interests outside of work?
- What accomplishment gave you the greatest satisfaction?
- Why did you leave your last job?
- Why were you fired (if you were)?
- Where do you see yourself five years from now?
- What are your goals in life?
- How much did you make at your last job?

But really there are only *five basic questions* that you need pay atten
tion to. The people-who-have-the-power-to-hire-you need to know the
answers to these five, which they may ask directly or try to find out
obliquely:

1. **"Why are you here?"** *This means "Why are you knocking on my
   door, rather than someone else's door?"*

2. **"What can you do for us?"** *This means "If I were to hire you, would
   you be part of the challenges I already have, or would you be a part of
   the solution to those challenges? What are your skills, and how much do
   you know about the subject or field that we are in?"*

3. **"What kind of person are you?"** *This means "Will you fit in? Do
   you have the kind of personality that makes it easy for people to work
   with you, and do you share the values that we have at this place?"*

4. **"What distinguishes you from nineteen or nine hundred other
   people who are applying for this job?"** *This means "Do you have
   better work habits than the others, do you show up earlier, stay later,
   work more thoroughly, work faster, maintain higher standards, go the
   extra mile, or . . . what?"*

5. **"Can I afford you?"** *This means "If we decide we want you here,
   how much will it take to get you, and are we willing and able to pay
   that amount—governed, as we are, by our budget, and by our inability
   to pay you as much as the person who would be next above you, on our
   organizational chart?"*

These are the five principal questions that employers need to know the answers to. *This is the case, even if the interview begins and ends with these five questions never once being mentioned explicitly by the employer.* The questions are still *floating* beneath the surface of the conversation, beneath all the things being discussed. Anything you can do, during the interview, to help the employer answer these five questions, will make the interview more helpful to the employer. And you can do a lot, if you did the Flower Exercise (chapter 5) in this book. You will *know* the answers.

Of course, it's not just the employer who has questions. You have some too—inevitably. And—surprise—they are basically the same questions (in only slightly different form) *as the employer's:*

1. **"What does this job involve?"** *You want to understand exactly what tasks will be asked of you, so that you can determine if these are the kinds of tasks you would really like to do, and can do.*

2. **"What are the skills a top employee in this job would have to have?"** *You want to find out if your skills match those that the employer thinks a top employee in this job has to have, in order to do this job well.*

3. **"Are these the kinds of people I would like to work with, or not?"** *Do not ignore your intuition if it tells you that you would not be comfortable working with these people!! You want to know if they have the kind of personalities that would enable you to accomplish your best work. If these people aren't it, keep looking!*

4. **"If we like each other, and we both want to work together, can I persuade them there is something unique about me, that makes me different from nineteen or nine hundred other people who are applying for this job?"** *You need to think out, way ahead of time, what does make you different from other people who can do the same job. For example, if you are good at analyzing problems, how do you do that? Painstakingly? Intuitively, in a flash? By consulting with greater authorities in the field? You see the point. You are trying to put your finger on the "style" or "manner" in which you do your work, that is distinctive and hopefully appealing, to* this *employer.*

5. **"Can I persuade them to hire me at the salary I need or want?"** *This requires some knowledge on your part of how to conduct salary negotiation. (Key things to know: it should always take place at the end*

of the interviews there, and whoever mentions a salary figure first, gen-erally loses, in the negotiation.) That's covered in chapter 11.

You will probably want to ask questions one and two out loud. You will *observe* quietly the answer to question three. You will be prepared to make the case for questions four and five, when the *appropriate* time in the interview arises.

How do you first raise these questions of yours? If you initiated the interview, you might begin by reporting just exactly how you've been conducting your job-hunt, and what impressed you so much about *their* organization during your research, that you decided to come in and talk to them about a job. From there, and thereafter, you can fix your attention on these five questions—in the employer's mind, and in yours.[4]

Incidentally, let's not leave this tip without observing that these five questions pop up (yet again), if you're there to talk *not* about a job that already exists, but rather, one that you hope they will *create* for you. In that case, these five questions change form slightly again. They get changed into six *statements*, that you make to the person-who-has-the-power-to-*create*-this-job:

1. What you **like** about this organization.

2. What sorts of **needs** you find intriguing in this field, in general, and in this organization, in particular (unless you first hear the word coming out of their mouth, don't use the word *"problems,"* as most employers prefer synonyms that sound gentler to their ears, such as *"challenges"* or *"needs"*).

3. What **skills** seem to you to be necessary in order to meet such needs.

4. **Evidence** from your past experience that demonstrates you have those very skills. Employers, in these days of "behavioral inter-views," are looking for *examples* from your past performance and

---

4. To help you explore these five, you may want to ask:
   What significant changes has this company gone through in the past five years?
   What values are sacred to this company?
   What characterizes the most successful employees this company has?
   What future changes do you see in the work here?
   Who do you see as your allies, colleagues, or competitors in this business?

achievement—your behavior—not just vague statements like: "I'm good at . . ." They want concrete examples, specifically of any transferable skills, work content skills, or self-management skills, i.e., traits, that you claim to have.

It's helpful to pose the question to yourself before you ever go in there: "What are *the three most important* competencies, for this job?" Then, of course, you need to demonstrate during the interview that you *have* those three—for the job that you want them to create.

5. What is **unique** about the way *you* perform those skills. Every prospective employer wants to know *what makes you different* from nineteen or nine hundred other people who can do the same kind of work as you. You *have* to know what that is. And then not merely talk about it, but actually demonstrate it by the way you conduct your side of the hiring-interview.

6. How the hiring of you will not cost them, in the long run. You need to be prepared to demonstrate that you will, in the long run, end up costing them nothing, as you will bring in more money than the salary they paid you. Emphasize this!

Tip #11

Throughout the interview, keep in mind: employers don't really care about your past; they only ask about it, in order to try to predict your future (behavior) with them, if they decide to hire you.

Legally, U.S. employers may only ask you questions that are related to the requirements and expectations of the job. They cannot ask about such things as your creed, religion, race, age, sexual orientation, or marital status. But, any other questions about your past are *fair game*. And they *will* ask them, if they know what they're doing.

Therefore, during the hiring-interview, before you answer any question the employer asks you about your past, you should pause to think, "What fear about the *future* caused them to ask this question about my past?" and then address *that fear*, obliquely or directly.

Here are some *examples*:

Employer's Question	The Fear Behind the Question	The Point You Try to Get Across	Phrases You Might Use to Get This Across
"Tell me about yourself."	The employer is afraid he/she isn't going to conduct a very good interview, by failing to ask the right questions. Or is afraid there is something wrong with you, and is hoping you will blurt it out.	You are a good employee, as you have proved in the past at your other jobs. (Give the briefest history of who you are, where born and raised, interests, hobbies, and kind of work you have enjoyed the most to date.) Keep it to two minutes, max.	In describing your work history, use any honest phrases you can about your work history, that are self-complimentary: "Hard worker." "Came in early, left late." "Always did more than was expected of me." Etc.
"What kind of work are you looking for?"	The employer is afraid that you are looking for a different job than that which the employer is trying to fill. E.g., he/she wants an assistant, but you want to be an office supervisor, etc.	You are looking for precisely the kind of work the employer is offering (but don't say that, if it isn't true). Repeat back to the employer, in your own words, what he/she has said about the job, and emphasize the skills you have to do that.	If the employer hasn't described the job at all, say, "I'd be happy to answer that, but first I need to understand exactly what kind of work this job involves." Then answer, as at left.
"Have you ever done this kind of work before?"	The employer is afraid you don't possess the necessary skills and experience to do this job.	You have skills that are transferable, from whatever you used to do; and you did it well.	"I pick up stuff very quickly." "I have quickly mastered any job I have ever done."

Employer's Question	The Fear Behind the Question	The Point You Try to Get Across	Phrases You Might Use to Get This Across
"Why did you leave your last job?"—or "How did you get along with your former boss and co-workers?"	The employer is afraid you don't get along well with people, especially bosses, and is just waiting for you to "bad-mouth" your previous boss or co-workers, as proof of that.	Say whatever positive things you possibly can about your former boss and co-workers (with-out telling lies). Emphasize you usually get along very well with people—and then let your gracious attitude toward your previous boss(es) and co-workers prove it, right before this employer's very eyes (and ears).	If you left voluntarily: "My boss and I both felt I would be happier and more effective in a job where [here describe your strong points, such as] I would have more room to use my initiative and creativ-ity." If you were fired: "Usually, I get along well with everyone, but in this particular case the boss and I just didn't get along with each other. Difficult to say why." You don't need to say anything more than that. If you were laid off and your job wasn't filled after you left: "My job was terminated."
"How is your health?"—or "How much were you absent from work during your last job?"	The employer is afraid you will be absent from work a lot, if they hire you. Unfortu-nately for them, and fortunately for you, this is a question they cannot legally ask you.	Just because the question is illegal, doesn't mean you can't address their hidden fear. Even if they never mention it, you can try to disarm that fear.	You can find a way to say, "My productivity always exceeded other workers, in my previ-ous jobs."
"Can you explain why you've been out of work so long?"—or "Can you tell me why there are these gaps in your work history?" (Usually said after studying your resume.)	The employer is afraid that you are the kind of person who quits a job the minute he/she doesn't like something at it; in other words, that you have no "stick-to-it-iveness."	You love to work, and you regard times when things aren't going well as challenges, which you enjoy learning how to conquer.	"During the gaps in my work record, I was studying/doing volun-teer work/doing some hard thinking about my mission in life/finding redirection." (Choose one.)

Employer's Question	The Fear Behind the Question	The Point You Try to Get Across	Phrases You Might Use to Get This Across
"Wouldn't this job represent a step down for you?"—or "I think this job would be way beneath your talents and experience."—or "Don't you think you would be underemployed if you took this job?"	The employer is afraid you could command a bigger salary, somewhere else, and will therefore leave him/her as soon as something better turns up.	You will stick with this job as long as you and the employer agree this is where you should be.	"This job isn't a step down for me. It's a step up—from welfare." "We have mutual fears; every employer is afraid a good employee will leave too soon, and every employee is afraid the employer might fire him/her, for no good reason." "I like to work, and I give my best to every job I've ever had."
And, last, "Tell me, what is your greatest weakness?"	The employer is afraid you have some character flaw, and hopes you will now rashly blurt it out, or confess it.	You have limitations just like anyone else, but you work constantly to improve yourself and be a more and more effective worker.	Mention a weakness and then stress its positive aspect, e.g., "I don't like to be over-supervised, because I have a great deal of initiative, and I like to anticipate problems before they even arise."

Tip #12

As the interview proceeds, you want to quietly notice the time-frame of the questions the employer is asking, because it's a way of measuring how the interview is going. If it's going favorably for you, the timeframe of the employer's questions will often move—*however slowly*—through the following stages.

1. Distant past: *e.g., "Where did you attend high school?"*

2. Immediate past: *e.g., "Tell me about your most recent job."*

3. Present: *e.g., "What kind of a job are you looking for?"*

4. Immediate future: *e.g., "Would you be able to come back for another interview next week?"*

5. Distant future: *e.g., "Where would you like to be five years from now?"*

Well, you get the point. The more the timeframe of the interviewer's questions moves from the past to the future, the more favorably you may assume the interview is going for you. On the other hand, if the interviewer's questions stay firmly in the past, the outlook is not so good. *Ah well, ya can't win them all!*

When the timeframe of the interviewer's questions moves firmly into the future, *then* is the time for you to get more specific about the job in question. Experts say it is essential for you to ask, at that point, these kinds of questions, *if* you don't already know the answers:

What is the job, specifically, that I am being considered for?

If I were hired, what duties would I be performing?

What responsibilities would I have?

What would you be hiring me to accomplish?

Would I be working with a team, or group? To whom would I report?

Whose responsibility is it to see that I get the training I need, here, to get up to speed?

How would I be evaluated, how often, and by whom?

What were the strengths and weaknesses of previous people in this position?

If you don't mind my asking, I'm curious as to why *you* yourself decided to work at this organization?

What do you wish you had known about this company before you started here?

May I meet the persons I would be working with and for (if it isn't you)?

Tip #13

After all this careful, rational approach, I hate to tell you but sometimes interviews are lost for the darnedest reasons, that would never occur to you in a million years. I think of this as losing to mosquitoes when you were prepared to fight dragons. And losing in the first two minutes (ouch)!

So let us look at *what* mosquitoes (*as it were*) can fly in, during the first thirty seconds to two minutes of your interview so that *the person-who-has-the-power-to-hire-you* starts muttering to themselves, "*I sure hope we have some other candidates besides this one*":

1. **Your appearance and personal habits.** Interview after interview has revealed that *you are much more likely to get the job if.*

   - you have obviously freshly bathed; if a male that you have your face freshly shaved or your hair and beard freshly trimmed, have clean fingernails, and are using a deodorant; if a female that you have not got tons of makeup on your face, have had your hair newly cut or styled, have clean or nicely manicured fingernails, that don't stick out ten inches from your fingers, are using deodorant, and are not wearing clothes so daring that they call *a lot* of attention to themselves; *and that*

   - you have on freshly laundered clothes, pants, or pantsuits with a sharp crease, and shoes, not flip-flops, freshly polished; *and*

   - you do not have bad breath, do not dispense the odor of garlic, onion, stale tobacco, or strong drink, into the enclosed office air, but have brushed and flossed your teeth; *and equally*

   - you are not wafting tons of aftershave cologne or overwhelming perfume fifteen feet ahead of you, as you enter the room. Employers are super-sensitive these days to the fact that many of their employees are allergic.

2. **Nervous mannerisms.** *It is a turnoff for employers if:*

   - you continually avoid eye contact with the employer (in fact, this is a *big, big* no-no), *or*

   - you give a limp handshake, *or*

   - you slouch in your chair, or endlessly fidget with your hands, or crack your knuckles, or constantly play with your hair during the interview.

3. **Lack of self-confidence.** *It is a turnoff for employers if:*

   - you are speaking so softly you cannot be heard, or so loudly you can be heard two rooms away, *or*

- you are giving answers in an extremely hesitant fashion, *or*

- you are giving one-word answers to all the employer's questions, *or*

- you are constantly interrupting the employer, *or*

- you are downplaying your achievements or abilities, or are continuously being self-critical in comments you make about yourself during the interview.

4. **The consideration you show to other people.** *It is a turnoff for employers if:*

- you show a lack of courtesy to the receptionist, secretary, and (if at lunch) to the waiter or waitress, *or*

- you display extreme criticalness toward your previous employers and places of work, *or*

- you drink strong stuff during the interview process. Ordering a drink if the employer takes you to lunch is *always* a no-no, as it raises the question in the employer's mind, *Do they normally stop with one, or do they normally keep on going?* Don't . . . do . . . it! . . . even if they do; *or*

- you forget to thank the interviewer as you're leaving, or forget to send a thank-you note afterward. Says one human resources expert: "A prompt, brief, faxed business letter thanking me for my time along with a (brief!) synopsis of his/her unique qualities communicates to me that this person is an assertive, motivated, customer-service-oriented salesperson who utilizes technology and knows the rules of the 'game.' These are qualities I am looking for. . . . At the moment I receive approximately one such letter . . . for every fifteen candidates interviewed."

- Incidentally, *many* an employer will watch to see if you smoke, either in the office or at lunch. *In a race between two equally qualified people, the nonsmoker will win out over the smoker 94 percent of the time, according to a study done by a professor of business at Seattle University.* Sorry to report this, but there it is!

5. **Your values.** *It is a complete turnoff for most employers, if they see in you:*

- any sign of arrogance or excessive aggressiveness; any sign of tardiness or failure to keep appointments and commitments on time, including this hiring-interview; *or*

- any sign of laziness or lack of motivation; *or*

- any sign of constant complaining or blaming things on others; *or*

- any signs of dishonesty or lying—especially on your resume or during the interview; *or*

- any signs of irresponsibility or tendency to goof off; *or*

- any sign of not following instructions or obeying rules; *or*

- any sign of a lack of enthusiasm for this organization and what it is trying to do; *or*

- any sign of instability, inappropriate response, and the like; *or*

- the other ways in which you evidence your *values,* such as: what things impress you or don't impress you in their office; *or* what you are willing to sacrifice in order to get this job *and* what you are *not* willing to sacrifice in order to get this job; *or* your enthusiasm for work; *or* the carefulness with which you did or didn't research this company before you came in; and blah, blah, blah.

There you have it: the *mosquitoes* that can kill you, when you're on the watch only for dragons, during the hiring-interview. One favor I ask of you: do not write me, telling me how picayune or asinine some of this is. Believe me, I *know* that. I'm not reporting the world as it *should* be, and certainly not as I would like it to be. I'm only reporting what study after study has revealed about the hiring world as it *is*.

But here's the good news, when all is said and done: you can *kill* all these mosquitoes. Yes, you control and can change *every one* of these factors. Go back and read the list; see!

Tip #14

Before you let the (final) interview end, there are five questions you should *always* ask:

1. *"Can you offer me this job?"* **I know this seems stupid, but it is astonishing (at least to me) how many job-hunters have secured a job simply by being bold enough to ask for it, at the end of the (final) interview, in language they feel comfortable with.** I don't know *why* this is. I only know that it is. Anyway, if after hearing all about this job at this place, you decide you'd really like to have it, you must *ask for it.* The worst thing the employer can say is "No," or "We need some time to think about all the interviews we're conducting."

2. *"When may I expect to hear from you?"* If the employer says, *"We need some time to think about this,"* or *"We will be calling you for a second interview,"* you don't want to leave this as a vague good intention on the employer's part. You want to nail it down.

3. *"Might I ask what would be* the latest *I can expect to hear from you?"* The employer has probably given you their best guess, in answer to your previous question. Now you want to know: *what is the worst-case* scenario? Incidentally, when I was job-hunting once, and I asked my interviewer when was the latest I might expect to hear from him, he replied, *"Never!"* I thought he had a great sense of humor. Turned out he was dead serious.

4. *"May I contact you after that date, if for any reason you haven't gotten back to me by that time?"* Some employers resent this question. You'll know that is the case if they snap at you. But most employers appreciate your offering them what is in essence a safety-net. They know they can get busy, become overwhelmed with other things, forget their promise to you. It's reassuring, in such a case, for you to offer to rescue them.

(Optional: #5. *"Can you think of anyone else who* might *be interested in hiring me?"* This question is invoked *only* if they replied *"No,"* to your first question, above.)

Jot down any answers they give you, then stand up, thank them sincerely for their time, give a firm handshake, and leave.

In the following days, rigorously keep to all that you said, and don't contact them except with that mandatory thank-you note, until after the latest deadline you two agreed upon, in answer to question #4. If you do have to contact them after that date, and if they tell you things are still up in the air, you should gently ask questions #2, #3, and #4, all over again.

Incidentally, it is a good idea for you to insert a thank-you note into the running stream, after *each* interview or telephone contact. Just keep it brief.

Tip #15

Every expert on interviewing will tell you two things:

(1) Thank-you notes *must* be sent after *every* interview, by every job-hunter; and (2) most job-hunters ignore this advice.

Indeed, it is safe to say that **it is the most overlooked step in the entire job-hunting process.**

If you want to stand out from the others applying for the same job, send thank-you notes—to *everyone* you met there, that day. Ask if they have a business card, and if not, ask them to write out their name and address. Do this with secretaries (who often hold the keys to the kingdom) as well as with your interviewer.

If you need any additional encouragement to send thank-you letters (*besides the fact that it may get you the job*), here are six more reasons for sending a thank-you note, especially to the one who interviewed you:

First, you were presenting yourself as one who has good skills with people. Your actions with respect to the job-interview must back this claim up. Sending a thank-you note does that. The employer can see you are good with people; you remembered to thank them.

Second, it helps the employer recall who you are. Very helpful if they've seen a dozen people that day.

Third, if a committee will be involved in the hiring process, the man or woman who first interviewed you has something to show the others on the committee.

Fourth, if the interview went rather well, and the employer seemed to show an interest in further talks, the thank-you letter can reiterate *your* interest in further talks.

Fifth, the thank-you note gives you an opportunity to correct any wrong impression you left behind. You can add anything you forgot to tell them, that you want them to know. And from among all the things you two discussed, you can underline the two or three points that you most want to stand out in their minds.

Lastly, if the interview did not go well, or you lost all interest in working there, and this thank-you note is sort of *"goodbye, and thanks,"* keep in mind that they may hear of openings elsewhere, that would be of interest to you. In the thank-you note, you can mention this, and ask them to please let you know if they hear of anything anywhere. If this was a kind man or woman who interviewed you, they may send you additional leads.

Tip #16

Remember, despite all your careful preparation, and all your thoughtful questions, you may not be offered the job. I remind you of what I said at the beginning of this chapter: *the hiring process is more like choosing a mate, than it is like deciding whether or not to buy a car.* "Choosing a mate" here is a metaphor. To elaborate upon the metaphor just a bit, it means that *the mechanisms* by which human nature decides to hire someone, are *similar* to the mechanisms by which human nature decides whether or not to marry someone. Those mechanisms, of course, are often impulsive, intuitive, nonrational, unfathomable, and made on the spur of the moment.

There is no magic in job-hunting. No techniques work all the time. I hear regularly from job-hunters who report that they paid attention to all the tips I have mentioned in this chapter and book, and are quite successful at securing interviews—but they never get hired. And they want to know what they're doing wrong.

Well, unfortunately, the answer *sometimes* is: "Maybe you're doing nothing wrong." I don't know *how often* this happens, but I know it *does* happen: namely, *some* employers play despicable tricks on job-hunters, whereby they invite you in for an interview despite the fact that they have already hired someone for the position in question, and they know from the beginning that they have absolutely no intention of hiring you—not in a million years!

You are cheered, of course, by the ease with which you get these interviews. But unbeknownst to you, the manager who is interviewing you (we'll say it's a *he*) has a personal friend he already agreed to give the job to. Only one small problem remains: the state or the federal government gives funds to this organization, and has mandated that this position be opened to all. So this manager must *pretend* to interview ten candidates, including his favorite, *as though* the job opening were still available. But, he intended, from the beginning, to reject the other nine and give the job to his favorite. You were selected for the honor of being among those nine *rejectees*.

You will, of course, be baffled as to *why* you got turned down. Trouble is, they will *never* confess it to you.

On the other hand, there is always the chance that no games are being played. You are getting rejected, at place after place, because there is something really wrong with the way you are coming across, during these hiring-interviews.

Employers will rarely ever tell you this. You will never hear them say something like, "You came across as just too cocky and arrogant during the interview." You will almost always be left in the dark as to *what* it is you're doing wrong.

If you've been interviewed by a whole bunch of employers, one way around this deadly silence, is to ask for *generalized* feedback from whoever was the *friendliest* employer that you saw. You can always try phoning, reminding them of who you are, and then asking the following question—**deliberately kept generalized, vague, unrelated to just** *that* **place, and above all, future-directed**. Something like: *"I'd appreciate some advice. I've been on several interviews at several different places now. From what you've seen, is there something about me in an interview, that you think might be causing me not to get hired at those places? If so, I'd really appreciate your giving me some pointers so I can do better in my future hiring-interviews."*

Most of the time they'll *still* duck saying anything hurtful or helpful. Their legal advisor, if they have one, will certainly advise against it. First of all, they're afraid of lawsuits. Second, they don't know how you will use what they might have to say. (Said an old military veteran to me one day, "I used to think it was my duty to tell everyone the truth. Now I only give it to those who can use it.")

But *occasionally* you will run into an employer who is willing to risk giving you the truth, because they think you will know how to use it wisely. If so, thank them from the bottom of your heart, no matter how painful their feedback is. Such advice, seriously heeded, can bring about just the changes in your interviewing strategy that you most need, in order to win interviews in the future.

In the absence of any such help from employers who interviewed you, you might want to get a good business friend of yours to role-play a mock hiring-interview with you, in case they immediately see something glaringly wrong with how you're "coming across."

When all else fails, I would recommend you go to a career coach who charges by the hour, and put yourself in their tender knowledgeable hands. Role-play an interview with them, and take their advice seriously (you've just paid for it, after all).

Conclusion

I have left out the subject of salary negotiation in this chapter. It requires a chapter of its own (chapter 11).

Hopefully, however, with these tips you will do well in your interviews. And if you do get hired, make one resolution to yourself right there on the spot: plan to keep track of your accomplishments at this new job, on a weekly basis—jotting them down, every weekend, in your own private log. Career experts recommend you do this without fail. You can then summarize these accomplishments annually on a one-page sheet, for your boss's eyes, when the question of a raise or promotion comes up.[5]

---

5. In any good-size organization, you will often be amazed at how little attention your superiors pay to your noteworthy accomplishments, and how little they are aware at the end of the year that you really are entitled to a raise, based on the profits you have brought in. Noteworthy your accomplishments may be, but no one is taking notes . . . unless you do. You may even need to be the one who brings up the subject of a raise or promotion. Waiting for the employer to bring this up may never happen.

THE TEN COMMANDMENTS
FOR JOB-INTERVIEWS

Whereby Your Chances of Finding a Job Are Vastly Increased

I. Go after new small organizations with twenty or fewer employees, since they create two-thirds of all new jobs. Only if you turn up nothing should you broaden the search to slightly larger organizations.

II. Hunt for places to interview using the aid of, say, eighty friends and acquaintances— because a job-hunt requires eighty pairs of eyes and ears. But first do homework on yourself so you can tell them exactly what you are looking for.

III. As for who to interview, once you've identified a place that interests you, you really need to find out who has the power to hire you there, for the position you want, and use "bridge-people" (those who know you and also know them) to get an introduction to that person. Employ LinkedIn.com and similar, to find these people.

IV. Do thorough homework on an organization before going there, using Informational Interviews plus the Internet to find out as much about them as you possibly can. If you have a public library in town, ask there too.

V. Then prepare for the interview with your own agenda, your own questions and curiosities about whether or not this job fits you. This will always impress employers.

VI. If you initiated the appointment, ask for just twenty minutes of their time, and keep to your word strictly. Watch your watch.

VII. When answering a question of theirs, talk only between twenty seconds to two minutes, at any one time. Try to be succinct. Don't keep rattling on, out of nervousness.

VIII. Basically approach them not as a "job-beggar" but humbly as a resource person, able to produce better work for that organization than any of the people who worked in that position, previously.

IX. At the end of the interviewing process, ask for the job: "Given all that we have discussed, can you offer me this job?" Salary negotiation should only happen when they have definitely said they want you; prior to that, it's pointless.

X. Always write a thank-you note the same evening as the interview, and mail it at the latest by early next morning. You may also e-mail it.

God, grant me the serenity
To accept the things I cannot change,
The courage to change the things I can,
And the wisdom to know the difference.

—Reinhold Niebuhr (1892–1971)

Chapter 10 How to Deal with Handicaps (Real or Imagined)

I know what you're thinking. If you got a job-interview (or interviews), and got turned down, you're thinking that there is some handicap (hidden or obvious) that is keeping you from getting hired.

Maybe you're thinking this, even before you go in for an interview. (*You turned to this chapter straightaway, didn't you?*)

You're thinking, I'm getting turned down (or *I will be turned down*) because:

I have a physical handicap *or*
I have a mental handicap *or*
I never graduated from high school *or*
I never graduated from college *or*

I am just graduating *or*

I just graduated two years ago and am still unemployed *or*

I graduated way too long ago *or*

I am too beautiful or handsome *or*

I am too ugly *or*

I am too fat *or*

I am too thin *or*

I am too old *or*

I am too young *or*

I am too near retirement *or*

I have only had one employer in life *or*

I have hopped from job to job all my life *or*

I have been out of the job-market too long *or*

I have been in the job-market far too long *or*

I am too inexperienced *or*

I have a prison record *or*

I have a psychiatric history *or*

I have not had enough education and am underqualified *or*

I have too much education and am overqualified *or*

I am Hispanic *or*

I am Black *or*

I am Asian *or*

My English is not very good *or*

I speak heavily accented English *or*

I am too much of a specialist *or*

I am too much of a generalist *or*

I am ex-clergy *or*

I am ex-military *or*

I am too assertive *or*

I am too shy *or*

I have only worked for volunteer organizations *or*

I have only worked for small organizations *or*

I have only worked for a large organization *or*

I have only worked for the government *or*

I come from a very different culture or background *or*

I come from another industry *or*

I come from another planet.

In other words, you are thinking that there are only three weeks in our life when we are employable!

Okay, fine! But if you think you have a handicap that will keep employers from hiring you, take heart! No matter what handicap you have, or think you have, it cannot possibly keep you from getting hired. It can only keep you from getting hired *at some places.*

So, here are a couple of things to keep in mind, all during your job-hunt.

You Cannot Generalize About Employers

You must always keep in mind something we talked about, back in chapter 2:

> There is no such thing as "employers." They are not all the same tribe. Each of them is an individual. But so far as you are concerned, you need think of only two kinds of employers: employers who are interested in hiring you for what you *can* do; vs. employers who are bothered by what you *can't* do. With the latter you should thank them for their time, and ask if they know of any other employers who might be interested in someone with your skills. Then, gently take your leave. And write and mail them a thank-you note that very night. Keep going until you find the other kind of employer: the one who only looks at what you *can* do, not at what you *can't.*

The second thing you want to keep in mind, is that "handicap" is a hazy concept. It can refer to either job-hunters or employers. That is, either to job-hunters' *disabilities* or employers' *prejudices.* There is a difference, and you need to remember that.

Suppose you cannot hear. If you are considering a job that requires acute hearing, then that is a disability: it means there are certain skills you don't have, that are essential, at least for *that* job.

But now let us suppose you can hear perfectly, but you are way overweight. If you are applying for that same job, overweight is not a disability unless it interferes with your ability to do that work.

Nonetheless a particular employer may be prejudiced against overweight people, and simply won't hire you, even though this has nothing to do with your ability to do the job.

So, here's the difference: a **disability** is something within *you*. A **prejudice** is something within *the employer*.

Both may technically be handicaps, because both may keep you from getting hired, but it is important to understand that *a real handicap* is a disability you have—you cannot do some important task required in that particular job. On the other hand, a prejudice is *a phantom handicap*. It may raise its ugly head in one particular interview or more, but if you keep on going, find the right employer, then poof! the so-called handicap vanishes.

You must just be sure you don't share some employers' prejudices. That is, don't look at yourself through *their* eyes. Look at yourself through your own eyes.

The Key Employer Prejudice

The employer prejudice that is getting increasing scrutiny now is *age*. Reason? Millions of baby boomers (*the 76 million people born 1946–1964*) are beginning to enter the so-called "retirement years." A lot of *them*—no, make that *us*—are not going to find generous pensions waiting, but are going to have to keep working long after we ever thought we would have to. What are employers going to think about you? Well you know what they're going to think, at least some of them. They will think you're too old for them to hire. Why? Handicap? No, *prejudice!*

Prejudices are often not about age but about money. Given all your years of experience, many of them think you will expect a high salary—*and* they could hire two less-experienced workers in their twenties for what it would cost them to hire just you. Also, there's the matter of *bennies* (benefits). You would cost them too much if they're a company that still has a generous pension plan—though that is increasingly a vanishing breed these days. Or you may cost them too much if age does bring with it more medical problems, and they are mandated to have a medical plan.

Prejudice *plus* the bottom line! Tough to overcome. And yet, despite all this, there are still employers out there who *will* hire you, regardless of your age, if . . . (and here we have a lot of "*if*"s—all of which lie within your control, thank heaven).

They *will* hire you:

If you choose to approach a small company and they don't have to put you late into a pension plan; and

If you come with a positive attitude toward your aging. For example, thinking of your current age not in terms of work but in terms of music—particularly a symphony. A symphony, traditionally, has four movements, as they're called. So does Life. There is the first movement, infancy; then the second movement, the time of learning; the long third movement follows, the time of working; and finally, a fourth movement. It is traditionally spoken of, in terms of work: hence, we call it *retirement*. It is much better to think of it as the Fourth Movement, a triumphant, powerful ending to the symphony of our life here on earth. Go listen to Beethoven's Third Symphony, the Eroica.

And

If you convey energy, even in this period of your life. Ask any employer what they are looking for, when they interview a job candidate who is fifty years or older, and they will tell you: *energy*. Okay, but where shall we find energy, after fifty? When we were younger, energy came from the *physical* side of our nature. We were "feeling our oats," as they say. We could go all day, and all night. "My, where do you get all your energy?" our grandmother would ask us. We were a dynamo . . . of *physical* energy. But after fifty, physical energy may be harder to come by, despite workouts, exercise, and marathons. Increasingly, our energy must spring not from our muscles but from our excitement about Life; there are inevitably *some* employers dying to have that excitement in their organization; and

If you have done some life/work planning, and you know alternative ways to describe who you are and what you can do, because you did the homework on Who You Are, in chapter 5; and

If you keep going on interviews until you encounter an employer or two who share this understanding of age. What do I mean by *keep going*? Well, here is a job-hunter's actual records (the "process" she is referring to, is the PIE method, described back in chapter 6):

"Here are the figures you wanted: In the course of my surveying, September through November, I was referred to 120+ people. Of these I contacted 84 and actually met with 50. I met most people at their offices, a few for lunch, a couple for dinner, and one for breakfast! The process worked so well for me, I am really excited about my new prospects."

Job-hunting success, regardless of your age, often requires this kind of persistence, keeping at it, working at your job-hunt far longer and far harder than the average job-hunter would ever dream of doing, because you know you will be valuable to any organization that is able to see you clearly, without prejudice.

Another Employer Prejudice: Concerning Ex-Offenders

With any employer prejudice, Google it by name on the Internet, and see what you turn up. What you turn up, may prove very interesting. This is the case if you are (*or work with*) an ex-offender. The most detailed help I know of, is found on the website run by a man named Dick Gaither. Let me tell you about him. He is head of Job Search Training Systems in Indiana, and has worked with ex-offenders a lot, over many years. Email Dick at **workwizard@aol.com** and he will send you 126 pages of useful information and guidance that you can print out. Incredibly helpful, and . . . **it's free.** A great public service, from a tremendous human being.

Everyone Is Handicapped

Turning from the subject of *prejudices* to that of genuine *handicaps*, this is the point where I need to remind you that *everyone* looking for work is handicapped. *What!* Well, sure. As we have seen, a real handicap means *dis-ability*: there are some things a person does not have the ability to do. To see what that means here, let's start with how many skills there are, in the whole world. Nobody knows the number, so let's make one up. Let's say there are 4,341 **transferable skills** in the world.

How many of those 4,341 do you think the average person has? Nobody knows that number either, so let's again make one up. Let's say the average person has 1,341 skills. That's a lot. That would be 1,341 things the average person can do.

But 4,341 skills in all the world minus 1,341 that the average person has, leaves 3,000 things the average person *can't* do. Of course, what those 3,000 are, will vary from person to person. But, in the end, *everybody* is handicapped. Everybody.

So when you go job-hunting, if you have a real handicap, but it doesn't keep you from performing the tasks in the job or career you are targeting, what's so special about *your* handicap, compared with others'? The answer is *Nothing.*

Unless—*unless*—you are so disheartened by the fact that you are handicapped, and so focused on what you *can't* do, that you have forgotten all the things you *can* do.

Unless you're thinking of all the reasons why employers might not hire you, instead of all the reasons why employers would be lucky to get you.

Unless you're going about your job-hunt feeling like *a job-beggar,* rather than standing tall to offer yourself as *a helpful resource* for this employer.

What You Can Do, What You Can't

To focus our attention on what we can do, not what we can't, here's a useful exercise. Take a piece of notebook paper and divide it into two columns, viz,

I have this skill:	I don't have this skill:

Then, get a list of transferable skills from somewhere. You could use The Skills Grid in chapter 5. Or, if you prefer, use the famous *A List of 246 Skills as Verbs*, on the next page. Whichever list you use, copy as many skills as you choose onto that piece of paper, putting each skill in the proper column, depending on whether you *can* do the skill, or *cannot.* (*Or not yet, anyway.*) Use additional sheets, as needed. If you decline to use paper, use your iPad or similar.

When you are done with these two columns, *can, can't,* pick out your favorite five things that you *can* do, and *love* to do; and write out some examples of how you actually demonstrated that, sometime in your recent past.

Incidentally, if you want a longer list than either of the two referred to, above, Canadian career-expert Martin Buckland has a free mega list of 2,010 action verbs at Elite Resumes (**http://aneliteresume.com**).

Put No Limits on Your Dreams

What about a *disability* that seems to negate all your dreams: something you simply *can't* do, but really want to be able to do? Maybe someone has invented a technology or simple strategy that helps you get around that disability. You never know. There are some very clever people in the world. How to find them? If your particular disability has a name, look it up on the Internet. Put its name into a search engine like Google, and see what turns up. Look particularly on the list it gives you for any professional association that deals with your disability. Contact them, and ask them what information they have.

An alternative way of dealing with this is to search for *related* jobs. Example: one career counselor in Europe was working with a young teenager who wanted to be a pilot. Problem: his eyesight was too poor. So the counselor sent him out to the large airport nearby, with a pad of yellow paper and a pen, and told him to spend the day listing every different kind of occupation that he saw or heard about, there at the airport—besides pilot. The next day he showed his list to his counselor. It was very long. When asked if he'd come across any occupation that interested him, he said, "Yes. I love the idea of making the seats that they put inside new airplanes." So, that's the job he pursued. He ended up in the airline industry, even though he couldn't be a pilot.

A List of 246 Skills as Verbs

achieving	acting	adapting	addressing	administering
advising	analyzing	anticipating	arbitrating	arranging
ascertaining	assembling	assessing	attaining	auditing
budgeting	building	calculating	charting	checking
classifying	coaching	collecting	communicating	compiling
completing	composing	computing	conceptualizing	conducting
conserving	consolidating	constructing	controlling	coordinating
coping	counseling	creating	deciding	defining
delivering	designing	detailing	detecting	determining
developing	devising	diagnosing	digging	directing
discovering	dispensing	displaying	disproving	dissecting
distributing	diverting	dramatizing	drawing	driving
editing	eliminating	empathizing	enforcing	establishing
estimating	evaluating	examining	expanding	experimenting
explaining	expressing	extracting	filing	financing
fixing	following	formulating	founding	gathering
generating	getting	giving	guiding	handling
having responsibility	heading	helping	hypothesizing	identifying
illustrating	imagining	implementing	improving	improvising
increasing	influencing	informing	initiating	innovating
inspecting	inspiring	installing	instituting	instructing
integrating	interpreting	interviewing	intuiting	inventing
inventorying	investigating	judging	keeping	leading
learning	lecturing	lifting	listening	logging
maintaining	making	managing	manipulating	mediating
meeting	memorizing	mentoring	modeling	monitoring
motivating	navigating	negotiating	observing	obtaining
offering	operating	ordering	organizing	originating
overseeing	painting	perceiving	performing	persuading
photographing	piloting	planning	playing	predicting
preparing	prescribing	presenting	printing	problem solving
processing	producing	programming	projecting	promoting
proofreading	protecting	providing	publicizing	purchasing
questioning	raising	reading	realizing	reasoning
receiving	recommending	reconciling	recording	recruiting
reducing	referring	rehabilitating	relating	remembering
rendering	repairing	reporting	representing	researching
resolving	responding	restoring	retrieving	reviewing
risking	scheduling	selecting	selling	sensing
separating	serving	setting	setting-up	sewing
shaping	sharing	showing	singing	sketching
solving	sorting	speaking	studying	summarizing
supervising	supplying	symbolizing	synergizing	synthesizing
systematizing	taking instructions	talking	teaching	team-building
telling	tending	testing & proving	training	transcribing
translating	traveling	treating	trouble-shooting	tutoring
typing	umpiring	understanding	understudying	undertaking
unifying	uniting	upgrading	using	utilizing
verbalizing	washing	weighing	winning	working
writing				

Self-Esteem Versus Egotism

As most of us know, the proper attitude toward ourselves is called "good self-esteem." But self-esteem is an art. An art of *balance*. A balance between thinking too little of ourselves, and thinking too much of ourselves.

The name for thinking too much of ourselves is "egotism." We have all run into that, at some point in our lives, so we know what it looks like. Some of us have even caught a passing glimpse of it in the mirror.

In our culture and others, we are taught to recoil from this in horror. We even have mythologies warning us against it; the story of Narcissus comes to mind. Poor guy! *(See* **http://tinyurl.com/a3a33** *if you are unfamiliar with the myth.)*

In order to avoid egotism, a lot of us go way overboard in the other direction. We shrink from ever declaring that we have any virtue, any excellency, any special gifts, lest we be accused of boasting. And so we fall into that opposite pit from egotism, namely, ingratitude. We appear ungrateful for the gifts that life, the universe, God—you name it—has already given us.

So, how do we adopt the proper attitude toward our gifts—speaking of them honestly, humbly, gratefully—without sounding egotistical? Just this: the more you see your own gifts clearly, the more you must pay attention to the gifts that others have. The more sensitive you become to how unusual you are, the more you must become sensitive to how unusual those around you are. The more you pay attention to yourself, the more you must pay attention to others. The more you ponder the mystery of You, the more you must ponder the mystery of all those you encounter, every loved one, every friend, every acquaintance, every stranger.

Self-esteem is an art. It is the art of balance. A balance between thinking too little of ourselves, and thinking too much of ourselves. But we can only think too much of ourselves if we lose sight of others. Look at yourself, but equally look at them—with wonder.

That is the proper attitude we all should set as our goal.

Good self-esteem is a precondition for salary negotiation. You cannot just set some monetary target for salary negotiation. You have to believe you are genuinely worth *that salary* or that salary *range*. So, it is to salary negotiation that we now turn, in our next chapter.

Discussion

Job-hunter: I never thought of egotism this way. I always thought that if you talked about yourself being good at something, that was boasting. I'd heard about "the tall poppy" theory of life, with its implication that you shouldn't stand taller than others in your field.

Career-counselor: Well, I think that's true. But you make yourself equal to others not by lowering yourself but by raising them. I ask you, what are the favorite skills of your best friend or mate? Do you know? Are you sure? Have you asked them what they think they are? Have you complimented them on these skills, during the past week?

Job-hunter: I've got to go now; I think I have work to do.

Career-counselor: No longer worried about being egotistical, eh?

Job-hunter: No, I'm just worried about them. I want them to know how excellent they are.

Career-counselor: Just remember, it's no sin to praise yourself as long as that heightens your awareness of what there is to praise in them. And you then express that praise directly to them.

If you pay peanuts, you get monkeys.

—James Goldsmith (1933–1997)

Chapter 11 The Six Secrets of Salary Negotiation

Let us rehearse what we've covered thus far: a *resume's* purpose is to get you a *first interview* somewhere; a first interview's purpose is to get you a second interview; a *second interview's* purpose is to answer *your* curiosities about them as well as *their* curiosities about you, and into this by-play come your *handicaps* (discussed) and the employer's *prejudices* (not discussed); and once that's settled, if you both decide you want to work there, then you come to *salary negotiation*. That's where we are now.

Salary. It must be negotiated. It must be discussed. I hope you know that. I remember once talking to a breathless high school graduate, who was elated at having just landed her first job. "How much are they going to pay you?" I asked. She looked startled. "I don't know," she said, "I never asked. I just assume they will pay me a fair wage." *Boy!* did she get a rude awakening when she received her first paycheck. It was so miserably *low*, she couldn't believe her eyes. And thus did she learn, painfully, what you must learn too: *Before accepting a job offer, always ask about salary*. Indeed, *ask and then negotiate*.

It's the "**negotiate**" that throws fear into our hearts. We feel ill prepared to do this. Well, set your mind at ease; it's not all that difficult. While whole books can be—and have been—written on this subject, there are basically just six secrets to keep in mind.

The First Secret of Salary Negotiation

Never Discuss Salary Until the End of the Interviewing Process When (and If) They Have Definitely Said They Want You

"The end of the interviewing process" is difficult to define. It's the point at which the employer says, or thinks, "We've got to get this person!" That may be at the end of the first (and therefore the last) interview; or it may be at the end of a whole series of interviews, often with different people within the same company or organization. But assuming things are going favorably for you, whether after the first, or second, or third, or fourth interview, if *you* like them and *they* increasingly like you, a job offer *will* be made. Then, and only then, is it time to deal with the question that is inevitably on any employer's mind: *how much is this person going to cost me?* And the question that is on *your* mind: *how much does this job pay?*

If the employer raises the salary question earlier, say near the beginning of the interview, innocently asking, "What kind of salary are you looking for?" you should have three responses ready at your fingertips.

Response #1: If the employer seems like a kindly man or woman, your best and most tactful reply might be: "Until you've decided you definitely want me, and I've decided I definitely could help you with your tasks here, I feel any discussion of salary is premature."

That will work, in most cases. There are instances, however, where that doesn't work. Then you need:

Response #2: You may be face-to-face with an employer who will not be put off so easily, and demands within the first two minutes of the interview to know what salary you are looking for. At this point, you may need your second response: "I'll gladly answer that, but could you first help me understand what this job involves?"

That is a good response, in most cases. But what if it doesn't work? Then you need:

Response #3: The employer with rising voice says, "Come, come, don't play games with me. I want to know what salary you're looking for." You have your third response ready at hand for *this very eventuality*. You answer in terms of a *range*. For example, "I'm looking for a salary in the range of $35,000 to $45,000 a year."

If that still doesn't satisfy them, then consider what this means. Clearly, you are being interviewed by an employer who has no range in mind. Their beginning figure is their ending figure. No negotiation is possible.[1] This happens, when it happens, because many employers in this post-Recessionary period of history are making salary their major criterion for deciding who to hire, and who not to hire. *It's an old game, now played with new determination by many employers, which runs,* "among two equally qualified candidates, the one who is willing to work for the least pay, *wins.*"

If you run into this situation, and if you want that job badly enough, you will have no choice but to give in. Ask what salary they have in mind, and make your decision. (Of course you can always postpone announcing your decision by saying, *"I need a little time, to think about this."*)

However, all the foregoing is merely the *worst-case scenario.* Usually, things won't go this badly. In most interviews these days, the employer *will* be willing to save salary negotiation until they've finally decided they want you (and you've decided you want them). And at that point, the salary *will be* negotiable.

When You Should Be Willing to Discuss Salary

Not until all of the following conditions have been fulfilled—

- *Not until they've gotten to know you, at your best, so they can see how you stand out above the other applicants.*
- *Not until you've gotten to know them, as completely as you can, so you can tell when they're being firm, or when they're flexible.*
- *Not until you've found out exactly what the job entails.*
- *Not until they've had a chance to find out how well you match the job requirements.*
- *Not until you're in the final interview at that place, for that job.*

---

1. One job-hunter said his interviews *always* began with the salary question, and no matter what he answered, that ended the interview. Turned out, this job-hunter was doing all the interviewing over the phone. That was the problem. Once he went face to face, salary was no longer the first thing discussed in the interview.

- *Not until you've decided, "I'd really like to work here."*
- *Not until they've said, "We want you."*
- *Not until they've said, "We've got to have you."*

—should you get into salary discussion with any employer.

If you'd prefer this be put in the form of a diagram, here it is:

WHEN TO NEGOTIATE SALARY

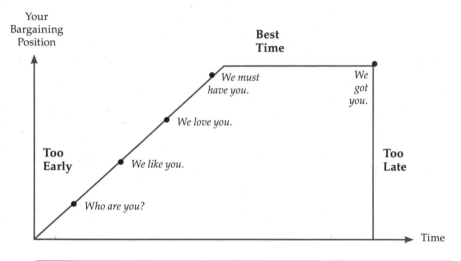

Why is it to your advantage to delay salary discussion? Because, if you really *shine* during the hiring-interview, they may—at the end— offer you a higher salary than they originally had in mind when the interview started—and this is particularly the case when the interview has gone so well, that they're now *determined* to obtain your services.

The Second Secret of Salary Negotiation

The Purpose of Salary Negotiation Is to Uncover the Most That an Employer Is Willing to Pay to Get You

Salary negotiation would never happen if *every* employer in *every* hiring-interview were to mention, right from the start, the top figure they are willing to pay for that position. *Some* employers do, as I mentioned. And that's the end of any salary negotiation. But, of course, most employers don't. Hoping they'll be able to get you for less, they start *lower* than they're ultimately willing to go. **This creates *a range*. And that range is what salary negotiation is all about.**

For example, if the employer wants to hire somebody for no more than $20 an hour, they may start *the bidding* at $12 an hour. In which case, their *range* runs between $12 and $20 an hour.

So, why do you want to negotiate? Because, if a range *is* thus involved, you have every right to try to discover the highest salary that employer is willing to pay you *within that range.*

The employer's goal is to save money, if possible. Your goal is to bring home to your family, your partner, or your own household the most money that you can, for the work you will be doing. Nothing's wrong with the goals of either of you. But it does mean that, where the employer starts lower, salary negotiation is legitimate, and expected.

The Third Secret of Salary Negotiation

During Salary Discussion, Never Be the First One to Mention a Salary Figure

Where salary negotiation has been kept *offstage* for much of the interview process, when it finally does come *onstage* you want the employer to be the first one to mention *a figure*, if you possibly can.

Nobody knows why, but it has been observed over the years that where the goals are opposite, as in this case—you are trying to get the employer to pay the most they can, and the employer is trying to pay the least they can—whoever mentions a salary *figure* first, generally loses. You can speculate from now until the cows come home, as to *why* this is so; all we know is *that* it is.

Inexperienced employer/interviewers often don't know this quirky rule. But experienced ones are very aware of it; that's why they will *always* toss the ball to you first, with some innocent-sounding question, such as: "What kind of salary are you looking for?" *Well, how kind of them to ask me what I want*—you may be thinking. No, no, no. Kindness has nothing to do with it. They are hoping *you* will be the first to mention a figure, because they know this strange and idiotic truth: *whoever mentions a salary figure first, generally loses salary negotiation, at the end.*

Accordingly, if they ask you to name a figure, the *countermove* on your part should be: "Well, you created this position, so you must have some figure in mind, and I'd be interested in knowing what that figure is."

The Fourth Secret of Salary Negotiation

Before You Go to the Interview, Do Some Careful Research on Typical Salaries for Your Field and in That Organization

As I said, salary negotiation is required *anytime* the employer does not open discussion of salary by naming the top figure they have in mind, but starts instead with a lower figure.

Okay, so here is our $64,000 question: how do you tell whether the figure the employer first offers you is only their *starting bid*, or is their *final final offer*? The answer is: by doing some research on the field *and* that organization, before you go to the interview.

Oh, come on! I can hear you say. *Isn't this more trouble than it's worth?* No, not if you want to win the salary negotiation.

Trust me, salary research pays off *handsomely*. Let's say it takes you from one to three days to run down this sort of information on the three or four organizations that interest you the most. And let us say

that because you've done this research, when you finally come to the
end of the (final) hiring-interview you are able to ask for and obtain
a salary that is $15,000 a year higher than you would otherwise have
gotten. In just the next three years, you will be earning $45,000 extra,
because of your salary research. *Not bad pay, for one to three days' work!*
And it can be even more. I know *many* job-hunters and career-changers
to whom this has happened.

There is a financial penalty exacted from those who are too lazy,
or in too much of a hurry, to go gather this information. In plain language: *if you don't do this research, it'll cost ya!*

Okay, then, how do you do this research? Well, there are two ways
to go: on the Internet, and off the Internet. Let's look at each, in turn:

Salary Research on the Internet

If you have access to the Internet, and you want to research salaries
for particular geographical regions, positions, occupations, or industries, or even (sometimes) organizations, here are some free sites that
may give you just what you're looking for:

- **http://jobstar.org/tools/salary/index.cfm**: This site is a treasure
  trove. It links to 300 different sites that maintain salary lists, and
  joy, joy, it is kept updated. It's one of the largest and most complete lists of salary reviews on the Web, maintained by a genius
  named Mary Ellen Mort. This is a treasure.

- **www.salary.com**: The most visited of all the salary-specific job-
  sites, with a wide variety of information about salaries. It was
  started by Kent Plunkett, and acquired by Kenexa Corporation,
  in August 2010. It has expanded a lot, over the years. Roll over the
  green navigation bar at the top to see all its resources.

- **www.bls.gov/ooh**: The Bureau of Labor Statistics' survey of salaries in individual **occupations**, from *The Occupational Outlook
  Handbook 2012–2013*.

- **http://stats.bls.gov/oes/oes_emp.htm**: The Bureau of Labor Statistics' survey of salaries in individual industries (it's a companion
  piece to *The Occupational Outlook Handbook*). This site is up-to-date
  as of May 2011.

- **MyPlan.com** has a list of the 300 highest-paying jobs that don't require a college degree, at **http://tinyurl.com/bo2a7so**.

- **www.salaryexpert.com**: When you need a salary expert, it makes sense to go to "the Salary Expert." Lots of stuff on the subject of salaries here, including a free "Salary Report" for hundreds of job-titles, varying by area, skill level, and experience. Also has some salary calculators.

If you "strike out" on all the above sites, then you're going to have to get a little more clever, and work a little harder, and pound the pavement, as I shall describe below.

Salary Research off the Internet

Offline, how do you go about doing salary research? Well, there's a simple rule: generally speaking, abandon **books**, and go talk to **people**. Use books and libraries only as a *second*, or *last*, resort. Their information is often just way too outdated.

You can get much more complete and up-to-date information from people who are doing the kind of job you're interested in, but *at another company or organization*. If you don't know where to find them, talk to people at a nearby university or college who *train* such people, whatever their department may be. Teachers and professors will usually know what their graduates are making.

How to you research salaries at particular places? Let's look at some concrete examples:

First Example: Working at your first entry-level job, say at a fast-food place. You may not need to do any salary research. They pay what they pay. You can walk in, ask for a job application, and interview with the manager. He or she will usually tell you the pay, outright. It's usually set in concrete. But at least it's easy to discover what the pay is. *(Incidentally, filling out an application, or having an interview there, doesn't force you to take the job—but you probably already know that. You can always decline an offer from any place. That's what makes this approach harmless.)*

Second Example: Working at a place where you can't discover what the pay is, say, *at a construction company*. If that construction company where you would *hope* to get a job is difficult to research, go visit a *different* construction company in the same town—one that isn't of much interest to you—and ask what they make *there*. Or, if you don't know who to talk to there, fill out one of *their* applications, and talk to the hiring person about what kinds of jobs they have (or might have in the future), at which time prospective wages you would be paid, is a legitimate subject of discussion. Then, having done this research on a place you don't care about, go back to the place that *really* interests you, and apply. You still don't know *exactly* what they pay, but you do know what their competitor pays—which will usually be *close* to what you're trying to find out.

Third Example: Working in a one-person office, say *as an administrative assistant.* Here you can often find useful salary information by perusing the Help Wanted ads in the local newspaper for a week or two, assuming you still have a local paper! Most of the ads won't mention a salary figure, but a few may. Among those that do, note what the lowest salary offering is, and what the highest is, and see if the ad reveals any reasons for the difference. It's interesting how much you can learn about administrative assistants' salaries, with this approach. I know, because I was an administrative assistant myself, once upon a time.

There's a lot you can find out by talking to people. But another way to do salary research—if you're out of work and have time on your hands—is to find a *Temporary Work Agency* that places different kinds of workers, and let yourself be farmed out to various organizations: the more, the merrier. It's relatively easy to do salary research when you're *inside* a place. *(Study what that place pays the agency, not what the agency pays you after they've taken their "cut.")* If you're working temporarily at a place where the other workers *like* you, you'll be able to ask questions about a lot of things there, including salary.

The Fifth Secret of Salary Negotiation

Research the Range That the Employer Likely Has in Mind, and Then Define an Interrelated Range for Yourself, Relative to the Employer's Range

Before you go into any organization for your final interview, you want more than just *one* salary figure at your fingertips. You want *a range:* what's the *least* the employer may offer you, and what's the *most* the employer may be willing to offer you. In any organization that has more than five employees, that range is comparatively easy to figure out. **It will be less than what the person who would be above you makes, and more than what the person who would be below you makes.** Examples:

If the Person Who Would Be Below You Makes	And the Person Who Would Be Above You Makes	The Range for Your Job Would Be
$45,000	$55,000	$47,000–$53,000
$30,000	$35,500	$32,500–$34,000

One teensy-tiny little problem here: *how* do you find out the salary of those who would be above and below you? Well, first you have to find out their **names** or the names of their **positions**. If it is a small organization you are going after—one with twenty or fewer employees—finding out this information should be *duck soup.* Any employee who works there is likely to know the answer, and you can usually get in touch with one of those employees, or even an ex-employee, through your own personal "bridge-people"—people who know you and also know them. Since up to two-thirds of all new jobs are created by small companies of that size, that's the size organization you are likely to be researching, anyway.

If you are going after a larger organization, then you fall back on that familiar life preserver, namely **every person you know** (family, friend, relative, business, or spiritual acquaintance) and ask them who they know that might know the company in question, and therefore, the information you seek. LinkedIn should prove immensely helpful to you here, in locating such people. If you're not already on it, get on it. (**LinkedIn.com**.)

If, in the end, you absolutely run into a blank wall at a particular organization (everyone who works there is pledged to secrecy, and they have shipped all their ex-employees to Siberia), then seek out information on their nearest *competitor* in the same geographic area. *For example,* let us say you were trying to find out managerial salaries at Bank X, and that place was proving to be inscrutable about what they pay their managers. You would then turn to Bank Y as your research base, to see if the information were easier to come by, there. And if it were, you can then assume the two are basically similar in their pay scales, and that what you learned about Bank Y is probably applicable to Bank X.

Experts say that in researching salaries, you should also take note of the fact that most governmental agencies have civil service positions paralleling those in private industry—and government job descriptions and pay ranges are available to the public. Go to the nearest city, county, regional, state, or federal civil service office, find the job description nearest what you are seeking in private industry, and then ask the starting salary.

Once you've made a guess at what the employer's range might be, for the job you have in mind, you then define your own range *accordingly*. Let me give an example. Suppose you guess that the employer's range is $36,500 to $47,200. Accordingly, you now *invent* an "asking" range for yourself, where your *minimum* "hooks in" just below that employer's *maximum*.

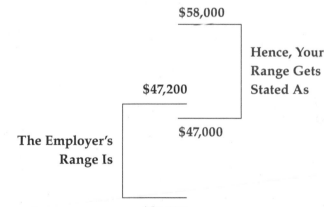

And so, when the employer has stated a figure (probably around his or her *lowest*—i.e., $36,500), you will be ready to respond with something along these lines: "I understand, of course, the constraints under which all organizations are operating these days, but I am confident that my productivity is going to be such, that it will *justify a salary*"— *and here you mention a* **range** *whose bottom figure hooks in just below the top of their range, and goes up from there, as shown on the diagram above*—"in the **range** of $47,000 to $58,000."

It will help a lot during this discussion, if you are prepared to show in what ways you will *make money* or in what ways you will *save money* for that organization, such as would justify the higher salary you are seeking. Hopefully, this will get you at least near the salary you want.

What if this just doesn't work? The employer has a ceiling they *have to* work with, it's above what you're asking, and you are unwilling to lower your definition of what you're worth? Daniel Porot, the job-expert in Europe, suggests that if you're *dying* to work there, but they cannot afford the salary you need and deserve, consider offering them part of your time. If you need, and believe you deserve, say $50,000 annually, but they can only afford $30,000, you might consider offering them three days a week of your time for that $30,000 (30/50 = 3/5). This leaves you free to take work elsewhere during those other two days. You will *of course* determine to produce so much work during those three days per week you are there, that they will be ecstatic about this bargain—won't you?

The Sixth Secret of Salary Negotiation

Know How to Bring the Salary Negotiation to a Close; Don't Leave It "Just Hanging"

Salary negotiation with this employer is not finished until you've addressed both salary and so-called **fringe benefits**. "Fringes" such as life insurance, health benefits or health plans, vacation or holiday plans, and retirement programs typically add anywhere from 15 to 28 percent to many workers' salaries. That is to say, if an employee receives $3,000 salary per week, the fringe benefits are worth another $450 to $840 per week.

Before you walk into the interview, you should decide what benefits are particularly important to you, so after the basic salary discussion, when you ask them what benefits are on offer, you can negotiate for the benefits you particularly care about. Thinking this out ahead of time makes that negotiating easier, by far.

Finally, under the subject of closing the interview, you want to get *everything they're offering* summarized, in writing. Always request **a letter of agreement**—or employment contract.

Many executives unfortunately "forget" what they told you during the hiring-interview, or even deny they ever said such a thing.

Also, many executives leave a company abruptly and unexpectedly, and their successor or the top boss may disown any *unwritten* promises: *"I don't know what caused them to say that to you, but they clearly exceeded their authority, and of course we can't be held to that."*

Conclusion: The Greatest Secret

We are hoping, of course, that your interview and salary negotiation end up well. There are times, however, when all seems to be going well, and then without any warning it suddenly comes totally unraveled. You're hired, told to report next Monday, and then get a phone call on Friday telling you that all hiring has been put, mysteriously, "on hold." You're therefore back out "on the street." Having seen this happen so many times, over the years, I remind you of the truth we began with, in chapter 1: *successful* job-hunters and career-changers *always have alternatives.*

Alternative ideas of what they could do with their life.

Alternative ways of describing what they want to do right now.

Alternative ways of going about the job-hunt (not just the Internet, not just resumes, agencies, and ads).

Alternative job prospects.

Alternative "target" organizations that they go after.

Alternative ways of approaching employers.

And, of course, alternative job offers. Make sure you are continuing to pursue more than just one employer, until after that new job starts.

Remember, job-hunting always involves luck, to some degree. But with a little bit of luck, and a lot of hard work, and determination, these instructions about how to get hired and negotiate a salary, should work for you, as they have worked for so many hundreds of thousands before you.

Take heart from those who have gone before you, such as this determined job-hunter, who wrote me this heartfelt letter, with which I close this chapter:

> *Before I read this book, I was depressed and lost in the futile job-hunt using Want Ads only. I did not receive even one phone call from any ad I answered, over a total of four months. I felt that I was the most useless person on earth. I am female, with a two-and-a-half-year-old daughter, a former professor in China, with no working experience at all in the U.S. We came here seven months ago because my husband had a job offer here.*
>
> *Then, on June 11th of last year, I saw your book in a local bookstore. Subsequently, I spent three weeks, ten hours a day except Sunday, reading every single word of your book and doing all of the flower petals in the Flower Exercise. After getting to know myself much better, I felt I was ready to try the job-hunt again. I used* Parachute *throughout as my guide, from the very beginning to the very end, namely, salary negotiation.*
>
> *In just two weeks I secured (you guessed it) two job offers, one of which I am taking, as it is an excellent job, with very good pay. It is (you guessed it again) a small company, with twenty or so employees. It is also a career-change: I was a professor of English; now I am to be a controller!*
>
> *I am so glad I believed your advice: there are jobs out there, and there are two types of employers out there, and truly there are!*
>
> *I hope you will be happy to hear my story.*

You've got to be careful
If you don't know where you're going,
Because you might not get there.

      —Yogi Berra (b. 1925)

Chapter 12 Starting Your Own Business

If you're unemployed, and just can't find any job-openings, no matter how hard you try, you're probably going to think about starting your own business. According to some surveys, 50 percent of all workers toy with this idea at some point in their lives. According to official statistics, only 10 percent actually do it, in any given year. But if you're seriously considering it, you should do your research carefully beforehand; and, you should try to find a business that really fits *You*.

So, I want to do two things in this chapter. I want to tell you about the existing business opportunities there are, which you may want to look at to see if there is a fit. But I also want to sound warning notes about each of them, so that you will go in with your eyes wide open, if you decide it might be a fit. We live in a world of spams and scams these days, and consequently the pathway to creating your own job has its perils, as well as its rewards. Anyway, here are three ideas for creating your own job:

Finding a Fit, Idea #1: Consider a business already existing that you could start a branch of. Franchises, as they are called, exist because some people want to start their own business, but don't want to go through the agony of starting from scratch. They want to *buy in* on an already established business, and they have some money in their savings with which to do that. Fortunately for them, there are a lot of such franchises. To find the range of possibilities, to decide if any one of them might be a fit for you, start with the following sites:

www.franchiseopportunities.com

www.franchisedirect.com

www.franchisegenius.com

Now, here's the rub. Franchises require you, generally speaking, to have a bundle of cash, if you wish to buy in. And you may not be able to take much money out, the first year. And they are very risky businesses. Their failure rate is high, particularly in these difficult economic times. You have to guess what kind of services or products the public wants. And the public is tremendously fickle.

So, if you start out thinking that maybe, just maybe, a franchise might fit you—not only creating a job for you, but also for others—you owe it to yourself to investigate the whole idea, and that particular franchise, thoroughly. That's: thoroughly. *Thoroughly.*

Start that homework with these sites:

> http://tinyurl.com/64gda2: Interesting checklist from *Entrepreneur Magazine* on "Are You Suited to Be a Franchisee?"

> http://tinyurl.com/4286yju: The best franchises in 2012 according to their owners' ratings.

> http://tinyurl.com/23kuwp: The Ten Riskiest Businesses to Start, according to Fair Isaac Corporation, popularly known as FICO (2007 data).

> http://thefranchisehound.com/2011/01/25/the-best-and-worst-franchises-to-own: This has very current data (from 2011) on the best and the worst, plus news items about retirement as a vanishing dream, etc.

> www.bbb.org/us/article/4580: An article by the Better Business Bureau on the things you should beware of when considering a franchise.

> http://tinyurl.com/97zy3a: You want specifics about home business offers that are scams? The government will be glad to help you. Here they list the business offers to avoid like the plague.

> http://tinyurl.com/3vv97lw: This site goes over all the things you need to know the answers to, if you're going to come up with a business plan.

> www.bestfranchise.org: A new site on finding the best franchise opportunities (2011 data).

> http://tinyurl.com/3bzbrxw: This site cleverly lists franchises whose owners have defaulted most frequently on their SBA

(Small Business Administration) loans, as well as those franchises whose owners have defaulted the least frequently.

http://tinyurl.com/44yxdvh: Nolo Press has a good article here about *fit*, called "Starting the Right Business for You."

After doing this homework please note that there isn't a franchising book, or site, that doesn't warn you eighteen times to go talk to people who have *already* bought that same franchise, before you ever decide to go with them. And I mean *several* people, not just one. Most experts also warn you to go talk to *other* franchises in the same field, not just the kind you're thinking about signing up with. Maybe there's something better, which your research can uncover.

You want to keep in mind that some *types* of franchises have a failure rate *far* greater than others.

And you want to keep in mind also that some individual franchises are *terrible*—and that includes well-known names. They charge too much for you to *get on board*, and often they don't do the advertising or other commitments that they promised they would.

If you are in a hurry, and you don't want to do this homework first, *'cause it's just too much trouble,* you will deserve what you get, believe me. You will rue the day.

Finding a Fit, Idea #2: Starting a home business. A home seems like an excellent place to create your own job. Low rent (ha!). Short commute! Low overhead. That's the vision. Sounds like it might be a fit, for you.

So let's start out with a dose of reality. It *can* be a great idea (I have a home business myself). But be aware that there are three major problems with home businesses:

1. The first major problem of home businesses is that this is a rich playground for scams, that can cost you lots of money but never give any back. A lot of people like the idea of a home business, so vultures have taken advantage of that. You will run into ads on TV and on the Web and in your e-mail, offering you a home business "buy-in." They sound enticing. But, as AARP's Bulletin of March 23, 2009, pointed out: of the more than 3 million Web entries that surface from a Google search on the terms "work at home," more than 95 percent of the results are scams, links to

scams, or other dead ends. Even the sites that claim to be scam-free often feature ads that link to scams. The statistic is: a 48 to 1 scam ratio among ads offering you a nice home business. That's 48 scams for every one true ad. *This swamp is filled with alligators!*

2. The second major problem of home businesses is that even if you start a legitimate one, be it as writer, artist, business expert, lawyer, accountant (doing people's taxes), consultant, childcare, or the like, out of your home, it's often difficult to maintain a balance between business and family time. Sometimes the *family* time gets shortchanged, while in other cases the demands of family (particularly with small children) may become so interruptive, that the *business* gets shortchanged. So, do think out thoroughly ahead of time *how* you would go about doing this *well*.

3. The third major problem of home businesses is that it puts you into a perpetual job-hunt. Yes, I know. You like the idea of a home business because you *hate* job-hunting. You are attracted to the idea of a home business because this seems like an ideal way to cut short your job-hunt, by creating your own job.

   The irony is, that a home business makes you in a very real sense a *perpetual* job-hunter—because you have to be *always* seeking new clients or customers—which is to say, new *employers*. Yes, they are *employers* because they *pay* you for the work you are doing. The only difference between this and a full-time job is that here *the contract is limited*. But if you are running your own business, you will have to *continually* beat the bushes for new clients or customers. Some of us have absolutely no appetite for that aspect of home businesses. *Forewarned is forearmed.*

Of course, the dream of most budding home business people is that you will become so well known, and so in demand, that clients or customers will be literally beating down your doors, and you will be able to stop this endless job-hunt. But that only happens to a relative minority, sorry to report. The greater likelihood is that you will *always* have to beat the bushes for employers/clients. It may get easier as you get better at it, or it may get harder, if the economy goes further south. But you must learn to make your peace with it—however grudgingly. Otherwise, you're probably going to find *a home business* is just a glamorous synonym for *"starving."* I know *many* home business people to whom this has happened, and it happened precisely because they couldn't stomach going out to beat the bushes for clients or customers. If that's true for you, but you're still determined to start a home business, then for heaven's sake start out by *hiring* someone part-time, who is willing to do this for you—one who, in fact, "eats it up."

Anyway, there are a bunch of resources on the Web, to help you make a home business succeed, such as:

> **www.ahbbo.com; www.ahbbo.com/articles.html**: This is a great site, with lots of information for you if you want to learn more about a home-based business. There are more than a hundred articles at that second URL.

Finding a Fit, Idea #3: Starting your own business, outside the home. It may be that, in thinking about creating your own job, you know exactly *what* business you'd like to start, because you've been thinking about it for *years*, and may even have been *doing* it for years—but in the employ of someone else.

But now, you're thinking about doing this kind of work for yourself, whether it be business services, consultancy, or repair work, or some kind of craft, or some kind of product, or service. Maybe your dream is: *I want to run a bed-and-breakfast place.* Or *I want a horse ranch, where I can raise and sell horses.* Or *I want to grow lavender and sell soap and perfume made from it.* Stuff like that.

The first thing you should do is read up on all the virtues and perils of running your own business. The Internet has lots of stuff about this. For example:

> **Business Owner's Toolkit**
>
> **www.toolkit.com/small_business_guide/index.aspx**
>
> Yikes, there is a lot of information here for the small business owner. Everything about your business: starting, planning, financing, marketing, hiring, managing, getting government contracts, taxes—all that stuff.

Small Business Administration

www.sba.gov

The SBA has endured some bad press in the face of the multiple natural catastrophes that have been striking the U.S. in the past five years, from hurricanes to tornadoes to floods. But keep in mind that it was established to help start, manage, and grow small businesses. Lots of useful articles and advice are online, here. Also, check out its *Starting a Business* resources at http://tinyurl.com/24h59yy.

The Business Owner's Idea Café

www.businessownersideacafe.com

Great, fun site for the small business owner.

A Small Business Expert

http://asmallbusinessexpert.com

Scott Steinberg, a hugely popular analyst and industry insider for all the major TV networks, has just produced a free—yes I said free—*Business Experts Guidebook*, for those considering starting their own business. You can download it from his website (above). Unbelievably comprehensive!! He will also allow you to download a free 2012 Online Marketing Guide.

Free Agent Nation

www.fastcompany.com/online/12/freeagent.html

Daniel Pink, before he became famous for such books as *Drive* and *A Whole New Mind*, was the first to call attention to how many people were refusing to work for any employer. This is his classic work, written in 1997, on the site of the popular magazine *Fast Company*. It's still regarded as timeless, though of course its statistics *are* outdated. His basic thesis: self-employment has become a broader concept than it was in another age. The concept now includes not only those who own their own business but also free agents: independent contractors who work for several clients; temps and contract employees who work each day through temporary agencies; limited-timeframe workers who work only for a set time, as on a project, then move on to another company; consultants; and so on. This is a fascinating article to help you decide if you want to be a "free agent."

Working Solo

www.workingsolo.com/faqstarting.html

www.workingsolo.com/resources/resources.html

Working Solo is a good site for the small business worker. The first url, above, is a series of questions to help you determine if you have it in you to be an entrepreneur. The second url gives you a whole bunch of resources if you decide *Yes*.

Nolo's Business, LLCs & Corporations

www.nolo.com/legal-encyclopedia/business-llcs-corporations

Lots of helpful legal stuff here, about how to form an LLC, and other stuff you'll really need to know.

Entrepreneur

www.entrepreneurmag.com

Entrepreneur magazine's website. It has lists of home-based businesses, start-up ideas, how to raise money, shoestring start-ups, small business myths, a franchise and business opportunity site-seeing guide, how to research a business opportunity—and more.

World Wide Web Tax

www.wwwebtax.com/miscellaneous/self_employment_tax.htm

Wow. If you're going to be self-employed, you *really really* want this site. One of the banes of being self-employed is dealing with taxes; this site has more than 1,300 pages to help you handle all of that: articles, resources, links, downloadable tax forms (going back ten years!), in PDF format, of course. The site is selling something (e-filing tax returns), but it has a lot of free information about what self-employed people have to do vis-à-vis taxes, in the United States at least.

When You're Operating
on a Shoestring

Finding clients or customers: With the Internet came globalization. And this changed everything for the self-employed. You now have a much larger market at your disposal where you can sell your skills, knowledge, services, and products, worldwide.

Finding employees or vendors: In this global age if you're operating on a shoestring, and you need, let us say, to have something printed or produced as inexpensively as possible, you can search for an inexpensive printer, vendor, or manufacturer anywhere in the world, and solicit bids. All you have to do is type in the name of the skill-set you need, plus the word "overseas," and the word "jobs"—and see what you can find. For example, if you try "overseas cartoonist jobs" this will turn up a list of sites to try.

There are lots of books and magazines that are filled with ideas for home businesses. The best books on home businesses are written by Paul Edwards and Sarah Edwards. Their most recent one (2010) is called *Home-Based Business for Dummies*. Earlier works include (2008) *Middle-Class Lifeboat: Careers and Life Choices for Navigating a Changing Economy*; (2004) *Best Home Businesses for People 50+*; and (2001) *The Best Home Businesses for the Twenty-First Century*. For other titles, browse the business shelves in your local independent bookstore or Barnes & Noble, or go online at Amazon.com.

Doing Your Homework,
Doing Your Homework

With this research behind you, if you still want to go ahead with the idea of your own business, then the next step would be this: once you've decided what kind of business you want to start, you *must* go talk to other people who have already done what you are thinking of doing. You *must* pick their brains for everything they're worth. You *must* avoid stepping on the same *land mines* that they did.

One job-hunter told me she started a home-based soap business, without ever talking to anyone who had started a similar endeavor before her. Not surprisingly, her business went belly-up within a year and a half. She falsely then concluded: no one should go into such a business. Ah, but Paula Gibbons created "Paula's Soaps" very success-fully twenty-two years ago in Seattle, Washington.[1] *Someone is already doing the work you are dreaming of. The key to your success, is go talk to them.*

Starting up your own business outside the home without first lis-tening to the experience of those who have gone before you, and prof-iting from their mistakes, is just nuts. Yet millions of people do just that, every year. And then they wonder why it didn't work out. As one woman said to me, "Yes, I knew I was being foolish, but I thought I'd get lucky." P.S. She didn't.

But you are wiser. And you intend to do the research I am recom-mending, I know. All you want is just some guidance as to how to go about picking other people's brains. Okay, here it is: the key lies in a simple formula:

$$A - B = C$$

You have a great idea for starting your own business. But you want to interview others who have started the same kind of business, so you don't make the same mistakes they did. Your interviewing, then, should have three steps to it:

1. Finding out what skills, knowledge, or experience it takes to make this kind of business idea work, from several business owners. *This is "A."*

2. Then making a list of the skills, knowledge, or experience that you have. *This is "B."*

3. Then subtracting "B" from "A," we arrive at a list of skills, etc., required for success in such a business, that you *don't* have. And you must go out and hire someone with those missing skills. *This is "C."*

---

1. http://paulassoap.com

Let me explain this in a little more detail:

1. You first write out *in as much detail as you can* just exactly what kind of business you are thinking about starting. Do you want to be a freelance writer, or a craftsperson, or a consultant, independent screenwriter, copywriter, digital artist, songwriter, photographer, illustrator, interior designer, video person, videographer, film person, filmmaker, counselor, therapist, plumber, electrician, agent, soap maker, bicycle repairer, public speaker, or *what*?

2. You then identify towns or cities that are at least fifty to seventy-five miles away (so they won't feel you are in competition with them directly down the block, as it were) and by using the Yellow Pages or the chamber of commerce, or some smartphone apps, try to identify at least three businesses in those towns, that are identical or at least similar to the business you are thinking of starting. You drive to that town or city, and talk to the founder or owner of each such business.

3. When you talk to them, you explain that you're exploring the possibility of starting your own business, similar to theirs, but seventy-five miles away. You ask them if they would mind sharing something of their own history, so you can better understand what pitfalls or obstacles one runs into, when starting this kind of business. You ask them what skills, knowledge, or experience they think are necessary to making this kind of business successful.

   Will they give you such information? Yes, most of the time. People love to help others get started in their same business, *if* they love the way their business turned out—although, let's face it, occasionally you may run into owners who are of an ungenerous nature. But if that happens, thank them politely for their time, and go on to the next name on your list. When you've found three people willing to help you by relating their own history, you should now know enough to make a list of the necessary skills, knowledge, and experience they all agree are essential. If not, go visit another city and find some more fellow business owners. When you have a list you're satisfied with, give this list a name. Call it "A" of course.

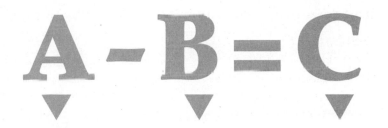

Skills and Knowledge Needed to Run This Kind of Business Successfully	Skills and Knowledge That I Have	Skills and Knowledge Needed, Which I Don't Have, So I'm Going to Go Out and Hire Someone Who Has Them
Precision-working with tools and instruments	Precision-working with tools and instruments	
Planning and directing an entire project	Planning and directing an entire project	
Programming computers, inventing programs that solve physical problems		Programming computers, inventing programs that solve physical problems
Problem solving: evaluating why a particular design or process isn't working	Problem solving: evaluating why a particular design or process isn't working	
Being self-motivated, resourceful, patient, persevering, accurate, methodical, and thorough	Being self-motivated, resourceful, patient, persevering, accurate, methodical, and thorough	
Thorough knowledge of: Principles of electronics		*Thorough knowledge of:* Principles of electronics
Physics of strings	Physics of strings	
Principles of vibration	Principles of vibration	
Properties of woods	Properties of woods	
Accounting		Accounting

4. Back home you sit down and inventory your own skills, knowledge, and experience, by doing the self-inventory described in chapter 5, the Flower Exercise. Give this list a name, also. Call it "B."

5. Having done this, subtract "B" from "A." This gives you another new list, which you should name "C." "C" is by definition a list of the skills or knowledge that you *don't* have, but *must* find—either by taking courses yourself, or by hiring someone with those skills, or by getting a friend or family member (who has those skills) to volunteer to help you for a while.

6. For example, if your investigation revealed that it takes good accounting practices in order to turn a profit, and you don't know a thing about accounting, you now know enough to go out and hire a part-time accountant *immediately*—or, if you absolutely have no money, maybe you can talk an accountant friend of yours into giving you some volunteer time, for a while.

I can illustrate this whole process with a case history. Our job-hunter is a woman who has been making harps for some employer, but now is thinking about going into business for herself, not only *making* harps at home, but also *designing* harps, with the aid of a computer. After interviewing several home-based harp makers and harp designers, and finishing her own self-assessment, her chart of A – B = C came out looking like the previous page.

If she decides she does indeed want to try her hand at becoming an independent harp maker and harp designer, she now knows what she needs *but lacks*: computer programming, knowledge of the principles of electronics, and accounting. In other words, List C. These she must either go to school to acquire for herself, OR enlist from some friends of hers in those fields, on a volunteer basis, OR go out and hire, part-time.

It is *always* possible—with a little blood, sweat, and imagination—to find out what A – B = C is, for any business you're dreaming of doing.

But let's say you've come up with a business idea that you're just sure no one else has ever thought of. Who do you go interview, then? *Parallel businesses.* Let's take a ridiculous example. You want to start a business of using computers to monitor the growth of plants at the Antarctic(!). A parallel business, in this case, would be:

someone who's *used computers with plants here in the States,*

or someone who's *used computers in the Antarctic,*

or someone who has *worked with plants in the Antarctic,* etc.

You would get names of these people, go talk to them, and along the way you might even discover that there *is* actually someone who has used computers to monitor the growth of plants at the South Pole. Then again, you might not.

But what you *would* get, for certain, is an awareness of most of the pitfalls that wait for you, by learning from the experience of those who are in these *parallel* businesses or careers.

"YES, THE BUSINESS HAS BECOME BIGGER, BUT FRED STILL LIKES TO WORK AT HOME."

Conclusion: "Can I Create My Own Job by Creating My Own Business?"

It takes a lot of guts to try ANYTHING new (*to you*) in today's brutal economy. It's easier, however, if you keep these things in mind:

1. There is always some risk, in trying something new. Your goal, I hope, is not to avoid risk—there is no way to do that—but to make sure ahead of time that the risks are *manageable*.

2. You find this out before you start, by first talking to others who have already done what you are thinking of doing; then you evaluate whether or not you still want to go ahead and try it.

3. Have a Plan b, laid out, *before you start*, as to what you will do if it doesn't work out; i.e., know where you are going to go, next. Don't wait, *puh-leaze!* Write it out, now. *This is what I'm going to do, if this doesn't work out.*

4. If you're sharing your life with someone, be sure to sit down with that partner or spouse and ask what the implications are *for them* if you try this new thing. Will they have to give up things? If so, what? Are they willing to make those sacrifices? And so on. You have a responsibility to make them full partners in any decision you're facing. Love demands it!

It is up to you to do your research thoroughly, weigh the risks, decide if they're *manageable* risks, count the costs, get counsel from those intimately involved with you, and then if you decide you still want to create your own job by starting this kind of business, go ahead and try—no matter what your well-meaning but cautious friends or family may say. They love you, they're concerned for you, and you should thank them for that; but come on, you only have one life here on this Earth, and that life is *yours* (under God) to say how it will be spent, or not spent. Parents, well-meaning friends, etc., can give loving advice, but in the end they get no vote. Just you . . . and God.

THE PINK PAGES

Appendix A Finding Your Mission in Life

Introduction to Finding Your Mission in Life

There are those who think that belief in God is just some fairy tale that mankind (or humankind) invented, to comfort themselves against the darkness. Naturally, therefore, they think that anyone who says they believe in God is demonstrably feebleminded, or a pathetic child who has never grown up intellectually.

Given this view, they are horrified to find a section on faith or religion in a job-hunting book. They have written to me, and said so.

Well, here it is, anyway.

That's because the percentage of the world's population that says they don't believe in God is less than 3 percent (it varies from country to country: here in the U.S. the figure is 9 percent, while in Canada that figure is 19–30 percent)[1] Still, that leaves us with an overwhelming percentage of the U.S. population (91 percent) believing in God. And my ten million readers are a pretty typical cross-section of this country.

So, leaving out a section that 91 percent of my readers might be interested in, and helped by, in order to please 9 percent of my readers, seems to me insane.

But you are welcome to skip this section, if you wish. It's not mandatory reading; that's why it is an Appendix to this book.

As I started writing this section, I toyed at first with the idea of following what might be described as an "all-paths approach" to religion: trying to stay as general and nonspecific as I could. But, after much thought, I decided not to try that. This, because I have read many other writers who tried, and I felt the approach failed miserably. An "all-paths" approach to religion ends up being a "no-paths" approach, just

---

1. See "Demographics of Atheism" in Wikipedia. Also see the Pew Research Center findings (2010 data), at http://tinyurl.com/3kk78zu.

as a woman or man who tries to please everyone ends up pleasing no one. It is the old story of the "universal" vs. the "particular."

Those of us who do career counseling could predict, ahead of time, that trying to stay universal is not likely to be helpful, in writing about faith. We know well from our own field that truly helpful career counseling depends upon defining the particularity or uniqueness of each person we try to help. No employer wants to know what you have in common with everyone else. He or she wants to know what makes you unique and individual. As I have argued throughout this book, the inventory of your uniqueness or *particularity* is crucial if you are ever to find meaningful work.

This particularity invades *everything* a person does; it is not suddenly "jettisonable" when he or she turns to matters of faith. Therefore, when I or anyone else writes about faith I believe we must write out of our own particularity—which *starts,* in my case, with the fact that I write, and think, and breathe as a Christian—as you might expect from the fact that I was an ordained Episcopalian minister for many years. Understandably, then, this chapter speaks from a Christian perspective. I want you to be aware of that, at the outset.

Balanced against this is the fact that I have always been acutely sensitive to the fact that this is a pluralistic society in which we live, and that I in particular owe a great deal to my readers who have religious convictions quite different from my own. It has turned out that the people who work or have worked here in my office with me, over the years, have been predominantly of other faiths. Furthermore, *Parachute*'s more than ten million readers have included not only Christians of every variety and persuasion, Christian Scientists, Jews, Hindus, Buddhists, and adherents of Islam, but also believers in "new age" religions, secularists, humanists, agnostics, atheists, and many others. I have therefore tried to be very courteous toward the feelings of all my readers, *while at the same time* counting on them to translate my Christian thought-forms into their own. This ability to thus translate is the indispensable *sine qua non* of anyone who wants to communicate helpfully with others in this pluralistic society of ours.

In the Judeo-Christian tradition from which I come, one of the indignant biblical questions was, "Has God forgotten to be gracious?" The answer was a clear "No." I think it is important *for all of us* also to seek the same goal. I have therefore labored to make this chapter gracious as well as thought-provoking.

R.N.B.

Turning Point

For many of us, the job-hunt offers a chance to make some fundamental changes in our whole life. It marks a turning point in how we live our life.

It gives us a chance to ponder and reflect, to extend our mental horizons, to go deeper into the subsoil of our soul.

It gives us a chance to wrestle with the question, "Why am I here on Earth?" We don't want to feel that we are just another grain of sand lying on the beach called humanity, unnumbered and lost in the billions of other human beings.

We want to do more than plod through life, going to work, coming home from work. We want to find that special joy, "that no one can take from us," which comes from having a sense of Mission in our life.

We want to feel we were put here on Earth for some special purpose, to do some unique work that only we can accomplish.

We want to know what our Mission is.

"WHAT DO YOU MEAN 'DON'T EXPECT MIRACLES'?
WHY SHOULDN'T I EXPECT MIRACLES??"

The Meaning of the Word "Mission"

When used with respect to our life and work, *Mission* has always been a religious concept, from beginning to end. It is defined by *Webster's* as "a continuing task or responsibility that one is destined or fitted to do or specially called upon to undertake," and historically has had two major synonyms: *Calling* and *Vocation*. These, of course, are the same word in two different languages, English and Latin. Both imply God.

To be given a Vocation or Calling implies *Someone who* calls. To have a Destiny implies *Someone who determined the destination for us.* Thus, the concept of Mission lands us inevitably in the lap of God, before we have hardly begun.

I emphasize this, because there is an increasing trend in our culture to try to speak about religious subjects without reference to God. This is true of "spirituality," "soul," and "Mission," in particular. More and more books talk about Mission as though it were simply "a purpose you choose for your own life, by identifying your enthusiasms."

This attempt to obliterate all reference to God from the originally religious concept of Mission, is particularly ironic because the proposed substitute word—enthusiasms—is derived from two Greek words, "en theos," and means "God in us."

In the midst of this increasingly secular culture, we find an oasis that—along with athletics—is very hospitable toward belief in God. That oasis is *job-hunting.* Most of the leaders who have evolved creative job-hunting ideas were—from the beginning—people who believed firmly in God, and said so: Sidney Fine, Bernard Haldane, and John Crystal (all of whom have departed this life), plus Arthur and Marie Kirn, Arthur Miller, Tom and Ellie Jackson, Ralph Matson, and of course myself.

I mentioned at the beginning of this Appendix that 91 percent of us in the U.S. believe in God. According to the Gallup Organization, 90 percent of us pray, 88 percent of us believe God loves us, and 33 percent of us report that we have had a life-changing religious experience.

However, it is not clear that we have made much connection between our belief in God and our work. Often our spiritual beliefs and our attitude toward our work live in separate mental ghettos, within our mind.

A dialogue between these two *is* opened up inside our head, and heart, when we are out of work. Unemployment, particularly in this brutal economy, gives us a chance to contemplate why we are here on Earth, and what our Calling, Vocation, or Mission is, uniquely, for each of us.

Unemployment becomes *life transition*, when we can't find a job doing the same work we've always done. Since we have to rethink one thing, many of us elect to rethink *everything.*

Something awakens within us. Call it *yearning.* Call it *hope.* We come to realize the dream we dreamed has never died. And we go back to get it. We decide to resume our search . . . for the life we know within our heart that we were meant to live.

Now we have a chance to marry our work and our religious beliefs, to talk about Calling, and Vocation, and Mission in life—to think out why we are here, and what plans God has for us.

That's why a period of unemployment can absolutely change our life.

The Secret of Finding Your Mission in Life: Taking It in Stages

I will explain the steps toward finding your Mission in life that I have learned in all my years on Earth. Just remember two things. First, I speak from a lifelong Christian perspective, and trust you to translate this into your own thought-forms.

Second, I know that these steps are not the only Way. Many people have discovered their Mission by taking other paths. And you may, too. But hopefully what I have to say may shed some light upon whatever path you take.

I have learned that if you want to figure out what your Mission in life is, it will likely take some time. It is not a *problem* to be solved in a day and a night. It is a *learning process* that has steps to it, much like the process by which we all learned to eat. As a baby, we did not tackle adult food right off. As we all recall, there were three stages: first there had to be the mother's milk or bottle, then strained baby foods, and finally—after teeth and time—the stuff that grown-ups chew. Three stages—and the two earlier stages were not to be disparaged. It was all Eating, just different forms of Eating—appropriate to our development at the time. But each stage had to be mastered, in turn, before the next could be approached.

There are usually three stages also to learning what your Mission in life is, and the two earlier stages are likewise not to be disparaged. It is all "Mission"—just different forms of Mission, appropriate to your development at the time. But each stage has to be mastered, in turn, before the next can be approached.

Of course, there is a sense in which you never master any of these stages, but are always growing in understanding and mastery of them, throughout your whole life here on Earth.

As it has been impressed on me by observing many people over the years (admittedly through *Christian spectacles*), it appears that the three parts to your Mission here on Earth can be defined generally as follows:

1. *Your first Mission here on Earth* is one that you share with the rest of the human race, but it is no less your individual Mission for the fact that it is shared: and it is, **to seek to stand hour by hour in the conscious presence of God, the One from whom your Mission is derived**. *The Missioner before the Mission*, is the rule. In religious language, your Mission here is: *to know God, and enjoy Him forever, and to see His hand in all His works.*

2. Second, once you have begun doing that in an earnest way, *your second Mission here on Earth* is also one that you share with the rest of the human race, but it is no less your individual Mission for the fact that it is shared: and that is, **to do what you can, moment by moment, day by day, step by step, to make this world a better place, following the leading and guidance of God's Spirit within you and around you**.

3. Third, once you have begun doing that in a serious way, *your third Mission here on Earth* is one that is uniquely yours, and that is:

   a) **to exercise the Talent that you particularly came to Earth to use—your greatest gift, which you most delight to use,**

   b) **in the place(s) or setting(s) that God has caused to appeal to you the most,**

   c) **and for those purposes that God most needs to have done in the world.**

When fleshed out, and spelled out, I think you will find that there you have the definition of your Mission in life. Or, to put it another way, these are the three Missions that you have in life.

The Two Rhythms of the Dance of Mission: Unlearning, Learning, Unlearning, Learning

The distinctive characteristic of these three stages is that in each we are forced to *let go* of some fundamental assumptions that our culture has taught us, about the nature of Mission. In other words, throughout this quest and at each stage we find ourselves engaged not merely in a process of *Learning*. We are also engaged in a process of *Un*learning. Thus, we can restate the three Learnings, in terms of what we also need to *un*learn at each stage:

- We need in the first stage to *un*learn the idea that our Mission is primarily to keep busy *doing* something (here on Earth), and learn instead that our Mission is first of all to keep busy *being* something (here on Earth). In Christian language (and others as well), we might say that we were sent here to learn how *to be* sons of God, and daughters of God, before anything else. *"Our Father, who art in heaven . . ."*

- In the second stage, "Being" issues into "Doing." At this stage, we need to *un*learn the idea that everything about our Mission must be *unique* to us, and learn instead that some parts of our Mission here on Earth are *shared* by all human beings: e.g., we were all sent here to bring more gratitude, more kindness, more forgiveness, and more love, into the world. We share this Mission because the task is too large to be accomplished by just one individual.

- We need in the third stage to *un*learn the idea that the part of our Mission that is truly unique, and most truly ours, is something Our Creator just *orders* us to do, without any agreement from our spirit, mind, and heart. (On the other hand, neither is it something that each of us chooses and then merely asks God to bless.) We need to learn that God so honors our free will, that He has ordained that our unique Mission be something that we have some part in choosing.

- In this third stage we need also to *un*learn the idea that our unique Mission must consist of some achievement for all the world to see—and learn instead that as the stone does not always know what ripples it has caused in the pond whose surface it impacts, so neither we nor those who watch our life will always know *what we have achieved* by our life and by our Mission. *It may be* that by the grace of God we helped bring about a profound change for the better in the lives of other souls around us, but it also may be that this takes place beyond our sight, or after we have gone on. And we may never know what we have accomplished, until we see Him face to face after this life is past.

• Most finally, we need to *un*learn the idea that what we have accomplished is our doing, and ours alone. It is God's Spirit breathing in us and through us that helps us do whatever we do, and so the singular first-person pronoun is never appropriate, but only the plural. Not "*I* accomplished this" but "*We* accomplished this, God and I, working together. . . ."

That should give you a general overview. But I would like to add some random comments on my part about each of these three Missions of ours here on Earth.

Some Random Comments About Your First Mission in Life

Your first Mission here on Earth is one that you share with the rest of the human race, but it is no less your individual Mission for the fact that it is shared: and that is, **to seek to stand hour by hour in the conscious presence of God, the One from whom your Mission is derived**. The Missioner before the Mission, is the rule. In religious language, your Mission is: to know God, and enjoy Him forever, and to see His hand in all His works.

Comment 1:
How We Might Think of God

Each of us has to go about this primary Mission according to the tenets of our own particular religion. But I will speak what I know out of the context of my own particular faith, and you may perhaps translate and apply it to yours. I will speak as a Christian, who believes (passionately) that Christ is the Way and the Truth and the Life. But I also believe, with St. Peter, "that God shows no partiality, but in every nation any one who fears Him and does what is right is acceptable to Him" (Acts 10:34–35).

Now, Jesus claimed many unique things about Himself and His Mission; but He also spoke of Himself as the great prototype for us all. He called Himself "the Son of Man," and He said, "I assure you that the man who believes in me will do the same things that I have done, yes, and he will do even greater things than these . . ." (John 14:12).

Emboldened by His identification of us with His Life and His Mission, we might want to remember how He spoke about His Life here on Earth. He put it in this context: **"I came from the Father and have come into the world; again, I am leaving the world and going to the Father"** (John 16:28).

If there is a sense in which this is, in even the faintest way, true also of our lives (and I shall say in a moment in what sense I think it is true), then instead of calling our great Creator "God" or "Father" right off, we might begin our approach to the subject of religion by referring to the One Who gave us our Mission and sent us to this planet not as "God" or "Father" but—*just to help our thinking*—as: **"The One From Whom We Came and The One To Whom We Shall Return,"** when this life is done.

If our life here on Earth is to be at all like Christ's, then this is a true way to think about the One Who gave us our Mission. We are not some kind of eternal, preexistent *being*. We are **creatures**, who once did not exist, and then came into Being, and continue to have our Being, only at the will of our great Creator. But as creatures we are both body and soul; although we know our body was created in our mother's womb, our soul's origin is a great mystery. Where it came from, at what moment the Lord created it, is something we cannot know. It is not unreasonable to suppose, however, that the great God created our *soul* before it entered our body, and in that sense we did indeed stand before God before we were born; and He is indeed **"The One From Whom We Came and The One To Whom We Shall Return."**

Therefore, before we go searching for "what work was I sent here to do?" we need to establish—or in a truer sense *reestablish*—contact with **"The One From Whom We Came and The One To Whom We Shall Return."** Without this reaching out of the creature to the great Creator, without this reaching out of *the creature with a Mission* to *the One Who Gave Us That Mission*, the question *what is my Mission in life?* is void and null. The *what* is rooted in the *Who*; absent the Personal, one cannot meaningfully discuss The Thing. It is like the adult who cries, "I want to get married," without giving any consideration to *who* it is they want to marry.

Comment 2:
How We Might Think of Religion or Faith

In light of this larger view of our creatureliness, we can see that *religion* or *faith* is not a question of whether or not we choose to (*as it is so commonly put*) "have a relationship with God." Looking at our life in a larger context than just our life here on Earth, it becomes apparent that some sort of relationship with God is a given for us, about which we have absolutely no choice. God and we **were** and **are** related, during the time of our soul's existence before our birth and in the time of our soul's continued existence after our death. The only choice we have is what to do about **The Time In Between**, i.e., what we want the nature of our relationship with God to be during our time here on Earth and how that will affect the *nature* of the relationship, then, after death.

One of the corollaries of all this is that by the very act of being born into a human body, it is inevitable that we undergo a kind of *amnesia*— an amnesia that typically embraces not only our nine months in the womb, our baby years, and almost one-third of each day (sleeping), but more important any memory of our origin or our destiny. We wander on Earth as an amnesia victim. To seek after Faith, therefore, is to seek to climb back out of that amnesia. Religion or Faith is **the hard reclaiming of knowledge we once knew as a certainty.**

Comment 3:
The First Obstacle to Executing This Mission

This first Mission of ours here on Earth is not the easiest of Missions, simply because it is the first. Indeed, in many ways, it is the most difficult. All we can see is that our life here on Earth is a very physical life. We eat, we drink, we sleep, we long to be held, and to hold. We inherit a physical body, with very physical appetites, we walk on the physical earth, and we acquire physical possessions. It is the most alluring of temptations, *in our amnesia*, to come up with just a *Physical* interpretation of this life: to think that the Universe is merely interested in the survival of species. Given this interpretation, the story of our individual life could be simply told: we are born, grow up, procreate, and die.

But we are ever recalled to do what we came here to do: that without rejecting the joy of the Physicalness of this life, such as the love of the blue sky and the green grass, we are to reach out beyond all this to **recall** and recover a *Spiritual* interpretation of our life. *Beyond* the physical and *within* the physicalness of this life, to detect a Spirit and a Person from beyond this Earth who is with us and in us—the very real and loving and awesome Presence of the great Creator from whom we came—and the One to whom we once again shall go.

Comment 4:
The Second Obstacle to Executing
This Mission

It is one of the conditions of our earthly amnesia and our creatureliness that, sadly enough, some very *human* and very *rebellious* part of us *likes* the idea of living in a world where we can be our own god—and therefore loves the purely Physical interpretation of life, and finds it *anguish* to relinquish it. Traditional Christian vocabulary calls this "**sin**" and has a lot to say about the difficulty it poses for this first part of our Mission. All who live a thoughtful life know that it is true: our greatest enemy in carrying out this first Mission of ours is indeed *our own* heart and our own rebellion.

Comment 5:
Further Thoughts About What Makes Us Special and Unique

As I said earlier, many of us come to this issue of our Mission in life, because we want to feel that we are unique. And what we mean by that, is that we hope to discover some "specialness" intrinsic to us, which is our birthright, and which no one can take from us. What we, however, discover from a thorough exploration of this topic, is that we are indeed special—but only because God thinks us so. Our specialness and uniqueness reside in Him, and His love, rather than in anything intrinsic to our own *being*. The proper appreciation of this distinction causes our feet to carry us in the end not to the City called Pride, but to the Temple called Gratitude.

> What is religion? Religion is the service of God out of grateful love for what God has done for us. The Christian religion, more particularly, is the service of God out of grateful love for what God has done for us in Christ.
> —PHILLIPS BROOKS, author of *O Little Town of Bethlehem*

Comment 6:
The Unconscious Doing of the Work We Came to Do

You may have *already* wrestled with this first part of your Mission here on Earth. You may not have called it that. You may have called it simply "learning to believe in God." But if you ask what your Mission is in life, this one was and is the precondition of all else that you came here to do. Absent this Mission, it is folly to talk about the rest. So, if you have been seeking faith, or seeking to strengthen your faith, you have—willy-nilly—already been about *the doing of the Mission you were given*. Born into **This Time In Between**, you have found His hand again, and reclasped it. You are therefore ready to go on with His Spirit to tackle together what you came here to do—the other parts of your Mission.

Some Random Comments About Your Second Mission in Life

Your second Mission here on Earth is also one that you share with the rest of the human race, but it is no less your individual Mission for the fact that it is shared: and that is, **to do what you can moment by moment, day by day, step by step, to make this world a better place—following the leading and guidance of God's Spirit within you and around you.**

Comment 1: The Uncomfortableness of One Step at a Time

Imagine yourself out walking in your neighborhood one night, and suddenly you find yourself surrounded by such a dense fog, that you have lost your bearings and cannot find your way. Suddenly, a friend appears out of the fog, and asks you to put your hand in theirs, and they will lead you home. And you, not being able to tell where you are going, trustingly follow them, even though you can only see one step at a time. Eventually you arrive safely home, filled with gratitude. But as you reflect upon the experience the next day, you realize how unsettling it was to have to keep walking when you could see only one step at a time, even though you had guidance you knew you could trust.

Now I have asked you to imagine all of this, because this is the essence of the second Mission to which *you* are called—and *I* am called—in this life. It is all very different than we had imagined. When the question, *"What is your Mission in life?"* is first broached, and we have put our hand in God's, as it were, we imagine that we will be taken up to *some mountaintop*, from which we can see far into the distance. And that we will hear a voice in our ear, saying, "Look, look, see that distant city? That is the goal of your Mission; that is where everything is leading, every step of your way."

But instead of the mountaintop, we find ourselves in *the valley*—wandering often in a fog. And the voice in our ear says something quite different from what we thought we would hear. It says, **"Your Mission is to take one step at a time, even when you don't yet see where it all** is leading, or what the Grand Plan is, or what your overall Mission in life is. Trust Me; I will lead you."

Comment 2:
The Nature of This Step-by-Step Mission

As I said, in every situation you find yourself, you have been sent here to do whatever you can—moment by moment—that will bring more gratitude, more kindness, more forgiveness, more honesty, and more love into this world.

There are dozens of such moments every day. Moments when you stand—as it were—at a spiritual crossroads, with two ways lying before you. Such moments are typically called "**moments of decision.**" It does not matter what the frame or content of each particular decision is. It all devolves, in the end, into just two roads before you, *every time*. **The one** will lead to *less* gratitude, *less* kindness, *less* forgiveness, *less* honesty, or *less* love in the world. **The other** will lead to *more* gratitude, *more* kindness, *more* forgiveness, *more* honesty, or *more* love in the world. Your Mission, each moment, is to seek to choose the latter spiritual road, rather than the former, *every time*.

Comment 3:
Some Examples of This Step-by-Step Mission

I will give a few examples, so that the nature of this part of your Mission may be unmistakably clear.

You are out on the freeway, in your car. Someone has gotten into the wrong lane, to the right of *your* lane, and needs to move over into the lane you are in. You *see* their need to cut in, ahead of you. **Decision time.** In your mind's eye you see two spiritual roads lying before you: the one leading to less kindness in the world (you speed up, to shut this driver out, and don't let them move over), the other leading to more kindness in the world (you let the driver cut in). **Since you know this is part of your Mission, part of the reason why you came to Earth, your calling is clear. You know which road to take, which decision to make.**

You are hard at work at your desk, when suddenly an interruption comes. The phone rings, or someone is at the door. They need something from you, a question of some of your time and attention. **Decision time.** In your mind's eye you see two spiritual roads lying before you: the one leading to less love in the world (you tell them you're just too busy to be bothered), the other leading to more love in the world (you put aside your work, decide that God may have sent this person to you, and say, "Yes, what can I do to help you?"). **Since you know this is part of your Mission, part of the reason why you came to Earth, your calling is clear. You know which road to take, which decision to make.**

Your mate does something that hurts your feelings. **Decision time.** In your mind's eye you see two spiritual roads lying before you: the one leading to less forgiveness in the world (you institute an icy silence between the two of you, and think of how you can punish them or otherwise get even), the other leading to more forgiveness in the world (you go over and take them in your arms, speak the truth about your hurt feelings, and assure them of your love). **Since you know this is part of your Mission, part of the reason why you came to Earth, your calling is clear. You know which road to take, which decision to make.**

You have not behaved at your most noble, recently. And now you are face to face with someone who asks you a question about what happened. **Decision time.** In your mind's eye you see two spiritual roads lying before you: the one leading to less honesty in the world (you lie about what happened, or what you were feeling, because you fear losing their respect or their love), the other leading to more honesty in the world (you tell the truth, together with how you feel about it, in retrospect). **Since you know this is part of your Mission, part of the reason why you came to Earth, your calling is clear. You know which road to take, which decision to make.**

Comment 4:
The Spectacle That Makes the Angels Laugh

It is necessary to explain this part of our Mission in some detail, because so many times you will see people wringing their hands, and saying, "*I want to know what my Mission in life is*," all the while they are cutting people off on the highway, refusing to give time to people, punishing their mate for having hurt their feelings, and lying about what they did. And it will seem to you that the angels must laugh to see this spectacle. *For these people wringing their hands*, their Mission was right there, on the freeway, in the interruption, in the hurt, and at the confrontation.

Comment 5:
The Valley Versus the Mountaintop

At some point in your life your Mission may involve some grand *mountaintop experience*, where you say to yourself, "This, this, is why I came into the world. I know it. I know it." *But until then*, your Mission is here in *the valley*, and the fog, and the little callings moment by moment, day by day. More to the point, it is likely you cannot ever get to your mountaintop Mission unless you have first exercised your stewardship faithfully in the valley.

It is an ancient principle, to which Jesus alluded often, that if you don't use the information the Universe has already given you, you cannot expect it will give you any more. If you aren't being faithful in small things, how can you expect to be given charge over larger things? (Luke 16:10–12, 19:11–24). If you aren't trying to bring more gratitude, kindness, forgiveness, honesty, and love into the world each day, you can hardly expect that you will be entrusted with the Mission to help bring peace into the world or anything else large and important. If we do not live out our day-by-day Mission in the valley, we cannot expect we are yet ready for a larger *mountaintop* Mission.

Comment 6:
The Importance of Not Thinking of
This Mission as "Just a Training Camp"

The valley is not just a kind of "training camp." There is in your imagination even now an invisible *spiritual* mountaintop to which you may go, if you wish to see where all this is leading. And what will you see there, in the imagination of your heart, but the goal toward which all this is pointed: **that Earth might be more like heaven. That human life might be more like God's**. That is the large achievement toward which all our day-by-day Missions *in the valley* are moving. This is a *large* order, but it is accomplished by faithful attention to the doing of our great Creator's **will** in little things as well as in large. It is much like the building of the pyramids in Egypt, which was accomplished by the dragging of a lot of individual pieces of stone by a lot of individual men.

The valley, the fog, the going step by step, is no mere training camp. The goal is real, however large. **"Thy Kingdom come, Thy will be done, on Earth, as it is in heaven."**

Some Random Comments About Your Third Mission in Life

Your third Mission here on Earth is one that is uniquely yours, and that is:

a) **to exercise the Talent that you particularly came to Earth to use—your greatest gift that you most delight to use,**

b) **in those place(s) or setting(s) that God has caused to appeal to you the most,**

c) **and for those purposes that God most needs to have done in the world.**

Comment 1:
Our Mission Is Already Written, "in Our Members"

It is customary in trying to identify this part of our Mission, to advise that we should ask God, in prayer, to speak to us—and **tell us** plainly what our Mission is. We look for a voice in the air, a thought in our head, a dream in the night, a sign in the events of the day, to reveal this thing that is otherwise *(it is said)* completely hidden. Sometimes, from just such answered prayer, people do indeed discover what their Mission is, beyond all doubt and uncertainty.

But having to wait for the voice of God to reveal what our Mission is, is not the truest picture of our situation. St. Paul, in Romans, speaks of a law "written in our members"—and this phrase has a telling application to the question of **how** God reveals to each of us our unique

Mission in life. Read again the definition of our third Mission (on the previous page) and you will see: the clear implication of the definition is that God has **already** revealed His will to us concerning our vocation and Mission, by causing it to be "**written in our members**" We are to begin deciphering our unique Mission by studying our talents and skills, and more particularly which ones (or one) we most rejoice to use.

God actually has written His will *twice* in our members: *first in the talents* that He lodged there, and second *in His guidance of our heart*, as to which Talent gives us the greatest pleasure from its exercise (**it is usually the one that, when we use it, causes us to lose all sense of time**).

Even as the anthropologist can examine ancient inscriptions, and divine from them the daily life of a long-lost people, so we by examining **our talents** and **our heart** can *more often than we dream* divine the Will of the Living God. For true it is, our Mission is not something He **will** reveal; it is something He **has already** revealed. It is not to be found written in the sky; it is to be found written in our members.

Comment 2:
Career Counseling: We Need You

Arguably, our first two Missions in life could be learned from religion alone—without any reference whatsoever to career counseling, the subject of this book. Why, then, should career counseling claim that this question about our Mission in life is its proper concern, *in any way?*

It is when we come to this third Mission, which hinges so crucially on the question of our Talents, skills, and gifts, that we see the answer. If you've read the body of this book, before turning to this section, then you know without my even saying it, how much the identification of Talents, gifts, or skills is the province of career counseling. Its expertise, indeed its *raison d'être*, lies precisely in the identification, classification, and (forgive me) "prioritization" of Talents, skills, and gifts. To put the matter quite simply, career counseling knows how to do this better than any other discipline—**including** traditional religion. This is not a defect of religion, but the fulfillment of something Jesus promised: "When the Spirit of truth comes, He will guide you into all truth" (John 16:12). Career counseling is part (we may hope) of that promised late-coming truth. It can therefore be of inestimable help to the pilgrim who is trying to figure out what their greatest, and most enjoyable, Talent is, as a step toward identifying their unique Mission in life.

If career counseling needs religion as its helpmate in the first two stages of identifying our Mission in life, then religion repays the compliment by clearly needing career counseling as **its** helpmate here in the third stage.

And this place where you are in your life right now—facing the job-hunt and all its anxiety—is the perfect time to seek the union within your own mind and heart of both career counseling (as in the pages of this book) and your faith in God.

Comment 3:
How Our Mission Got Chosen:
A Scenario for the Romantic

It is a mystery that we cannot fathom, in this life at least, as to why one of us has this Talent, and the other one has that; why God chose to give one gift—and Mission—to one person; and a different gift—and Mission—to another. Since we do not know, and in some degree cannot know, we are certainly left free to speculate, and imagine.

We may imagine that before we came to Earth, our souls, *our Breath, our Light*, stood before the great Creator and volunteered for this Mission. And God and we, together, chose what that Mission would be and what particular gifts would be needed, which He then agreed to give us, after our birth. Thus, our Mission was not a command given preemptorily by an unloving Creator to a reluctant slave without a vote, but was a task jointly designed by us both, in which as fast as the great Creator said, "I wish" our hearts responded, **"Oh, yes."** As mentioned in an earlier comment, it may be helpful to think of the condition of our becoming human as that we became amnesiac about any consciousness our soul had before birth—and therefore amnesiac about the nature or manner in which our Mission was designed.

Our searching for our Mission now is therefore a searching to recover the memory of something we ourselves had a part in designing.

I am admittedly a hopeless romantic, so of course I like this picture. If you also are a hopeless romantic, you may like it, too. There's also the chance that it just may be true. We will not know until we see Him face to face.

Comment 4:
Mission as Intersection

There are all different kinds of voices calling you to all different kinds of work, and the problem is to find out which is the voice of God rather than that of society, say, or the superego, or self-interest. By and large a good rule for finding out is this: the kind of work God usually calls you to is the kind of work a) that you need most to do and b) the world most needs to have done. If you really get a kick out of your work, you've presumably met requirement a), but if your work is writing TV deodorant commercials, the chances are you've missed requirement b). On the other hand, if your work is being a doctor in a leper colony, you have probably met b), but if most of the time you're bored and depressed by it, the chances are you haven't only bypassed a) but probably aren't helping your patients much either. Neither the hair shirt nor the soft birth will do. **The place God calls you to is the place where your deep gladness and the world's deep hunger meet.**

—FRED BUECHNER
Wishful Thinking—A Theological ABC

Excerpted from *Wishful Thinking—A Theological ABC* by Frederick Buechner, revised edition published by HarperOne. Copyright © 1973, 1993 by Frederick Buechner.

Comment 5:
Examples of Mission as Intersection

Your unique and individual Mission will most likely turn out to be a mission of Love, acted out in one or all of three arenas: either in the Kingdom of the Mind, whose goal is to bring more Truth into the world; or in the Kingdom of the Heart, whose goal is to bring more Beauty into the world; or in the Kingdom of the Will, whose goal is to bring more Perfection into the world, through Service.

Here are some examples:

"My mission is, out of the rich reservoir of love that God seems to have given me, to nurture and show love to others—most particularly to those who are suffering from incurable diseases."

"My mission is to draw maps for people to show them how to get to God."

"My mission is to create the purest foods I can, to help people's bodies not get in the way of their spiritual growth."

"My mission is to make the finest harps I can so that people can hear the voice of God in the wind."

"My mission is to make people laugh, so that the travail of this earthly life doesn't seem quite so hard to them."

"My mission is to help people know the truth, in love, about what is happening out in the world, so that there will be more honesty in the world."

"My mission is to weep with those who weep, so that in my arms they may feel themselves in the arms of that Eternal Love that sent me and that created them."

"My mission is to create beautiful gardens, so that in the lilies of the field people may behold the Beauty of God and be reminded of the Beauty of Holiness."

Comment 6:
Life as Long as Your Mission Requires

Knowing that you came to Earth for a reason, and knowing what that Mission is, throws an entirely different light upon your life from now on. You are, generally speaking, delivered from any further fear about how long you have to live. You may settle it in your heart that you are here until God chooses to think that you have accomplished your Mission, or until God has a greater Mission for you in another Realm. You need to be a good steward of what He has given you, while you are here; but you do not need to be an anxious steward or stewardess.

You need to attend to your health, *but you do not need to constantly worry about it.* You need to meditate on your death, *but you do not need to be constantly preoccupied with it.* To paraphrase the glorious words of

G. K. Chesterton: **"We now have a strong desire for living combined with a strange carelessness about dying. We desire life like water and yet are ready to drink death like wine."** We know that we are here to do what we came to do, and we need not worry about anything else.

Comment 7:
Using Internet Resources

There is a website that deals with news, etc., about all faiths, which you may want to look at: www.beliefnet.com.

Then there is a Jesuit site that leads you in a daily meditation for ten or more minutes (in more than twenty languages with a visual, but otherwise no sound or distraction): http://sacredspace.ie.

There is also a site that gives you a daily podcast of church bells, music, Scripture reading, and meditations or homily, with no visuals, but with sound, and an audio MP3 file that can be sent to your phone, computer, PDA, etc: www.pray-as-you-go.org.

There is a site dedicated to helping you keep a divine consciousness 24/7: by helping you link up to other people of faith, through prayer circles, sharing of personal stories of faith, etc., aimed especially, but not exclusively, toward young adults. Its ultimate message: you are not alone: www.24-7prayer.com/communities.

Lastly, there is a site dedicated to helping you find a spiritual counselor (or "spiritual director"), as well as retreat centers, in the Christian, Islamic, Buddhist, Jewish, or Interfaith faiths: www.sdiworld.org.

Final Comment

A Job-Hunt Done Well

If you approach your job-hunt as an opportunity to work on this issue as well as the issue of how you will keep body and soul together, then hopefully your job-hunt will end with your being able to say: "Life has deep meaning to me, now. I have discovered more than my ideal job; I have found my Mission, and the reason why I am here on Earth."

Appendix B A Guide to Dealing with Your Feelings While Out of Work

Introduction

Unemployment can take a terrible toll upon the human spirit. In a recent study of over 6,000 job-hunters, interviewed every week for up to 24 weeks, it was discovered

> *"that many workers become discouraged the longer they are unemployed. In particular, the unemployed express feeling more sad the longer they are unemployed, and sadness rises more quickly with unemployment duration during episodes of job search. In addition, reported life satisfaction is lower for the same individual following days in which comparatively more time was devoted to job search. . . . These findings suggest that the psychological cost of job search rises the longer someone is unemployed. . . One reason why job search assistance may have been found to consistently speed individuals' return to work in past studies is that it may help the unemployed to overcome feelings of anxiety and sadness that are associated with job search."[1]*

I know the truth of this from my own experience. I have been fired twice in my life. I remember how it felt each time I got the lousy news. I walked out of the building dazed, as though I had just emerged from a really bad train wreck. The sun was shining brightly, not a cloud in the sky; and, since it was lunch hour, as it happened, the streets were

---

1. Alan B. Krueger and Andreas Mueller, "Job Search, Emotional Well-Being and Job Finding in a Period of Mass Unemployment: Evidence from High-Frequency Longitudinal Data," *Brookings Papers on Economic Activity*, March 8, 2011. Found on the Web at http://tinyurl.com/4olmpj9.

filled with laughing happy people, who apparently had not a care in the world.

I remember thinking, "The world has just caved—my world at least. How can all these people act as though nothing has happened?"

And I remember the feelings. The overwhelming feelings, that only intensified in the weeks after that. Describe my state however you want—feeling sad, being in a funk, feeling despair, feeling hopeless, feeling like things "will always be this way," or feeling depressed—it doesn't matter. I was terribly unhappy. Unemployment was rocking my soul to its foundations. I needed to know what to do about my feelings.

I have since learned that my experience was not the least unusual. Many of us, if not most of us, when we are out of work for a long time feel weary and depressed.[2] Our greatest desire is to get rid of these depressed feelings. After talking to thousands of job-hunters, I think there are:

Ten Things We Can Do to Deal with Our Feelings, When We Are Unemployed

1. **We can catch up on our sleep,** even if it means we have to take naps during the day because our attempt to sleep at nighttime is, at the moment, a disaster. We tend to feel depressed if we are short on our sleep, or our body is otherwise run-down.

   There are two states that can be easily confused:

   First of all, the world never looks bright or happy to us when we are very short on sleep.

   Secondly, the world never looks bright or happy to us when we are feeling depressed.

   It is therefore easy to confuse the two feeling-states. Over the years, I have seen many job-hunters who first thought they were

---

2. Serious clinical depression often has a lifelong history, and requires treatment, particularly when a person is feeling endangering impulses, such as suicide. In such a case, you should seek competent psychological or psychiatric help. (For immediate help, this minute, call 1-800-273-8255 or go online to www.suicidepreventionlifeline.org. There are counselors 24/7 at both places who deal with anyone, including the military or veterans, in trouble.)

really depressed over their situation, later discover they were really depressed just because they were so tired. Or a bit of both. Anyway, sleep or nap, we often turn into happier, more upbeat people, just by catching up on our sleep. This can make us feel better—sometimes much better.

2. **There are other things that we can do to keep ourselves more physically fit while unemployed.** Job-hunters have told me they found it important to:

   • get regular exercise, involving a daily walk;

   • drink plenty of water each day (this seems silly, but I found out we tend to skip the water, and get dehydrated, when we're out of work);

   • eliminate sugar as much as possible from the diet;

   • take supplementary vitamins daily (no matter how many doctors and nutritionists try to tell us that we already get enough from our daily food);

   • eat balanced meals (not just pig out on junk food in front of the telly);

   • and all that other stuff that our mothers always told us to do.

3. **We can do something about the physical space around us.** Our surroundings often mirror how we feel about ourselves. If our physical environment looks like a disaster area, that in itself can make us depressed. When we are unemployed, we can vow we will live simpler—something that maybe we've wanted to do, for a long time. We can begin by taking care that each time we handle a thing, we take it all the way to its new destination; we don't just drop it on the counter, thinking that we will deal with it later. We can take care that when we take our clothes off at night, we don't just drop them on the floor, but hang them up or put them in a laundry-hamper. And that, when we finish eating, we put the dishes where they are going to be washed, and put our food back in the refrigerator. And we can determine that when we do such things as get a screwdriver out, to fix a screw that's dropped out of something, that we take the screwdriver all the way back to the tool box or wherever its final destination is. And so on.

When we determine to always put our things away in a timely fashion, neatness will start to appear in our physical environment; this can help lift our spirits immensely, as our physical space mirrors an upbeat life.

4. **We can get outdoors daily and take a good walk.** Hiding in our cave (figuratively speaking) will only make us feel more *down*. Seeing green trees (in season), sunlight, mountains, flowers, people, will do our heart good, each day.

5. **We can focus on other people** and their problems—not just our own. If our unemployment is dragging on and on, and we're starting to have a lot of time on our hands, we can find someplace in town that is dealing with people worse off than we are, and go volunteer there. I'm talking food banks, hospitals, housing aid, anything dealing with kids —especially deprived kids, or kids with tremendous handicaps—that sort of thing. We can do a search on Google, put in the name of our town or city plus the name of the problem we want to help with, and see what turns up. If we determine to help someone else in need, while we're unemployed, we won't feel so discarded by society.

And speaking of other people, we can renew our acquaintance with old friends. We can explore the friendships we already have, not because they are useful in our job-hunt, but just because they are valuable human beings. A wise man named Phillips Brooks used to say there are two kinds of exploration: one involves going out to explore new country; the other involves digging down more deeply into the country we already occupy. Do both, when you're feeling *down*.

6. **We can go on fun mini-adventures.** Often there are portions of our surroundings that we have never explored, but a tourist would "hit" on, the very first day they were there. I lived in New York City for a long time; never once went up in the Empire State Building. I lived in San Francisco for years; never once went out to the Zoo. You get the point. If I lived in either of these cities today, and was unemployed for any length of time, I would set out to visit places I'd never seen. We can stop obsessing about how much we lost from our past, and turn our face toward the future. There are new worlds to conquer, after all.

7. **We can deal with our feelings by expanding our mental horizons, and learning something new.** We can go read up on subjects that have always interested us, but we've never had enough time to explore. While we're unemployed, we have the time. If we can't think of any subject, there's always the human mind. The mind, after all, is what is trying hard to figure out what we should do next. The more we understand it, the better we can heal. If you're looking for suggestions, I'd read anything by Martin Seligman. There's *Learned Optimism: How to Change Your Mind and Your Life*, which, as one reviewer commented, "vaulted me out of my funk." It has excellent chapters on dealing with depression. Or there's Seligman's most recent book, *Flourish: A Visionary New Understanding of Happiness and Well-being*. If you want to delve into improving your memory, there's Joshua Foer's *Moonwalking with Einstein: The Art and Science of Remembering Everything*. And, last but not least, if you want to learn more about how one mind influences another mind, there is Robert B. Cialdini's *Influence: The Psychology of Persuasion*. All these authors have extensive videos on YouTube.

   Speaking of videos, there are a million *free* videos online, where you can learn just about anything. In addition to videos, there are videocasts, webcasts, podcasts, and every other kind of *-cast*. You can type the word "webcast," plus the subject in which you are interested, into your favorite browser like Google, and then pick through whatever turns up. There are also, of course, books. For our Kindle Fire or Nook or iPad, or from online bookstores like Amazon or Barnes & Noble, there are tons of eBooks available, running around ten bucks, or a little more.

   Another subject to explore is the world around us. I love *The Unofficial U.S. Census: Things the Official U.S. Census Doesn't Tell You About America*, by Les Krantz and Chris Smith. My favorite factoid there, because it's related to what I was talking about in our first suggestion: "More than one-third of Americans take naps." *Yes!*

8. **We can talk, talk, talk with our loved ones, or a close friend, about all the feelings we have.** It's amazing how giving voice to thoughts and feelings, particularly when we don't much care for those thoughts and those feelings, causes them to lose their

power over us. So we should do it, because otherwise stuff bottled up inside us tends to fester and grow. We don't want that. We must just take care that we don't pick *the town gossip* to confide in, nor a friend or loved one who just can't keep their mouth shut. You know who they are.

9. We can pound a punching bag or even some pillows, to get some of the angry energy out of us. I don't know why, but it's astonishing how many of the unemployed have told me this actually helps them get rid of some of their anger. And this helps lift our depression as well. Sometimes feeling *down*, and feeling *angry* seem almost to be two different sides of the same coin. If we don't have a gym in our life we can build one at home, simply by putting a pile of pillows on top of our bed, and then pounding the pillows repeatedly, as hard as we can—without breaking anything in our hands, wrists, or arms. This often really helps. We are strange creatures.

10. We can make a list each day of the things that make us grateful, glad, or even happy, day by day. There is a habit of mind that is deadly while we're out of work, and that is spending too much of our day, every day, brooding about what is wrong in our lives: what is wrong with people, what is wrong with our situation, what is wrong with anything and everything. By listing the things we are thankful for, we teach ourselves to focus on what precious gifts we still have, whether they be intelligence, health, or love.

If we want to get over being depressed, it is crucial that we give up endless complaint, it is crucial that we come to forgiveness for any past wrongs done to us, it is crucial that we, as Baltasar Gracián put it, "Get used to the failings of our friends, family, and acquaintances. . . ." We are all human. We are all capable of turning our face toward the future, rather than toward the past.

Postscript

Millions of people in this country have no religious beliefs. But untold millions do. And it is not uncommon that for them, unemployment turns out to be a major spiritual crisis in their life. They cry out, "How could God have let this happen to me—if He truly loved me?" Their faith, far from helping them out of depression, often plunges them into it. They write me and ask for some help and advice. Here is what I tell them.

We can revisit our picture of God and how He works in this world. In the Christian church, for example, the Creed does not begin with "I believe *there is a* God. . . ." It begins with "I believe *in* God. . . ." I think we all understand this distinction, between believing something about a friend of ours, say that she is tall, or smart, versus *believing in* that friend. To believe in someone is to trust them, and to trust that they feel toward us as they say they feel.

We can, instead of abandoning our faith, put some energy into rethinking our faith on a higher level. Some 91 percent of us in the U.S. say we believe in God, but the question is, What kind of God do we believe in? Half a century ago, a man wrote a book titled, *Your God Is Too Small.* Unemployment or any crisis often reveals how poor and small our concept of God is. It is small because it holds God responsible for everything that happens in the world.

Each of us has to figure this out for ourselves. But since people have asked me what I think, after eighty-five years on this Earth, my thoughts ramble along in this fashion: In the Christian faith, Jesus said the most important thing in the world, to God, was that we love Him. Robots can't love. He has to give us freedom so we can choose to love, or not. With that freedom, however, comes the possibility that we will make wrong choices, and thus introduce tragedy into the world. Look at the mess the world is in right now. Look at Congress. God didn't do that!

Well, then, what does God do? To what larger conception of God might we press? Let's try this: imagine that you have, in your dining room, a fine wooden chair, which one day has its back broken off completely—I mean, into smithereens—by a guest in your home. You run down the street, to summon a carpenter who lives nearby. He comes and examines the chair. He pronounces the back unrepairable. "But," he says, "I think I could make a fine wooden stool out of the remainder of the chair, for you." And so he spends much time, shaping, polishing and sanding it, and fashioning out of the former chair a fine stool, more resplendent than anything you have ever dreamed. He inlays it with precious metals, and soon it is the treasure of your house.

This is, of course, a parable. And I know you understand it. But let me underline a couple of key points in it. First of all, the carpenter did not break the chair. Your houseguest did that. But the carpenter came quickly, and with all his art and powers he tried, first of all, to see if he could repair it. Finding it was too late for that, he determined to make of it something even finer than it had been before. And, he labored mightily, to that end. A beautiful stool was the result.

A faith that thinks God is responsible for our unemployment, and He could have and should have prevented it, needs to grow up. It is too small a faith. It has too small a God.

While we are out of work, we can reach toward a larger conception of our God and of ourselves. For, "to believe in God" has the power to lift us out of depression, unless our God is too small.

We can, realize that religion isn't necessarily a blessing. Much depends on whether it is *healthy* religion, or *unhealthy* religion. Your choice. Here is the distinction between them:

Healthy Religion	Unhealthy Religion
Is obsessed with gratitude	Is obsessed with guilt
Focuses on the presence of God in the world; sees holiness everywhere	Focuses on the presence of evil in the world; sees contamination everywhere
Sees all the world as "us"	Sees all the world as "us vs. them"
Is closely related to mental health with its emphasis on repentance (metanoia) or "Most of my ills are self-inflicted."	Is distantly related to mental illness (paranoia) or "Most of my ills stem from what others are doing 'out there.'"
Unconsciously exhibits humility	Unconsciously exhibits arrogance
Treasures the differences in others	Wants everyone to be like them
Has a high sense of "all the saints" worshipping God together	Has a high sense of "the individual alone with his or her God"
Believes in learning from others	Believes in confronting others
Renounces manipulation of others, and lets them have their own beliefs	Desires to manipulate others into accepting their every belief
Wants God's forgiveness toward those who have harmed them or follow other gods; forgives readily	Wants God's vengeance toward those who have harmed them or follow other gods; often has low, long-simmering anger, masked beneath a smile
Focuses on what one can give, out of faith; anxious to give others benefits	Focuses on what one gets out of faith; anxious to get for themselves the benefits
Faith is primarily a matter of actions; words are used only to interpret one's actions	Faith is primarily a matter of words used as tests or orthodoxy. Shibboleth and sibboleth.
Is well aware that their faith may have some unhealthiness to it	Doesn't even dream their faith may be unhealthy

Feelings are often a messenger bringing gifts, if only we open our eyes to see them. If our feelings while we are out of work push us to get more sleep, drink more water, get more physically fit, get outdoors more, look harder at other people who are worse off than we are, renew old neglected friendships, embark on mini-adventures, expand the horizons of our mind, and get us to rethink our faith, then that is a gift indeed. A great gift.

Appendix C A Guide to Choosing a Career Coach or Counselor

If You Decide You Need One

All readers of this book divide into two families, or groups. The first group are those who find the book is all they need, particularly if they do the exercises in chapter 5 successfully, on their own.

The second group are those who find they need a little bit of extra help. Either they bog down in their effort to complete the whole book, or they start the exercises in chapter 5 and then get stuck, at some point. So they want some additional help.

Fortunately, there are a lot of people out there, anxious to help you with your job-hunt or career-change, in case this book isn't sufficient by itself. They go by various names: career coach, career counselor, career development specialist, you name it. They're willing to help you for a fee—because this is how they make their living. That fee will usually equal the fee charged by other types of counselors in town, say a good psychologist. That will range from about $40 an hour in rural areas, on up to . . . *you don't want to know*. The fee may be charged by the hour (recommended) or as one large lump sum up front (definitely not recommended). And most towns or cities of any size have free or almost-free help, too, even though it's likely to be in a group and not face-to-face with an individual counselor. For "free," or "almost free," see Susan Joyce's marvelous website (**job-hunt.org**, or as she likes to say, "job dash hunt dot org") for the section called *Networking and Job Search Support by State*, at **http://tinyurl.com/7a9xbb**.

Now, about those coaches or counselors who charge to help you. There are some simply excellent ones, out there. In fact, I wish I could

303

say that *everyone* who hangs out a sign in this business could be completely recommended. But—alas! and alack!—they can't all be. This career-coaching or career-counseling field is largely unregulated. And even where there is some kind of certification, resulting in their being able to put a lot of degree-soundin' initials after their name, that doesn't really tell you much. It means a lot *to them* of course; in many cases, they purchased those initials with their blood, sweat, and tears. (*Although a few, sad to say, got the initials after their name by mail-order or after one long weekend of training. Tsk, tsk. But, oh well, no different I suppose from a lot of other professions. Some people are always looking for shortcuts.*)

I used to try to explain what all those initials meant. There is a veritable alphabet-soup of them, with new ones born every year. But no more; I've learned, from more than forty years of experience in this field, that 99.4 percent of all job-hunters and career-changers don't care a fig about these initials. All they want to know is: *do you know how to help me find a job?* Or, more specifically, *do you know how to help me find my dream job—one that matches the gifts, skills, and experience that I have, one that makes me excited to get up in the morning, and excited to go to bed at night, knowing I helped make this Earth a little better place to be in? If so, I'll hire you. If not, I'll fire you.*

How to Lose Your Shirt (or Skirt)

So, *bye-bye initials!* Let us start, instead, with this basic truth: *All coaches and counselors divide basically into three groups:*

a) *those who are honest, compassionate, and caring, and know what they're doing;*

b) *those who are honest but don't know what they're doing; and*

c) *those who are dishonest, and merely want your money—large amounts, in a lump sum, and up front. These are often so-called executive counseling firms—***some*** executive counseling firms—rather than individual counselors.*

In other words, you've got compassionate, caring people in the same field with bums and crooks. Your job, if you want help and don't want to waste your money, is to learn how to distinguish the one from the other.

It would help, of course, if someone could just give you a list of those who are firmly in the first category—honest and know what they're doing. But unfortunately, no one (including me) has such a list, or ever has had. You've got to do your own homework or research here, and your own interviewing, in your chosen geographical area. *And if you're too lazy to take the time and trouble to do this research, you will deserve what you get.*

Why is it that *you* and only *you* can do this particular research? Well, let's say a friend tells you to go see so-and-so. He's a wonderful coach or counselor, but unhappily when you meet him he reminds you of your Uncle Harry, whom you detest. Bummer! But, no one except you knows that you've always disliked your Uncle Harry.

> That's why no one else can do this research for you—because the real question is not "Who is best?" but "Who is best for you?" Those last two words demand that it be you who "makes the call."

A special word, here, to those considering paying any firm that focuses on executives or people who make or would like to make a high salary. (This warning is regarding *firms*, not *individual* counselors.) If you are an executive you are considered a fair target for any scam the mind can imagine. New ones appear every year. I have consulted with the Federal Trade Commission in Washington, and States Attorneys General over the years, where they have described the scams to me in detail. I have collected news items, done individual interviews with those who got "taken," and I wish I could tell you about individual firms, but that's not my job. Do your own research. If you are considering signing up with any such firm, Google them first: you will come across timely research about *any* firm. Example: http://corcodilos.com/blog/3219/theladders-how-the-scam-works-2. If you are too lazy to do this research, and subsequently get "taken," let me share the words a Scotsman once said to me, when I got "taken": *"I'm sorry ya lost yer money, but ya dinna do your homework."*

Now, for all my other readers: your dilemma is between categories *a* and *b* on the previous page. How do you find an honest counselor *who knows what they're doing*, and can give you a little bit of help, if you bog down in using this book, most especially chapter 5?

The first bright idea that will occur to you might be something along the lines of "Well, I'll just see who Bolles recommends." Sorry, no such luck. I rarely if ever recommend anyone. Some of the coaches or counselors listed in the *Sampler* at the end of this Appendix, try to claim that their very listing here constitutes a recommendation from me. Oh, come on! They're there because they asked to be. I ask a few questions, but I don't have time to do any thorough research on them. This *Sampler* is more akin to the Yellow Pages, than it is to *Consumer Reports*. Let me repeat this—as I have for forty years now—and repeat it very loudly:

The listing of a career counselor or coach in this book does NOT constitute an endorsement or recommendation by me. Never has meant that. Never will. (Any counselor or coach listed here who claims that it does—either in their ads, or brochures, or publicity— gets permanently removed from this Sampler the following year after I find out about it, and without warning.) This is not "a hall of fame"; it is just a *Sampler* of names of those *who have* **asked** *to be listed, and have answered some reasonable questions.*

Consider the listings as just a starting point for your search. You must check them out. You.must do your own homework. You must do your own research.

A Guide to Choosing a Good Career Coach

So, how do you go about this research toward the goal of finding a good career coach or counselor, if you decide you need more help than this book can give you? Well, you start by collecting **three names** of career coaches or counselors in your geographical area.

How do you find those names? Several ways:

First, you can get names from your friends: ask if any of them have ever used a career coach or counselor. And if so, did they like 'em? And if so, what is that coach's or counselor's name? And how do you get in touch with them, so you can ask them some questions before deciding whether you want to sign up with them, or not?

Second, you can get some names from the aforementioned Sampler in Appendix D (which begins on page 319). See if there are any career coaches or counselors who are near you. They may know how you can find still other names in your community.

Need more names? Try your telephone book's Yellow Pages, under such headings as: *Aptitude and Employment Testing, Career and Vocational Counseling, Personnel Consultants*, and (if you are a woman) *Women's Organizations and Services*.

Once you have three names, it's time to go do some comparison shopping. You want to talk with all three of them and decide which of the three (if any) you want to hook up with.

What will this initial interview cost you, with each coach or counselor? The answer to that is easy: when first setting up an appointment, *ask*. You do have the right to inquire ahead of time how much they are going to have to charge you for the exploratory interview.

Some—a few—will charge you nothing for the initial interview. One of the brightest counselors I know says this: *I don't like to charge for the first interview because I want to be free to tell them I can't help them, if for some reason we just don't hit it off.*

However, do not expect that most coaches or counselors can afford to give you this exploratory interview for nothing! If they did that, and got a lot of requests like yours, they would never make a living.

If this is not an individual counselor, but *a firm* trying to sell you a "pay-me-first" package *up front*, I guarantee they will give you the initial interview for free. They plan to use that "intake" interview (as they call it) to sell you a much more expensive program. They will even ask you to bring your spouse or partner along. (If they can't persuade one of you, maybe they can persuade the other.)

The Questions to Ask

When you are face to face with the coach or counselor, you ask each of them the same questions, listed on the form on the next page. (Keep a little pad, notebook, or PDA with you, so you can write down their answers.)

After visiting the three places you chose for your comparison shopping, you can go home, sit down, put your feet up, look over your notes that evening, and compare those places. A chart like this, drawn in your notebook, may help:

MY SEARCH FOR A GOOD CAREER COUNSELOR

Questions I Will Ask Them	Answer from Counselor #1	Answer from Counselor #2	Answer from Counselor #3
1. What is your program?			
2. Who will be counseling? And how long has this person been counseling?			
3. What is your success rate?			
4. What is the cost of your services?			
5. Is there a contract up front? If so, may I see it please, and take it home with me?			

You need to decide a) whether you want **none** of the three, or b) **one** of the three (and if so, which one).

Remember, you don't have to choose *any* of the three coaches, if you didn't really care for any of them. If that is the case, go choose three new names out of the Yellow Pages or wherever, dust off the notebook, and go out again. It may take a few more hours to find what you want. But **the wallet, the purse, the job-hunt, and the life, you save will be your own.**

As you look over your notes, you will soon realize there is no definitive way for you to determine a career coach's intentions. It's something you'll have to *smell out*, as you go along. But here are some clues.

Bad Vibes, on Up to Real Bad Vibes

If they give you the feeling that everything will be done for you, by them (*including interpretation of tests, and decision making about what this means you should do, or where you should do it*)—rather than asserting that you are going to have to do almost all the work, with their basically being your coach,

(Give them 15 bad points)

You want to learn how to do this for yourself; you're going to be job-hunting again, you know. That's the nature of our world today. Job-hunting is a repetitive activity in human life.

If you don't like the counselor, period!,

(Give them 150 bad points)

I don't care what their expertise is, if you don't like them, you're going to have a rough time getting what you want. I guarantee it. Rapport is everything.

If you ask how long this particular counselor has been doing this, and they get huffy or give a double-barreled answer, such as: "I've had eighteen years' experience in the business and career counseling world,"

(Give them 20 bad points)

What that may mean is: seventeen and a half years as a fertilizer salesman, and one half year doing career counseling. Persist: "How long have you been with this firm, and how long have you been doing formal career coaching or counseling, as you are here?" You don't want someone who's brand new to advising job-hunters. They may call this "their practice," but what they mean is that they are practicing . . . on you.

If they try to answer the question of their experience by pointing to their degrees or credentials,

(Give them 3 bad points)

Degrees or credentials tell you they've passed certain tests of their qualifications, but often these tests bear more on their expertise at career assessment, than on their knowledge of creative job-hunting.

If, when you ask about that firm's success rate, they say they have never had a client who failed to find a job, no matter what,

(Give them 500 bad points)

They're lying. I have studied career counseling programs for more than forty years, have attended many, have studied records at state and federal offices, and have hardly ever seen a program that placed more than 86 percent of their clients, tops, in their best years. And it goes downhill from there. A prominent executive counseling firm was reported by the Attorney General's Office of New York State to have placed only 38 out of 550 clients (a 93 percent failure rate). On the other hand, if they make it clear that they have had a good success rate, but if you fail to work hard at the whole process, then there is no guarantee you are going to find a job, give them three stars.

If any counselor shows you letters from ecstatically happy former clients, but when you ask to talk to some of those clients, you get stonewalled,

(Give them 200 bad points)

Here is a job-hunter's letter about his experience with an executive counseling firm he was considering:

"I asked to speak to a former client or clients. You would have thought I asked to speak to Elvis. The counselor stammered and stuttered and gave me a million excuses why I couldn't talk to some of these 'satisfied' former clients. None of the excuses sounded legitimate to me. We went back and forth for about thirty minutes. Finally, he excused himself and went to speak to his boss, the owner. The next thing I knew I was called into the owner's office for a more 'personal' sales pitch. We spoke for about forty-five minutes as he tried to convince me to use his service. When I told him I was not ready to sign up, he became angry and asked my counselor why I had been put before 'the committee' if I wasn't ready to commit? The counselor claimed I had given a verbal commitment at our last meeting. The owner then turned to me and said I seemed to have a problem making a decision and that he did not want to do business with me. I was shocked. They had turned the whole story around to make it look like it was my fault. I felt humiliated. In retrospect, the whole process felt like dealing with a used car salesman. They used pressure tactics and intimidation to try to get what they wanted. As you have probably gathered, more than anything else this experience made me angry."

If you are dealing with a career counseling *firm*, and you ask what is the cost of their services, and they reply that it is a lump sum that must all be paid "up front" before you start or shortly after you start, all at once or in rapid installments,

(Give them 300 bad points)

We're talking about firms here, not the average individual counselor or coach. The basic problem with firms is that both "the good guys" and "the crooks" do this. The good guys operate on the theory that if you give them a large sum up front, you will then be really committed to the program. The crooks operate on the theory that if you give them a large sum up front, they don't have to give you anything back, except endless excuses and subterfuge, after a certain date (quickly reached).

And the trouble is that there is absolutely no way for you to distinguish crook from good guy, at first impression; they only reveal their true nature after they've got all your money. And by that time, you have no legal way to get it back, no matter what they verbally promised.[1]

Let me repeat: with firms that make you sign a contract and pay basically up front, there is no way to distinguish the good guys from the crooks. The only safe counseling is one with no contract, and you just pay for each hour, as you use it.

I have tried for years to think of some way around this dilemma, to be fair to the good guys, but there just is none. So if you decide to pay up front, be sure it is money you can afford to lose.

If Money Is a Problem for You: Hourly Coaching

Most career coaches or counselors charge by the hour. You pay only for each hour as you use it, according to their set rate. Each time you keep an appointment, you pay them at the end of that hour for their help,

---

1. Sometimes the written contract—there is *always* a written contract, when you are dealing with the bad guys, and they will probably ask your partner to sign it, too—will claim to provide for an almost complete refund, at any time, until you reach a cutoff date in the program, which the contract specifies. Unfortunately, fraudulent firms bend over backward to be extra nice, extra available, and extra helpful to you, from the time you first walk in, until that cutoff point is reached. Therefore, when the cutoff point for getting a refund has passed, you let it pass because you are very satisfied with their past services, and believe there will be many more weeks of the same. Only, there aren't. At fraudulent firms, once the cutoff point is passed, the career counselor suddenly becomes virtually impossible for you to get ahold of. Call after call will not be returned. You will say to yourself, "What happened?" Well, what happened, my friend, is that you paid up in full, they have all the money they're ever going to get out of you, and now, they want to move on.

according to that rate. Period. Finis. You never owe them any money (unless you made an appointment, and failed to keep it). You can stop seeing them at any time, if you feel you are not getting the help you wish. The fee will probably range from $40 an hour on up to $200 an hour or more. It varies *greatly*. Counselors in cities tend to charge more than counselors out in the country.

That fee is for *individual time* with the career coach or counselor. If you can't afford that fee, ask whether they also run groups. If they do, the fee will be much less. And, in one of those delightful ironies of life, since you get a chance to listen to problems that other job-hunters in your group are having, the group will often give you more help than an individual session with a counselor would have. Not always; but often. It's always ironic when *cheaper* and *more helpful* go hand in hand.

If the career counselor in question does offer groups, there should (again) never be a contract. The charge should be payable at the end of each session, and you should be able to drop out at any time, without further cost, if you decide you are not getting the help you want.

There are some career counselors who run free (or almost free) job-hunting workshops through local churches, synagogues, chambers of commerce, community colleges, adult education programs, and the like, as their community service or *pro bono* work (as it is technically called). I have had reports of workshops from a number of places in the U.S. and Canada. They exist in other parts of the world as well. If money is a problem for you, in getting help with your job-hunt, ask around to see if workshops exist in your community. Your chamber of commerce will know, or your church or synagogue.

As I mentioned earlier, you can find an incredibly useful list of all the job support groups in the U.S. compiled by Susan Joyce, on her site Job-Hunt.org: http://tinyurl.com/7a9xbb.

If Your Location Is a Problem for You: Distance-Coaching or Telephone-Counseling

The assumption, from the beginning, was that career counseling would always take place face to face. Both of you, counselor and job-hunter, together in the same room. Just like career counseling's close relatives: marriage counseling, or even AA.

Of course, a job-hunter might—on occasion—phone his or her counselor the day before an interview, to get some last-minute tips or to answer some questions that a prospective interviewer might ask, *tomorrow*.

What is different, today, is that in some cases, career counseling is being conducted exclusively over the phone from start to finish. Some counselors now report that they haven't laid eyes on over 90 percent of their clients, and wouldn't know them if they bumped into them on a street corner. I call this "distance-coaching" or "telephone-counseling."

With the invention of the Internet, with the invention of Internet *telephoning*, we are witnessing "the death of distance"—that is to say, the death of distance as an obstacle. The world, as the wonderful *New York Times* columnist Thomas Friedman has famously written, is in effect *flat*.

An increasing number of counselors or executive coaches are doing this *distance-counseling*.[2] I'll bet we see this increase, geometrically, now that Microsoft has bought Skype, and we are going to have video counseling at our disposal in many shapes and forms.

This increasing availability of "distance-counseling" is good news, and bad news.

Why good news? Well, in the old days you might be a job-hunter in some remote village, with a population of only eighty-five, back in the hills somewhere, or you might be living somewhere in France or in China, miles from any career counselor or coach, and so, be totally out of luck. Now, these days you can be anywhere in the world, but as long as you have the Internet on your desk, you can still connect with the best distance-counseling there is.

And the bad news?

Well, just because a counselor or coach does distance-counseling or phone-counseling, doesn't mean they are really good at doing it. Some are superb; but some are not. So, you're still going to have to research any *distance-counselor* very carefully.

It is altogether too easy for a counselor to get sloppy doing distance-counseling—for example, browsing the newspapers while you are telling some long personal story, etc., to which they are giving only

---

2. Two famous "distance coaches" are Joel Garfinkle in Oakland, California, www.dreamjobcoaching .com; and Marshall Goldsmith of www.marshallgoldsmithlibrary.com, international coach to the executive elite, and author (with Mark Reiter) of the popular book, *What Got You Here Won't Get You There*.

the briefest attention. (Of course, the increasingly wider use of video calling programs such as Skype may cure that!) To avoid any kind of sloppiness, *you* and the counselor need discipline. Experienced distance-counselors, such as Joel Garfinkle,[3] insist on forms being used, both before and after each phone session. With his permission, I have adapted his forms, and print them here. *And, P.S., they are equally useful for normal, face-to-face counseling, as well.*

Client Coaching Forms

1. Before You Start

Prior to beginning the counseling, it helps if your coach or counselor asks you to fill out the following kind of form, for you to give to him or her. They are written by the counselor, addressed to you, the potential counselee. (And if they don't ask for a form like this to be filled out, you might volunteer to give them such a form on your own.)

Questions to Understand You Better

(Copy this onto another sheet of paper, and leave lots of space on the form for your answer, after each question below.)

1. **Why have you decided to work with me?**
2. **How can I have the most impact on your life in the next ninety days (three months)?**
3. **List three key goals you want to accomplish through our work together.**
4. **What stops you from achieving what you want in question #2 or #3 above?**
5. **Project ahead one year: As you look back, and things went well, how did you benefit from our coaching relationship?**
6. **What are your expectations from our work together? How can we exceed these expectations?**

---

3. www.dreamjobcoaching.com/about

7. **What else is helpful for me to know about you?**

8. **Explain your background (use the same format as the examples below).**

Examples:

1. After thirty years as a commercial insurance broker, I hit a wall last May, and decided to change careers . . .

2. After twelve successful years in the high-tech industry, I found myself unfulfilled in finding a satisfying career. Over the years, I read countless books on the topic of finding one's true purpose in career pursuits, but was still missing a sense of purpose and clarity on what I wanted to do . . .

3. After working for twenty years in the investment industry I decided to start my own company . . .

4. Etc.

2. Before Each Session, Preparation Form

Please fill out this form #2 for each coaching session. It should be filled out and e-mailed to me twenty-four hours before the next coaching session to assist me in preparing for that session.

(Copy this onto another sheet of paper, and leave lots of space on the form for your answer, after each question below.)

1. **Commitments that I made to myself on the last coaching session and what I accomplished since we had the coaching session:**

2. **The challenges and opportunities I am facing now:**

3. **The one action I can take that will most affect my current goals and provide the highest payoff:**

4. **My agenda for the coaching session is:**

3. After Each Session: Reflection Form

Immediately after each coaching session e-mail me form #3.

(Copy this onto another sheet of paper, and leave lots of space on the form for your answer, after each question below.)

1. **This week's commitment:**

2. **My greatest insights during this session were:**

3. **What you, my coach, said or asked during the session that impacted me most:**

4. **What I'd like you, as my coach, to do differently/more of/less of:**

5. **How I feel I am evolving from our work together:**

What happens in a counseling session is our responsibility, not just the counselor's or coach's.

The forms, above, are one way of our taking responsibility. Another, is that when you first contact prospective coaches for distance-counseling in particular, you have a right to ask them: (1) "What training have you completed, relevant to distance-counseling, such as telephone skills, and supervised counseling?" (2) "How will our distance-counseling be organized and scheduled?" and (3) "What will the two of us do if and when interruptions occur during a session, at either end?"

You must always remember: distance-counseling, attractive as it will be for many, as necessary as it will be for some, definitely has its limits.

To the caveman, the technology that enables all this to happen in this twenty-first century, would be jaw-droppingly awesome. But, good career counseling or coaching *is not just about technology.* What is really truly awesome, in the end, is simply our power to help each other on this Earth. And how much that power resides, not in techniques or technology—though these things are important—but in each of us just being a good human being. A *loving* human being.

A Sampler

The following Appendix is exactly what its name implies: a Sampler. Were I to list all the career coaches and counselors there are in the U.S. (never mind the world), we would end up with an encyclopedia. Some states, in fact, have encyclopedic lists of counselors and businesses, in various books or directories, and your local bookstore or library should have these, in their Job-Hunting Section, under such titles as "How to Get a Job in . . ." or "Job-Hunting in . . ." Now, let me repeat this:

I did not choose the places listed in this Sampler; rather, they are listed at their own request, and I offer their information to you simply as suggestions of where you can begin your investigation—when you're trying to find decent help.

Do keep in mind that many truly helpful places and coaches are not listed here. If you discover such a coach or place, which is very good at helping people with *Parachute* and creative job-hunting or career-change, do send us their pertinent information. We will ask them, as we do all the listings here, a few intelligent questions, and if they sound okay, we will add that place as a suggestion in next year's edition.[4]

What kind of questions? This directory appears nowhere but in this book, so we may presume you are interested in this book's approach, and if you need a little help it is help with the process in this book. We tried being broader in the past—there are obviously excellent counselors out there who have never heard of this book—but it turned out that our readers wanted counselors and places that have some expertise with *Parachute*, and can help job-hunters or career-changers finish the job-hunt in this book.

So, if they've never even heard of *Parachute*, we don't list them anymore. But even among those who have, we can't automatically assume

---

4. Yearly readers of this book will notice that we do remove people from this Sampler, without warning. First of all, there are accidents: we drop places we didn't mean to, but a typographical error was made, somehow (it happens). *Oops!* Counselor or coach: call this to our attention; we'll put you back in next year.

But accidents aside, we do deliberately remove the following: places that have moved, and don't bother to send us their new address. *Coaches and counselors: If you are listed here, we expect you to be a professional at communication. When you move, your first priority should be to let us know, immediately. As one exemplary counselor wrote: "You are the first person I am contacting on my updated letterhead . . . hot off the press just today!" So it should always be, if you want to continue to be listed here. A number of places get removed every year, precisely because of their sloppiness in keeping us up-to-date with their phone and other contact information.*

Other causes for removal: Places that have disconnected their telephone, or otherwise suggest that they have gone out of business. Places that our readers lodge complaints against with us, as being unhelpful or even obnoxious. The complaints may be falsified, but we can't take that chance. Places that change their personnel, and the new person has never even heard of *Parachute*, or "creative job-search techniques." College services that we discover (belatedly) serve only "Their Own." Counseling firms that employ salespeople as the initial "intake" person that a job-hunter meets. If you discover that any of the places listed in this Sampler fall into any of the above categories, you would be doing a great service to our other readers by dropping us a line and telling us so (10 Stirling Drive, Danville, CA 94526-2921).

they're good at what they do, no matter how many questions we asked them. So we list them and leave the research to you.

You must do your own sharp questioning before you decide to go with anyone. If you don't take time to research two or three places, before choosing a counselor, you will deserve whatever you get (or, more to the point, don't get). So, please, do some research.

The listings that follow are alphabetical within each state, with counselors listed by their name in alphabetical order, according to their last name.

Some offer group career counseling, some offer testing, some offer access to job-banks, etc. Ask.

One final note: places and counselors listed here have said they counsel anyone. Ninety-nine percent of them can absolutely be trusted, in this. A few, however, may turn out to have restrictions unknown to us ("we counsel only women," or "we only deal with alumni," etc.). If that turns out to be the case, your time isn't wasted. They may be able to help you with a referral. So, ask them, "Who else in the area can you tell me about, who helps with job-searches, and are there any (among them) that you think are particularly effective?" (Also, write us and let us know they only counsel *some* people, so we can remove them from this Sampler next year.)

Area Codes

If you call a phone number in the Sampler that is any distance geographically from you, and they tell you "this number cannot be completed as dialed," the most likely explanation is that the area code was changed—maybe some time ago. Throughout the U.S. now, area codes are subdividing constantly, sometimes more than once during a short time span. (We ask counselors listed here to notify us when the area code changes, but some do and some don't.) Anyway, call Information and check, or look up their phone number on the Web.

Of course, if you're calling a local counselor, you won't need the area code (unless you live in one of the metropolitan areas in the U.S. that requires ten-digit dialing).

Appendix D Sampler List of Coaches

* Throughout this Sampler, an asterisk before their name, in red, means they offer religious counseling as well as secular—that is, they're not afraid to have you talk about God, if you're looking for some help in finding your Mission in life through faith.

UNITED STATES

Alabama
Chemsak, Maureen J., LPC, NCC, MCC
NorthStart Counseling and
Consulting, PC
P.O. Box 2065
Madison, AL 35758
Athens, AL 35611
Phone: 256-520-7650
E-mail: mjchemsak104@gmail.com

Vantage Associates Inc.
2100-B Southbridge Pkwy., Ste. 240
Birmingham, AL 35209
Phone: 205-879-0501
Cell: 205-533-0429
Contact: Ellen Glasgow
E-mail: info@vantageassociates.com
www.vantageassodiates.com

Alaska
Career Transitions
2600 Denali St., Ste. 430
Anchorage, AK 99503
Phone: 907-274-4500
Fax: 907-274-4510
Contact: Deeta Lonergan, President
E-mail: deeta@alaska.net
www.careertransitions.biz

Arizona
Boninger, Faith, PhD
10965 E. Mary Katherine Dr.
Scottsdale, AZ 85259
Phone: 480-390-6736
E-mail: faithboninger@cox.net

*Career Discovery Services, LLC
3145 E. Chandler Blvd., Ste. 110-212
Phoenix, AZ 85048
Phone: 480-706-1262
Contact: Sandy Somers, RN, MS, ACC
E-mail: careerdiscovery@msn.com
www.careerdiscoveryservices.com

Davenport Institute
10645 N. Tatum Blvd., Ste. 200-362
Phoenix, AZ 85028
Phone: 480-348-7875
Contact: Debra Davenport
E-mail: debradavenport@davenport
institute.com
www.davenportinstitute.com

Passport to Purpose
7744 East Knots Pass
Prescott Valley, AZ 86314
Phone: 928-775-4949
Contact: Cathy Severson, MS
E-mail: cathy@passporttopurpose.com
www.passporttopurpose.com
www.retirementlifematters.com

Renaissance Career Solutions
PO Box 30118
Phoenix, AZ 85046-0118
Phone: 602-867-4202
Contact: Betty Boza, MA, LCC
E-mail: bboza@att.net
http://bboza-ivil.tripod.com

California
Bauer, Lauralyn Larsen
Career Counselor & Coach
Napa, CA 94558
Phone: 707-363-7775
E-mail: lauralynbauer@hotmail.com

Berrett & Associates
533 E. Mariners Cir.
Fresno, CA 93730
Phone: 559-284-3549
Contact: Dwayne Berrett, MA, RPCC
E-mail: dberrett@me.com
www.berrett-associates.com

California Career Services
6024 Wilshire Blvd.
Los Angeles, CA 90036
Phone: 323-933-2900
Phone: 1-800-63CAREER
Fax: 323-933-9929
Contact: Susan Wise Miller, MA
E-mail: susan@californiacareer
services.com
www.californiacareerservices.com

Career Balance
215 Witham Rd.
Encinitas, CA 92024
Phone: 760-436-3994
Fax: 760-632-9871
Contact: Virginia Byrd, MEd
Career and Work-Life Consultant
E-mail: virginia@careerbalance.net
www.careerbalance.net

*Career Choices
Dublin, CA
Contact: Dana E. Ogden, MS Ed, CCDV
E-mail: dana@careerchoices.us
www.careerchoices.us

Career Counseling and Assessment Associates
9229 W. Sunset Blvd., Ste. 502
Los Angeles, CA 90069
Phone: 310-274-3423
Contact: Dianne Y. Sundby, PhD
Director and Psychologist
E-mail: DYSD99@aol.com
www.dscounseling.com

Career and Personal Development Institute
582 Market St., Ste. 410
San Francisco, CA 94104
Phone: 415-982-2636
Contact: Bob Chope
www.cpdicareercounseling.com

Career Possibilities
3009 Lantana Ave.
Fullerton, CA 92835-1945
Phone: 714-990-6014
Contact: Cheryl A. Heil, MEd, JCTC, CPCM
E-mail: keytosuccess1@sbcglobal.net

Center for Career Growth and Development
453 Alberto Way, Ste. 257D
Los Gatos, CA 95032
Phone: 408-354-7150
Contact: Steven E. Beasley
E-mail: stevenbeasley@verizon.net

*Center for Creativity and Work
2024 Vine St. #2D
Berkeley, CA 94709
Phone: 510-526-1600
Contact: Allie Roth, Career Coach
E-mail: allie@allieroth.com
www.allieroth.com

*Center for Life & Work Planning
1133 Second St.
Encinitas, CA 92024
Phone/Fax: 760-943-0747
Contact: Mary C. McIsaac,
Executive Director

*Cheney-Rice, Stephen, MS
2113 Westboro Ave.
Alhambra, CA 91803-3720
Phone: 626-824-5244
E-mail: sccheneyrice@earthlink.net

Christen, Carol
Consultant, Career & Job Search Strategy
Co-author, *What Color Is Your Parachute?*
For Teens
Atascadero, CA
Phone: 805-462-8795
E-mail: carol@carolchristen.com
www.parachute4teens.com

*Clear Change Group
1330 Lincoln Ave., Ste. 102C
San Rafael, CA 94901
Phone: 415-488-4998
Contact: Audrey Seymour, MA, PCC,
CPCC
E-mail: inquiry@clearchangegroup.com
www.clearchangegroup.com

Collaborative Solutions
3130 W. Fox Run Way
San Diego, CA 92111
Phone: 858-268-9340
Contact: Nancy Helgeson, MA, LMFT
E-mail: nhelgeson@san.rr.com

Dream Job Coaching
6918 Thornhill Dr.
Oakland, CA 94611
Phone: 510-339-3201
Contact: Joel Garfinkle
E-mail: joel@dreamjobcoaching.com
www.dreamjobcoaching.com
www.garfinkleexecutivecoaching.com

Experience Unlimited Job Clubs
There are many Experience Unlim-
ited clubs in California, found at the
Employment Development Depart-
ment (EDD) in the following locations:
Anaheim, Canoga Park, Contra Costa,
Fremont, Fresno, Irvine, Lancaster,
Manteca, Murietta, Pasadena, San
Francisco, San Rafael, Santa Barbara,
Santa Cruz/Capitola, Santa Maria, Simi
Valley, Sunnyvale, Torrance, and West
Covina.
Contact the chapter nearest you
through your local EDD office. Website:
http://tinyurl.com/lww4ux.

*Frangquist, Deborah Gavrin, MS
Chosen Futures
1801 Bush St., Ste. 121
San Francisco, CA 94109
Phone: 415-346-6171
E-mail: Deborah@ChosenFutures.com
www.ChosenFutures.com

Fritsen, Jan, MS, MFT
Career Counseling and Coaching
23181 La Cadena Dr., Ste. 103
Laguna Hills, CA 92653
Phone: 949-497-4869
E-mail: janfritsen@cox.net
www.janfritsen.com

Geary & Associates, Inc.
1100 Coddingtown Ctr., Ste. A
PO Box 3774
Santa Rosa, CA 95402
Phone: 707-525-8085
Fax: 707-528-8088
Contact: Jack Geary, MA
Edelweiss Geary, MEd, CRC
E-mail: esgeary@sbcglobal.net
www.gearyassociates.com

Hilliard, Larkin, MA
Counseling Psychology
250 Curtner Avenue, Apt. 3
Palo Alto, CA 94306
Phone: 805-680-3496
E-mail: larkinhilliard@yahoo.com
(English, French, German, and Russian)

HRS
4421 Alla Rd., #2
Marina del Rey, CA 90292
Phone: 310-577-0972
Contact: Nancy Mann, MBA
Career Coach
E-mail: nanmanhrs@aol.com

*Miller, Lizbeth, MS
Nationally Certified Career Counselor
3425 S. Bascom Ave., Ste. 250
Campbell, CA 95008
and 306 Esmeralda Dr.
Santa Cruz, CA 95060
Phone: 408-486-6763
Fax: 408-369-4990
E-mail: lizmillercareers@yahoo.com
www.lizmillercareers.com

Nemko, Marty, PhD
Career and Education Strategist
5936 Chabolyn Terr.
Oakland, CA 94618
Phone: 510-655-2777
E-mail: mnemko@comcast.net
www.martynemko.com

Piazzale, Steve, PhD
Career/Life Coach
Mountain View, CA
Phone: 650-964-4366
E-mail: Steve@BayAreaCareer
Coach.com
www.BayAreaCareerCoach.com

Saraf, Dilip G.
Career and Worklife Strategist
Career Transitions Unlimited
39159 Paseo Padre Pkwy., #221
Fremont, CA 94538
Phone: 510-791-7005
E-mail: dilip@7keys.org
www.7keys.org

*Schoenbeck, Mary Lynne, MA,
NCCC,
MCC, Career/Retirement Counselor,
Coach, Consultant
Schoenbeck & Associates
Los Altos, CA
Phone: 650-964-8370
E-mail: schoenbeck@mindspring.com

Struntz and Associates
Career & Job Search Consulting
Saint Helena, CA 94574
Phone: 707-963-0843
Contact: Wolfgang Struntz, MA
E-mail: Struntz@netwiz.net

Transitions Counseling Center
171 N. Van Ness Ave.
Fresno, CA 93701
Phone: 559-233-7250
Contact: Margot E. Tepperman, MA,
LCSW, ACC
E-mail: mtepperman@aol.com
www.transitionscoaching.com

Wilson, Patti
Career Company
PO Box 35633
Los Gatos, CA 95030
Phone: 408-354-1964
E-mail: patti@careercompany.com
www.pattiwilson.com

**Zitron Parham Career Counseling &
Life Coaching**
4724 25th St., Ste. A
San Francisco, CA 94114
Phone: 415-648-7377
Contact: Nick Parham,
Career & Life Coach
E-mail: npcoach@gmail.com
www.zitronparhamcareerservices.com

Colorado
Arapahoe Community College
Career Center
Career Planning Seminars
Job Postings
5900 S. Santa Fe Dr.
PO Box 9002
Littleton, CO 80160-9002
Phone: 303-797-5805
E-mail: careers@arapahoe.edu

Gary Ringler & Associates
1747 Washington St., #203
Denver, CO 80203
Phone: 303-863-0234
E-mail: garyringler@msn.com

Helmstaedter, Sherry, MS
Englewood, CO 80111-1122
Phone: 720-560-9601
E-mail: changegrow@aol.com

Pivotal Choices, Inc.
PO Box 1098
Durango, CO 81302
Phone: 970-385-9597
Contact: Mary Jane Ward, MEd, NCC,
NCCC
E-mail: mjw@pivotalchoices.com
www.pivotalchoices.com

Women's Resource Agency
750 Citadel Dr. E., Ste. 312B
Colorado Springs, CO 80909
Phone: 719-471-3170
www.wrainc.org

Connecticut
Accord Career Services, LLC
Salmon Brook Corporate Park
500 Winding Brook Dr
Glastonbury, CT 06033
Phone: 860-674-9654 or 860-508-1026
Contact: Tod Gerardo, MS, Director
E-mail: tod@accordcareerservices.com
www.accordcareerservices.com

Center for Professional Development
University of Hartford
50 Elizabeth St.
Hartford, CT 06105
Phone: 860-768-5619
Contact: Eleta Jones, PhD, LPC
E-mail: ejones@hartford.edu
www.hartford.edu/cpd

The Offerjost-Westcott Group
263 Main St., Ste. 100
Old Saybrook, CT 06475
Phone: 860-388-6094
Contact: Russ Westcott
E-mail: russwest@snet.net

Pannone, Bob, MA
Career Specialist
62 Lane St.
Huntington, CT 06484
Phone: 203-513-2290
E-mail: upstartinc@yahoo.com

Preis, Roger J.
RPE Career Dynamics
Stamford, CT
E-mail: rjpreis@rpecareers.com
www.rpecareers.com

Delaware
Bronson, Kris, PhD
1409 Foulk Rd., Ste. 204
Foulkstone Plaza
Wilmington, DE 19803
Phone: 302-477-0708, ext. 4
www.krisbronsonphd.com

District Of Columbia
Roggenkamp, Robin
Certified Career and Leadership Coach
Washington, DC area (NoVa)
Phone: 703-298-2964
E-mail: robin@myauthenticcareer.com
www.myauthenticcareer.com

The Women's Center
1025 Vermont Ave. NW, Ste. 310
Washington, DC 20005
Phone: 202-293-4580
www.thewomenscenter.org

Florida
Career Choices Unlimited
4465 Baymeadows Rd., Ste. 7
Jacksonville, FL 32217
Phone: 904-443-0059 or 904-262-9470
Contact: Marilyn A. Feldstein, MPA,
JCTC, MBTI, PHR,
Career Coach and Professional Speaker
www.careerchoicesunlimited.com

Chabon-Berger, Toby, MEd, NCC,
NCCC
Career and Professional
Development Coach
4900 Boxwood Circle
Boynton Beach, FL 33436
Phone: 561-596-3656
E-mail: tberger@chabongroup.com
www.tobycareer.com

The Clarity Group
PO Box 110084
Lakewood Ranch, FL 34211
Phone: 941-388-8108
Contact: George H. Schofield, PhD
E-mail: george.schofield@clarity-group
.com
or george@georgeschofield.com
or george@newbrightlife.com
www.clarity-group.com
www.georgeschofield.com
www.newbrightlife.com

Cohen, James, PhD
7177 Granville Ave.
Boynton Beach, FL 33437
Fax/Phone: 561-509-9150
E-mail: vocdoc56@yahoo.com

**Focus on the Future: Displaced
Homemaker Program**
Santa Fe College
3000 NW 83rd St., I-40
Gainesville, FL 32606
Phone: 352-395-5047
Contacts: Nancy Griffin
or JoAnn Wilkes
E-mail: focusonthefuture@sfcollege.edu
www.sfcollege.edu/Displaced
Homemakers
(Classes are free.)

Graduate to Success
Career Coach for Students and
Graduates
Orlando, FL 32836
Phone: 407-701-5510
Contact: Susan Havill
E-mail: SusanHavill@yahoo.com
www.GraduateToSuccess.com

Life Designs, Inc.
19526 E. Lake Dr.
Miami, FL 33015
Phone: 305-829-9008
Contact: Dulce Muccio Weisenborn
E-mail: dmw@lifedesigns-inc.com
www.lifedesigns-inc.com

TransitionWorks
Delray Beach, FL
Phone: 301-233-4287
Contact: Nancy K. Schlossberg, EdD,
Principal
E-mail: nancyks4@gmail.com
Contact: Stephanie Kay, MA, LCPC.
Principal
E-mail: stephaniekay4@gmail.com
(They also have offices in Rockville,
Maryland, and Sarasota, Florida.)

Georgia
Ashkin, Janis, MEd, MCC, NCC, NCCC
2365 Winthrope Way Dr.
Alpharetta, GA 30009
Phone: 678-319-0297
E-mail: jashkin@bellsouth.net

Career Quest/Job Search Workshop
St. Ann's Catholic Church
4905 Roswell Rd. NE
Marietta, GA 30062-6240
Phone: 770-552-6400 ext. 6104
Contact: John Marotto
E-mail: careerquest-sa@comcast.net
www.st-ann.org/career_quest.php
LinkedIn Group: Career Quest at St.
Ann's Church

D & B Consulting, Inc.
3355 Lenox Rd., Ste. 750
Atlanta, GA 30326
Phone: 404-504-7079
Contact: Deborah R. Brown, SPHR,
MBA, MSW, Career Consultant
E-mail: Debbie@DandBconsulting.com
www.dandbconsulting.com

Satterfield, Mark
720 Rio Grand Dr.
Alpharetta, GA 30022
Phone: 770-643-8566
E-mail: msatt@mindspring.com

Waldorf, William H., MBA, LPC
Path Unfolding Career Development
5755 North Point Parkway., Ste. 39
Alpharetta, GA 30022
Phone: 678-822-5505
E-mail: wwaldorf@earthlink.net

Idaho
*****Career Coaching 4U**
9882 W. View Dr.
Boise, ID 83704
Phone: 208-323-2462
Contact: Michael W. Reed, MEd, MS
Counseling, LPC
E-mail: michael@careercoaching4u.com
www.careercoaching4u.com

Illinois
Alumni Career Center
University of Illinois Alumni
Association
200 S. Wacker Dr., First Floor
Chicago, IL 60606
Phone: 312-575-7830
Contact: Julie Hays Bartimus,
Vice President
Bernice Allegretti, Assistant Director
E-mail: careers@uillinois.edu
www.uiaa.org/careers

Career Vision/The Ball Foundation
526 N. Main St.
Glen Ellyn, IL 60137
Phone: 800-469-8378
Contact: Peg Hendershot, Director;
Paula Kosin, MS, LCPC;
Mary Hanney, MSEd, MBA, LCPC;
Nancy Ryan Krane, PhD
E-mail: info@careervision.org
www.careervision.org

Davis, Jean, MA
Counseling Psychology, specializing in
adult career transitions
1405 Elmwood Ave.
Evanston, IL 60201
Phone: 847-492-1002
E-mail: jdavis@careertransitions.net
www.careertransitions.net

**Dolan Career & Rehabilitation
Consulting, Ltd.**
307 Henry St., Ste. 411
Alton, IL 62002
Phone: 618-474-5328
Fax: 618-462-3359
Contact: J. Stephen Dolan, MA, CRC,
Career & Rehabilitation Consultant
E-mail: dolanrehab@att.net

Grimard Wilson Consulting, Inc.
333 W. Wacker Dr., Ste. 500
Chicago, IL 60606
and
1140 W. Lake St., Ste. 302
Oak Park, IL 60301
Phone: 312-925-5176
Contact: Diane Wilson, LCPC, BCN
E-mail: diane.g.wilson@gmail.com
www.grimardwilson.com

**Harper College Community
Career Services**
1200 W. Algonquin Rd., Rm. A-347
Palatine, IL 60067
Phone: 847-925-6220
Contact: Kathleen Canfield, Director
E-mail: careercenter@harpercollege.edu
www.harpercollege.edu

Inspired Career Options
PO Box 7174
Buffalo Grove, IL 60089
Phone: 847-808-9982
Contact: Deb Morton, Certified Executive
Career & Entrepreneur Coach
E-mail: deb@inspiredcareeroptions.com
www.inspiredcareeroptions.com

***Lansky Career Consultants**
500 N. Michigan Ave. #820
Chicago, IL 60611
Phone: 312-494-0022
Contact: Judi Lansky, MA, MBA
E-mail: lanskycareers@yahoo.com

LeBrun, Peter
Career/Leadership Coach
Executive Career Management
4333 N. Hazel St., Ste. 100
Chicago, IL 60613
Phone: 773-281-7274
E-mail: peterlebrun@aol.com

Moraine Valley Community College
Job Resource Center
9000 College Pkwy.
Palos Hills, IL 60465
Phone: 708-974-5737
www.morainevalley.edu/jrc

Iowa
Sucher, Billie, MS, CTMS, CTSB,
JCTC, CCM,
Private Practice Career Transition
Consultant
7177 Hickman Rd., Ste. 10
Des Moines, IA 50322
Phone: 515-276-0061
E-mail: billie@billiesucher.com
www.billiesucher.com

Zilber, Suzanne, PhD
Licensed Psychologist
Catalyst Counseling
600 5th St., Ste. 302
Ames, IA 50010-6072
Phone: 515-232-5340
Fax: 515-232-2070
www.catalystcounseling.com

Kansas
Keeping the People, Inc.
12213 Westgate St.
Overland Park, KS 66213
Phone: 913-620-4645
Contact: Leigh Branham
E-mail: LB@keepingthepeople.com
www.keepingthepeople.com

Kentucky
Career Span, Inc.
620 Euclid Ave., Ste. 210
Lexington, KY 40502
Phone: 859-233-7726 (233-SPAN)
Contact: Carla Ockerman-Hunter, MA,
MCC, NCC
E-mail: careerspan@aol.com
www.careerspanUSA.com

Louisiana
Career Center
River Center Branch, EBR Parish Library
120 St. Louis St.
Baton Rouge, LA 70802
Phone: 225-381-8434
Fax: 225-389-8910
Contact: Anne Nowak, Program Director
E-mail: anowak@careercenterbr.com
www.careercenterbr.com

Maine
D. Gallant Management Associates
75 Pearl St., Ste. 211
Portland, ME 04101
Phone: 207-773-4800
Contact: Deborah L. Gallant, SPHR,
CBP, CCP
E-mail: dgma@dgallant.com
www.dgallant.com

**Heart at Work Career Counseling &
Second Half of Life Career Transitions**
25 Middle St.
Portland, ME 04101
Phone: 207-775-6400
Contact: Barbara Babkirk, Master
Career Counselor
E-mail: barb@barbarababkirk.com
www.barbarababkirk.com

Women's Worth Career Counseling
9 Village Ln.
Westbrook, ME 04092
Phone: 207-856-6666
Contact: Jacqueline Murphy,
Career Counselor
E-mail: wethepeople@maine.rr.com

Maryland
**The Career Evaluation and
Coaching Center**
21 West Rd., Ste. 150
Baltimore, MD 21204
Phone: 410-825-0042
Fax: 410-825-0310
Contact: Ralph D. Raphael, PhD
E-mail: drraphael@ralphraphael.com
www.ralphraphael.com

CTS Consulting, Inc.
3126 Berkshire Rd.
Baltimore, MD 21214-3404
Phone: 410-444-5857
Contact: Michael Bryant
E-mail: mb3126@gmail.com
www.go2ctsonline.com

Friedman, Lynn, PhD
Psychologist, Psychoanalyst,
Work-Life Consultant
Johns Hopkins University
5480 Wisconsin Ave.
Chevy Chase, MD 20815
Phone: 301-656-9050
E-mail: drlynnfriedman@verizon.net
www.washington-dc-psychologist.com
www.drlynnfriedman.com

Headley, Anne S., MA
6510 41st Ave.
University Park, MD 20782
Phone: 301-779-1917
E-mail: asheadley@verizon.net
www.anneheadley.com

Horizons Unlimited, Inc.
17501 McDade Ct.
Rockville, MD 20855
Phone: 301-258-9338
Contact: Marilyn Goldman,
LPC, NCCC, MCC
E-mail: horizons@career-counseling
.com
www.career-counseling.com

**Positive Passages Life/Career
Transition Counseling and Coaching**
4702 Falstone Ave.
Chevy Chase, MD 20815
Phone: 301-580-5162
Contact: Jeanette Kreiser, EdD
E-mail: jskreiser@yahoo.com

Prince George's Community College
Career Services
301 Largo Rd.
Largo, MD 20774
Phone: 301-322-0109
Contact: H. Randall Poole,
Manager of Career Services;
Stephanie Pair, Senior Career Advisor
E-mail: Career_Job@pgcc.edu
www.pgcc.edu

TransitionWorks
Rockville, MD
Phone: 301-233-4287
Contact: Nancy K. Schlossberg, EdD,
Principal
E-mail: nancyks4@gmail.com
Stephanie Kay, MA, LCPC, Principal
E-mail: stephaniekay4@gmail.com
(With offices in Delray and Sarasota, FL.)

Massachusetts
Berke & Price Associates
Newtown Way #6
Chelmsford, MA 01824
Phone: 978-256-0482
Contact: Judit E. Price, MS, CDFI, IJCTC,
CCM, CPRW,
Career Consultant, Certified Resume
Writer, and Brand Specialist
E-mail: jprice@careercampaign.com
www.careercampaign.com
www.careercampaign.com/blog
www.linkedin.com/in/juditprice

The Boston Career Coach
26 Shanley St.
Brighton, MA 02135
Phone: 617-254-0791
Contact: Tom Jackson
www.thebostoncareercoach.com

Career in Progress
2 Marie Ann Dr.
Westford, MA 01886
Phone: 617-925-5289
Fax: 781-407-0955
Contact: Heather Maietta, EdD, GCDF,
JCDC, CPRW,
Career and Professional
Development Coach
E-mail: info@careerinprogress.com
www.careerinprogress.com

*Career Management Consultants
108 Grove St., Ste. 204
Worcester, MA 01605
Phone: 508-756-9998
Contact: Patricia Stepanski Plouffe,
Founder/Consultant
E-mail: info@careermc.com

Career Source
186 Alewife Brook Pkwy., Ste. 310
Cambridge, MA 02138
Phone: 617-661-7867
www.yourcareersource.com

***Center for Career Development &
Ministry**
30 Milton St., Ste. 107
Dedham, MA 02026
Phone: 781-329-2100
Fax: 781-407-0955
Contact: Stephen Ott, Director
E-mail: info@ccdmin.org
www.ccdmin.org

Changes
Career Counseling and Job-Hunt
Training
2516 Massachusetts Ave.
Cambridge, MA 02140
Phone: 617-868-7775 or 617-868-0660
Contact: Carl J. Schneider
E-mail: carl@changescareerservices.com
www.changescareerservices.com

Hadlock, Joanne, EdD, NCCC
Career/Life Transitions
223 Sandy Pond Rd.
Lincoln, MA 01773
Phone: 781-259-3752
E-mail: joannehadlock@comcast.net
www.joannehadlock.us

**Jewish Vocational Service,
Career Moves**
29 Winter St., 5th Floor
Boston, MA 02108
Phone: 617-399-3131
Contact: Judy Sacks, Director
www.career-moves.org

**Jewish Vocational Service,
Career Moves**
Career Counseling and Testing
333 Nahanton St.
Newton, MA 02159
Phone: 617-965-7940
Contact: Amy Mazur, Career Counselor
E-mail: amazur@jvs-boston.org;
www.career-moves.org

*****Liebhaber, Gail**, MEd
40 Cottage St.
Lexington, MA 02420
Phone: 781-861-9949
Contact: Gail Liebhaber, MEd
E-mail: gail@yourcareerdirection.com
www.yourcareerdirection.com

Miller, Wynne W.
Leadership Coaching
Brookline, MA 02446-4707
Phone: 617-232-4848
E-mail: wynne@win-coaching.com
www.win-coaching.com

Szekely, Bill
10 Doral Dr.
N. Chelmsford, MA 01863
Phone: 978-251-3693
Cell: 978-423-3196
E-mail: Bill@LifeWorkDiscovery.com
www.lifeworkdiscovery.com

Michigan
*****Careers Through Faith**
3025 Boardwalk St.
Ann Arbor, MI 48108
Phone: 734-332-8800, ext. 228
Contact: Cathy Synko
E-mail: Cathy@CareersThroughFaith
.org
www.CareersThroughFaith.org

*****Keystone Coaching & Consulting,
LLC**
22 Cherry St.
Holland, MI 49423
Phone: 616-396-1517
Contact: Mark de Roo
E-mail: mderoo@keystonecoach.com
www.keystonecoach.com

*****LifeSteward/EaRN Employment &
Resource Network**
PO Box 888187
Grand Rapids, MI 49588-8187
Phone: 616-813-4998
Contact: Ken Soper, MDiv, MA, MCC,
NCCC
E-mail: kensoper@yahoo.com
www.kensoper.com
www.earn-network.org

**New Options Town & Country
Counseling**
Specializing in careers & education
Ann Arbor, MI
Phone: 734-973-0003 or 734-973-8699
Contact: Phyllis Perry, MSW, MFA
E-mail: pepstar27@yahoo.com

Synko Associates, LLC
3025 Boardwalk, Ste. 120
Ann Arbor, MI 48108
Phone: 734-332-8800, ext. 212
E-mail: csynko@SynkoAssociates.com
www.SynkoAssociates.com

Minnesota
*North Central Ministry Development Center
(an Interdenominational Church Career Development Center)
516 Mission House Ln.
New Brighton, MN 55112
Phone: 651-636-5120
Contact: Mark Sundby, MDiv, PhD, LP,
Executive Director
E-mail: ncmdc@comcast.net
www.ncmdc.org

Prototype Career Service
626 Armstrong Ave.
St. Paul, MN 55102
Phone: 800-368-3197
Contact: Amy Lindgren,
Job Search Strategist
E-mail: getajob@prototypecareerservice.com
www.prototypecareerservice.com

Missouri
Eigles, Lorrie, PCC, MSED, LPC
Authentic Communication
Life and Career Coach
432 W. 62nd Terr.
Kansas City, MO 64113
E-mail: Lorrie@myauthenticlife
coaching.com
http://myauthenticlifecoaching.com

The Job Doctor
505 S. Ewing Ave.
St. Louis, MO 63103
Phone: 314-863-1166
Contact: M. Rose Jonas, PhD
E-mail: jobdoc@aol.com
www.jobdoctoronline.com

MU Career Center
201 Student Success Center
909 Lowry Mall
University of Missouri
Columbia, MO 65211
Phone: 573-882-6801
Fax: 573-882-5440
Contact: Craig Benson
E-mail: career@missouri.edu
http://career.missouri.edu

Women's Center
University of Missouri-Kansas City
5100 Rockhill Rd., 105 Haag Hall
Kansas City, MO 64110
Phone: 816-235-1638
Contact: Brenda Bethman, Director
E-mail: umkc-womens-center@
unkc.edu
www.umkc.edu/womenc

Montana
Career Transitions
189 Arden Dr.
Belgrade, MT 59714
Phone: 406-388-6701
Contact: Darla Joyner,
Executive Director
E-mail: ct@careertransitions.com
www.careertransitions.com

New Hampshire
Individual Employment Services (I.E.S)
1 New Hampshire Ave., Ste. 125
Portsmouth, NH 03801
Phone: 603-570-4850
or 800-734-JOBS (5627)
Fax: 603-766-1901
Contact: James Otis, Principal Career
Counselor/Recruiter
Anita Labell, Certified Professional
Resume Writer/Career Coach
E-mail: ies@iosnh.com

Tucker, Janet, MEd
Career Counselor
10 String Bridge
Exeter, NH 03833
Phone: 603-772-8693
E-mail: jbtucker@comcast.net

New Jersey
*CareerQuest
2165 Morris Ave., Ste. 15
Union, NJ 07083
Phone: 908-686-8400
Contact: Don Sutaria, MS, IE (Prof.)
Founder, President, and Life-Work
Coach
E-mail: don@careerquestcentral.com
www.careerquestcentral.com

Creating Life Options
Mendham, NJ 07945
Phone: 201-874-3264 or 973-543-3458
Contact: Katie McGinty
E-mail: katie@creatinglifeoptions.com
www.creatinglifeoptions.com
www.linkedin.com/in/katiemcginty

Grundfest, Sandra, EdD
Certified Career Counselor, Licensed
Psychologist
601 Ewing St., C-1
Princeton, NJ 08540
Phone: 609-921-8401
and
35 Clyde Rd., Ste. 101
Somerset, NJ 08873
Phone: 732-873-1212

Job Seekers of Montclair
St. Luke's Episcopal Church
73 S. Fullerton Ave.
Montclair, NJ 07042
Phone: 973-783-3442
www.jobseekersofmontclair.org
(Meets Wednesdays, 7:30–9:15 p.m.,
free of charge)

JobSeekers in Princeton
Trinity Church
33 Mercer St.
Princeton, NJ 08540
Phone: 609-921-9427
www.trinityprinceton.org
(Meets Tuesdays, 7:30–9:30 p.m.)

Mercer County Community College
Career Services
Student Center Room 229
1200 Old Trenton Rd.
West Windsor, NJ 08550
Phone: 609-570-3399
Fax: 609-570-3880
Contact: Gail C. La France,
Career Counselor
www.mccc.edu/careerservices

*W. L. Nikel
459 Passaic Ave., Ste. 171
W. Caldwell, NJ 07006
Phone: 973-439-1850
Contact: William L. Nikel, MBA
E-mail: wnikel@verizon.net

New York
Bernstein, Alan B., LCSW, PC
122 E 82nd St.
New York, NY 10028
Phone: 212-288-4881
www.guidetoyourcareer.com
www.yourretirementyourway.com

*CareerQuest
c/o TRS, Inc., Professional Ste.
44 E. 32nd St.
New York, NY 10016
Phone: 908-686-8400
Contact: Don Sutaria, MS, IE (Prof.),
Founder, President, and Life-Work
Coach
E-mail: don@careerquestcentral.com
www.careerquestcentral.com
www.careerquestcentral.blogspot.com

Careers in Transition, LLC
Professional Career Services
and Counseling
11 Computer Dr. W., #112
Albany, NY 12205
Phone: 518-366-8451
Contact: Dr. Thomas J. Denham, MCDP,
Founder and Career Counselor
E-mail: careersintransition@yahoo.com
www.careersintransitionllc.com

*Center for Creativity and Work
19 W. 34th St., Penthouse Floor
New York, NY 10001
Phone: 212-490-9158
Contact: Allie Roth, Career Coach
E-mail: allie@allieroth.com
www.allieroth.com

*Greene, Kera, MEd, DTM
Board Member of the
Career Counselors Consortium,
Adjunct Lecturer, New York University
(NYU)
Career Counselor/Workshop Leader/
Lecturer
200 E. 24th St., #1008
New York, NY 10001
Cell: 917-496-1804
E-mail: KeraGr@gmail.com
www.keragreenecareers.com

*Judith Gerberg Associates
250 W. 57th St., Ste. 2315
New York, NY 10107
Phone: 212-315-2322
E-mail: judith@gerberg.com
www.gerberg.com

Optima Careers
575 Madison Ave., between 56th and
57th Streets, Tenth Floor
New York, NY 10019
Phone: 212-876-3488
Contact: Marianne Ruggiero, President
and Founder
E-mail: mcruggiero@optimacareers.com
www.optimacareers.com

Orange County Community College
Office of Career and Internship Services
115 South St.
Middletown, NY 10940
Phone: 845-341-4444
Contact: Petra Wege-Beers, Director
E-mail: pwtra.wegegeers@sunyorange
.edu
www.sunyorange.edu/careers

Personnel Sciences Center
140 Briarcliff Rd.
Westbury, NY 11590
Phone: 516-338-5340
Fax: 516-338-5341
Contact: Jeffrey A. Goldberg, PhD,
President, Licensed Psychologist
E-mail: jag_psc@juno.com
(Services also provided in Manhattan)

The Prager-Bernstein Group
122 E. 42nd St., Ste. 2815
New York, NY 10168
Phone: 212-697-0645
Contact: Leslie B. Prager, MA, CMP,
Senior Partner/Career Counselor
E-mail: Leslie-PBG@msn.com
www.prager-bernsteingroup.com

North Carolina
Career Focus Workshops
8301 Brittains Field Rd.
Oak Ridge, NC 27310
Phone: 336-643-1419
Contact: Glenn Wise, President
E-mail: gwise001@triad.rr.com
http://careerfocusworkshops.com

Crossroads Career Network
PO Box 49664
Charlotte, NC 28277
Phone: 800-941-3566
www.CrossroadsCareer.org
(Nonprofit Christian network of member
churches equipped to help people find
jobs, careers, calling)

Joyce Richman & Associates, Ltd.
2911 Shady Lawn Dr.
Greensboro, NC 27408
Phone: 336-288-1799
E-mail: jerichman@aol.com
www.joycerichman.com
www.richmanresources.com

Kochendofer, Sally, PhD
2218 Lilac Ln.
Indian Land, SC 29707
Phone: 803-396-0979
E-mail: westiefriend@comporium.net

*The Life/Career Institute
131 Chimney Rise Dr.
Cary, NC 27511
Phone: 919-469-5775
Contact: Mike Thomas, PhD
E-mail: mikethomas@nc.rr.com
www.LifeCareerInstitute.com

Ohio
Cuyahoga County Public Library
The Career Center
5225 Library Ln.
Maple Heights, OH 44137-1291
Phone: 216-475-2225
E-mail: beaston@cuyahogalibrary.org
www.cuyahogalibrary.org/careerexpert

*Flood, Kay Reynolds, MA
Minstry
3600 Parkhill Cir. NW
Canton, OH 44718
Phone: 330-493-1448
E-mail: nana1725@aol.com

New Career
328 Race St.
Dover, OH 44622
Phone: 330-364-5557
Contact: Marshall J. Karp, MA, NCC,
LPC, Career Counselor
E-mail: marshallkarp@hotmail.com

Oklahoma
Career Development Partners, Inc.
4137 S. Harvard Ave., Ste. A
Tulsa, OK 74135
Phone: 918-293-0500
Toll-free: 866-466-1162
Fax: 918-293-0503
E-mail: Nancy@cdpartnersinc.com
www.cdpartnersinc.com

Oregon
Careerful Counseling Services
12555 SW First St.
Beaverton, OR 97005
Phone: 503-997-9506
Contact: Andrea King, MS, NCC, MCC,
Career Counselor
E-mail: aking@careerful.com
www.careerful.com

*Exceptional Living Coach, LLC
1230 Arthur St.
Eugene, OR 97402
Phone: 541-484-6785
Contact: Lisa R. Anderson, MA, NCC,
GCDF
E-mail: lisa@ExceptionalLivingCoach
.com
www.ExceptionalLivingCoach.com
(English and Spanish)

Pennsylvania
*Bartholomew, Uda
Vocational Transformations/
Vocational Liberation Workshops
PO Box 2112
Center City Philadelphia, PA 19103
Phone: 215-618-1572
Contact: Uda Bartholomew,
Lead Facilitator
E-mail: VocTransVocLib@gmail.com

**Delaware Valley Family Business
Center**
340 N. Main St.
Telford, PA 18969
Phone: 215-723-8413, ext. 204
Contact: Henry D. Landes, Consultant
E-mail: henry@dvfbc.com
www.dvfbc.com

*Hannafin, Christine, PhD
Personal and Career Counseling
Bala Farm
380 Jenissa Dr.
West Chester, PA 19382
Phone: 610-431-0588
E-mail: chrishannafin@aol.com
www.christinehannafin.com

Haynes, Lathe, PhD
401 Shady Ave., Ste. C107
Pittsburgh, PA 15206
Phone: 412-361-6336

Kessler, Jane E., MA
Licensed Psychologist
252 W. Swamp Rd., Ste. 56
Doylestown, PA 18901
Phone: 215-348-8212, ext. 1
Fax: 215-348-0329
E-mail: jane@kesslerandclark.com

William D. Morgan and Associates
Career Counseling & Coaching Services
63 Chestnut Road, Ste. 3
Paoli, PA 19301
Phone: 610-644-8182
E-mail: info@Counseling4Careers.com
www.Counseling4Careers.com

South Carolina
Crystal-Barkley Corp.
(formerly the John C. Crystal Center)
293 E. Bay St.
Charleston, SC 29401
Phone: 800-333-9003
Fax: 800-560-5333
Contact: Nella G. Barkley, President
E-mail: crystalbarkley@careerlife.com
www.careerlife.com
(John Crystal, the founder of the John C.
Crystal Center, died in 1988; Nella, his
business partner for many years, now
continues his work throughout the U.S.
and in the UK and the Netherlands.)

**White Ridgely Associates, Success
Management**
26 River Bend Dr.
Okatie, SC 29909
Phone: 443-829-9014
Contact: Daisy Nelson White, PhD
E-mail: Daisy@whiteridgely.com
www.WhiteRidgely.com

Tennessee
*Career Resources, Inc.
208 Elmington Ave.
Nashville, TN 37205
Phone: 615-957-0404
Contact: Jane C. Hardy, Career
Strategist/Founder
E-mail: JHardy@CareerResources.net
www.CareerResources.net

Texas
Career Action Associates PC
8350 Meadow Rd., Ste. 272
Dallas, TX 75231
Contact: Joyce Shoop, M.S., LPC, CRC
Phone: 214-378-8350
E-mail: joyshoop@sbcglobal.net
Contact: Rebecca Hayes, MEd, CRC, LPC
Phone: 817-926-9941
E-mail: rhayescaa@aol.com

NB Careers
New Braunfels, TX 78130
Phone: 830-237-2735
Contact: Shell Mendelson, MS
E-mail: shell@passiontocareer.com
www.passiontocareer.com

*New Life Institute
PO Box 4487
Austin, TX 78765
Phone: 512-469-9447
Contact: Bob Breihan
E-mail: newlifetexas@sbcglobal.net
www.newlifetexas.org

Quereau, Jeanne, MA, LPC, CPC
Life/Career Coach & Psycotherapist
9500 Jollyville Rd., #121
Austin, TX 78759
Phone: 512-342-9552
E-mail: jeanneq19@gmail.com
www.journeywithjeanne.com

Utah
Lue, Keith
PO Box 971482
Orem, UT 84097-1482
Phone: 801-885-1389
E-mail: keithlue@keydiscovery.com
www.keydiscovery.com

Vermont
Career Networks, Inc.
1372 Old Stage Rd.
Williston, VT 05495
Phone: 802-872-1533
Contact: Markey Read
E-mail: markey@careernetworksvt.com
www.careernetworksvt.com

Preis, Roger J.
RPE Career Dynamics
PO Box 115
Shelburne, VT 05482
Phone: 802-985-3775
E-mail: rjpreis@rpecareers.com
www.rpecareers.com

Virginia
The BrownMiller Group
312 Granite Ave.
Richmond, VA 23226
Phone: 804-288-2157
Contact: Bonnie Miller
E-mail: brownmillergroup@gmail.com
www.BrownMiller.com

McCarthy & Company
Executive Coaching,
Career Transition Management
4201 S. 32nd Rd.
Arlington, VA 22206
Phone: 703-671-4300
Contact: Peter McCarthy, President
E-mail: mccarthy@careertran.com
www.careertran.com

The Women's Center
127 Park St. NE
Vienna, VA 22180
Phone: 703-281-2657
E-mail: twc@thewomenscenter.org
(Subject line should read,
"Attention: Lauren Kellar")
www.thewomenscenter.org

Washington State
Bridgeway Career Development
1611 116th Avenue NE, Ste. 219
Bellevue, WA 98004
Phone: 877-250-2103
Contact: Carolyn Kessler, Maria
Escobar-Bordyn, Partners
E-mail: services@bridgewaycareer.com
www.bridgewaycareer.com

Career Management Institute
8404 27th St. W.
University Place, WA 98466
Phone: 253-565-8818
Contact: Ruthann Reim McCaffree, MA,
NCC, LMHC, CPC
E-mail: careermi@nwrain.com
www.CareerMI.com

**Centerpoint Institute for Life and
Career Renewal**
4000 NE 41st St., Bldg. D West, Ste. 2
Seattle, WA 98105-5428
Phone: 206-686-LIFE (5433)
Contact: Carol Vecchio
www.centerpointseattle.org

West Virginia
Ticich, Frank E., MS, CRC, CVE,
Career Consultant
153 Tartan Dr.
Follansbee, WV 26037
Phone: 304-748-1772
E-mail: frankticich@comcast.net

Wisconsin
***Career Momentum, Inc.**
49 Kessel Court, Ste. 103,
Madison, WI 53711
Phone: 608-274-2430
Contact: Clara Hurd Nydam,
MDiv, MCC, SPHR
E-mail: Clara.Nydam@
CareerMomentum.com
www.CareerMomentum.com

Guarneri Associates
6670 Crystal Lake Rd.
Three Lakes, WI 54562
Phone: 715-546-4449 or 866-881-4055
Contact: Susan Guarneri, NCCC, MCC,
CERW, CPBS, COIMS
E-mail: Susan@AssessmentGoddess.com

Wyoming
University of Wyoming
The Center for Advising and Career
Services
1000 E. University Ave., Dept. 3195
Laramie, WY 82071-3195
Phone: 307-766-2398
E-mail: uwcacs@uwyo.edu
www.uwyo.edu/cacs

CANADA

British Columbia
CBD Network, Inc.
201-2033 Gordon Dr.
Kelowna, BC V1Y 3J2
Phone: 250-717-1821
E-mail: info@cbdnetwork.com
www.cbdnetwork.com

Curtis, Susan, MEd, RCC, CEAP
Vancouver, BC
Phone: 604-228-9618
E-mail: susancurtis@telus.net

Ontario
***Careers by Design**
Coaching and Counseling
80 Harrison Garden Blvd.
Toronto, ON, M2N 7E3
Phone: 416-519-8408
Contact: (Ms.) Shirin Khamisa, BA
Hons., BEd, ICF-Certified Coach and
Career Counselor, Licenced HeartMath
Coach
E-mail: shirin@careersbydesign.ca
www.careersbydesign.ca

***CareersPlus Inc.**
55 Village Pl., Ste. 203
Mississaugua, ON L4Z 1V9
Phone: 905-272-8258
Contact: Douglas H. Schmidt,
BA, MEd, EdD
E-mail: info@careersplusinc.com
www.careersplusinc.com

Career Strategy Counselling
2 Briarhill Pl.
London, ON N5Y 1P7
Phone: 519-455-4609
Contact: Ruth Clarke, BA
E-mail: rclarke4609@rogers.com
www.careerstrategycounselling.com

donnerwheeler
1 Belvedere Ct., Ste. 1207
Brampton, ON L6V 4M6
Phone: 905-450-1086
Contact: Mary M. Wheeler, RN, MEd,
PCC
E-mail: info@donnerwheeler.com
www.donnerwheeler.com

Human Achievement Associates
22 Cottonwood Crescent
London, ON N6G 2Y8
Phone: 519-657-3000 or 519-200-6301
Contact: Mr. Kerry A. Hill
E-mail: haa.no.1@rogers.com

Puttock, Judith, BBA, CHRP
Career Management Consultant
The Puttock Group
913 Southwind Ct.
Newmarket, ON L3Y 6J1
Phone: 905-717-1738
E-mail: j.puttock@rogers.com

**YMCA Career Planning &
Development**
2200 Yonge St.
Toronto, ON M4S 2B8
Phone: 416-928-3362
Contact: Mr. Franz Schmidt
E-mail: franz.schmidt@ymcagta.org
www.ymcagta.org/assessment services

Quebec
Agence Ometz
Employment, Family, and Immigration
Services
1 Cummings Square
Montreal, QC H3W 1M6
Phone: 514-342-0000
Fax: 514-342-2371
Contact: Howard Berger or Gail Small,
Co-Executive Directors
E-mail: info@ometz.ca
www.ometz.ca
(Uses both French and English versions
of *Parachute*. Utilise des versions Fran-
caises et Anglaises de *Parachute*.)

**La Passerelle Employment &
Career Transition Centre**
1255 Phillips Square, Ste. 903
Montreal, QC H3B 3G1
Phone: 514-866-5982
Contact: Leslie (Laszlo) Acs, Executive
Director
E-mail: info@lapasserelle.ca
www.lapasserelle.ca

New Career Options
80 Coolbreeze (Pointe Claire)
Montreal, QC H9R 3S7
Contact: Don Smith
Phone: 514-816-2803
E-mail: DonSmithnco@bell.net
www.NewCareerOptions.ca

OVERSEAS

Australia
Career Action Centre
5 Bronte Ave.
Burwood, Victoria 3125
Phone: 03 9808 5500
Cell: 0403 136 260
Contact: Jackie Rothberg
E-mail: jackie@careeractioncentre
.com.au
www.careeractioncentre.com.au

The Growth Connection
32 Grove St.
Earlwood, NSW 2206
Phone: 61 2 9787 2748
Fax: 612 9787 3185
Cell: 0407 477 225
Contact: Imogen Wareing, Director
E-mail: iwareing@growconnect.com.au
www.linkedin.com/in/imogenwareing
www.growconnect.com.au

Life by Design
PO Box 50
Newport Beach, NSW 2106
Phone: 61 2 9979 4949
Contact: Ian Hutchinson,
Lifestyle Strategist
E-mail: info@lifebydesign.com.au
www.lifebydesign.com.au

Milligan, Narelle
Career Consultant (regional NSW)
Phone: 2 6584 3271
Cell: 0411 236 124
E-mail: nmilligan2000@yahoo.com.au

Taccori, John, EdD
Career Counsellor
Blue Mountains, NSW 2777
Phone: 04 0093 8574
www.careersdoctor.net

France
Chavigny, Catherine
11 bis, rue Huyghens
75014 Paris
Phone: (33) 6 30 51 40 56
E-mail: catherine.chavigny@me.com

Germany
Buddensieg, Marc
Niemeyerstrasse 17a
30449 Hannover
Phone: 49 0 163 624 2639
Fax: 49 0 12120 277 627
E-mail: buddensieg@gmx.de
www.www.lwp-institut-hannover.de

Leitner, Madeleine, Dipl. Psych.
Ohmstrasse 8
80802 Munchen
Phone: 089 33079444
Fax: 089 33079445
E-mail: ML@Karriere-Management.de
www.Karriere-Management.de
(Madeleine is one of the best *Parachute*
counselors in Europe. She translated
Parachute into German.)

Webb, John Carl
Meinenkampstr 83a
48165 Munster-Hiltrup
Phone: +49 0 2501 92 16 96
E-mail: john@muenster.de
www.lifeworkplanning.de
(Universities offering Life/Work Plan-
ning courses designed by John, and
based on *Parachute*, are located in Berlin,
Bochum, Bremen, Freiburg, Hannover,
Konstanz, Leipzig, and Potsdam. John
was on staff at my international Two-
Week Workshops; he is a master of the
Parachute process.)

Ireland
Brian McIvor & Associates
Newgrange Mall, Unit 4B
Slane, County Meath
Phone: 353 41 988 4035
E-mail: brianmcivor@gmail.com
www.brianmcivor.com
(Brian was on staff at my international
Two-Week Workshop for five years.)

Israel
Mendel, Lori
PO Box 148
Caesarea, Israel 38900
Phone: 972 3 524 1068
Cell: 972 54 814 4442
E-mail: bizcom@bezeqint.net

Transitions & Resources, Ltd.
Tzipornit, 6/3
Modiin, 71808 Israel
Phone: 08 926 6102
U.S. phone line in Israel until 4 p.m.
EST: 516-216-4457
Fax: 08 926 6103
Contact: Judy Feierstein, CEO
E-mail: info@maavarim.biz
www.maavarim.biz

The Netherlands
Crystal-Barkley Corp.
Service in The Netherlands
Phone: 800-333-9003
E-mail: crystalbarkley@careerlife.com
www.careerlife.com

Pluym Career Consultants
Career Executive & Expats Coaching
Services
Boshoekerweg 16
NL/8167 LS EPE/OENE
Contact: Johan Veeninga,
Senior Consultant
E-mail: johan.veeninga@gmail.com or
info@careerconsultants.nl
www.careerconsultants.nl

New Zealand
Career Lifestyle
Auckland CBD
Contact: Paula Stenberg
www.cvstyle.co.nz

*CV.CO.NZ (NZ) Ltd.
373 Masters Rd.
Auckland 2682
Toll-Free: 0800 282 669
Phone: 09 235 8484
Contact: Tom O'Neil
E-mail: tom@cv.co.nz
www.cv.co.nz

Strategic Career Services
PO Box 27072
Hamilton 3257
Phone: 64 7 849 0909
Contact: Tui Needham
E-mail: tui@tuineedham.co.nz
www.tuineedham.co.nz

Poland
JC Coaching Justyna Ciecwierz
Tarniny 5a
05-515 Nowa Iwiczna
Cell: 48 600 327 163
Contact: Justyna Ciecwierz, ACCC,
Career Coaching, Work/Life Planning
E-mail: justyna.ciecwierz@jc-coaching
.pl
www.jc-coaching.pl

Singapore
Transformation Technologies
122 Thomson Green
574986 Singapore
Phone: 65 98197858
Contact: Anthony Tan, Director
E-mail: anthonyt@singnet.com.sg

South Africa
Andrew Bramley Career Consultants
12 Ridge Way
PO Box 1311
Proteaville, Durbanville 7550
Phone: 27 0 21 9755573
Fax: 27 0 88 0 21 9755573
Contact: Andrew Bramley
E-mail: info@andrewbramley.co.za
www.andrewbramley.co.za

South Korea
Byung Ju Cho, PhD
Professor of Business and Career
Ajou University
Suwon
Phone: 82 31 219 2709
Fax: 82 2 594 6236
Cell: 82 10 9084 6236
E-mail: chobju@ajou.ac.kr
(Byung Ju Cho is the translator of the
Korean version of *Parachute*.)

Spain
Analisi-Nic
Via Augusta, 120
Principal 1
08006 Barcelona
Phone: 34 932119303
Fax: 34 932172128
Contact: José Arnó
E-mail: analisi@arrakis.es

Switzerland
Baumgartner, Peter
Hummelwaldstrasse 18a
8645 Rapperswil-Jona
Phone: +41 0 55 534 14 47
E-mail: lebensunternehmer@bluewin.ch

KLB LifeDesigning
Alpenblickstrasse 33
8645 Jona-Kempraten
Phone: +41 0 55 211 09 77
Fax: +41 0 55 211 09 79
Contact: Peter Kessler, LifeDesigning
Coach
E-mail: p.kessler@bluewin.ch
www.LifeDesigning.ch

Porot & Partenaire
Rue de la Terrassière 8
1207 Genève-Suisse
Phone: +41 0 22 700 82 10
Fax: +41 0 22 700 82 14
Contact: Daniel Porot, Founder
E-mail: daniel@porot.com
www.porot.com
(Daniel is the premiere career expert in
Europe; for the twenty years that I did
two-week workshops each August,
Daniel was always co-leader with me
each summer.)

Sauser, Hans-U.
Beratung und Ausbildung
Im Bungert 2
5430 Wettingen
Phone: 056 426 64 09
E-mail: husauser@gmx.ch

Vollenweider, Peter A.
Career and Transition Coaching,
Work/Life Planning, Consulting
Kaepfnerweg 20
8810 Horgen/Zurich
Phone: +41 0 44 715 15 63
Cell: +41 0 78 626 11 58
Contact: Dr. Peter A. Vollenweider
E-mail: peter.vollenweider@gmail.com

United Kingdom
Can Do It Now
Contact: Janie Wilson
UK: London, Surrey, and Sussex;
France:
Languedoc
Phone: +44 (0)7968 027344
E-mail: janie@candoitnow.co.uk
or
Contact: Alix Nadelman
London, Cambridge, and East Counties
Phone: +44 (0)7977 930223
E-mail: alix@candoitnow.co.uk
www.candoitnow.co.uk
www.lepuget.com

Career Dovetail
4 E. Hill Court
Oxted, Surrey RH8 9AD
and
Hub Working Centre
5 Wormwood St.
London EC2M 1RW
Contact: Duncan Bolam, Dip. CG,
Director, Career Coach, and Founder
E-mail: duncanbolam@careerdovetail.
co.uk or enquiries@careerdovetail.co.uk
www.careerdovetail.co.uk

Crystal-Barkley Corp.
Service in the United Kingdom
Phone: 800-333-9003
E-mail: crystalbarkley@careerlife.com
www.careerlife.com

Hawkins, Dr. Peter
Mt. Pleasant
Liverpool, L3 5TF
Phone: 0044 0 151 709-1760
Fax: 0044 0 151 709-1576
E-mail: p.Hawkins@gieu.co.uk

John Lees Associates
37 Tatton St.
Knutsford, Cheshire WA16 6AE
Phone: 01565 631625
Contact: John Lees
E-mail: johnlees@johnleescareers.com
www.johnleescareers.com

Sherridan Hughes
Career Management Expert
110 Pretoria Rd.
London SW16 6RN
Phone: 020 8769 5737
E-mail: sherridan@sherridanhughes
.com
www.sherridan-hughes.co.uk

About the Author

DICK BOLLES—more formally known as Richard Nelson Bolles—is credited with founding the modern career counseling field (by such career experts as the late Bernard Haldane), and has been featured in *Time*, the *New York Times*, *BusinessWeek*, *Fortune*, *Money*, *Fast Company*, the *Economist*, and *Publishers Weekly*. He has appeared on the *Today* show, CNN, CBS, ABC, PBS, and other popular media. Bolles has keynoted hundreds of conferences including the American Society for Training & Development and the National Career Development Association. He is a member of Mensa and the Society for Human Resource Management. "He is the most recognized job-hunting authority on the planet" (*San Francisco Chronicle*) and "America's top career expert" (*AARP*).

Bolles is the author of *What Color Is Your Parachute?*, the most popular job-hunting book in the world. *Time* magazine chose it as one of the hundred best nonfiction books written since 1923. The Library of Congress chose it as one of twenty-five books down through history that have shaped people's lives. It is a *New York Times* best seller, appearing on its list for more than five years. The book has sold 10 million copies, to date, and is revised every year. It has been translated into twenty languages and is used in twenty-six countries.

Bolles was trained in chemical engineering at Massachusetts Institute of Technology, and holds a bachelor's degree cum laude in physics from Harvard University, a master's in sacred theology from General Theological (Episcopal) Seminary in New York City, and three honorary doctorates. He lives in the San Francisco Bay Area with his wife, Marci.

E-mail address: dickbolles40@gmail.com

Websites: www.jobhuntersbible.com; www.eparachute.com

Blog: http://jobhuntersbible.typepad.com

Facebook: http://tinyurl.com/4zwxws6

LinkedIn: http://tinyurl.com/24mtryz

Twitter: http://twitter.com/@ParachuteGuy

Index

Update 2013

To: PARACHUTE
10 Stirling Drive
Danville, CA 94526-2921

I think that the information in the 2013 edition needs to be changed, in your next revision, regarding (or, the following resource should be added):

_____

_____

_____

_____

_____

I cannot find the following resource, listed on page _____:

_____

_____

_____

_____

_____

_____

_____

Name _____

Address _____

_____

Please make a copy.
Submit this so as to reach us by February 1, 2013.
Thank you.

Foreign Editions
of *What Color Is Your Parachute?*

Recent Translations (available now)

Spanish (Santillana USA Publishing Company, 2012): *¿De Qué Color Es Tu Paracaídas?*

Dutch (Nieuwezijds Publishers, 2011): *Welke Kleur Heeft Jouw Parachute?*

German (Campus Verlag, 2011): *Durchstarten zum Traumjob Das Bewerbungshandbuch*

Turkish (Optimist/BZD Yayin ve Iletisim Hizmetleri, 2011): *En iyi is Nasil Bulunur?*

Polish (Studio Emka, 2010): *Jakiego Koloru Jest Twoj Spadochron?*

Simplified Chinese (China CITIC Press, 2010): 這樣求職才能成功?

Portuguese (Actual Editora, 2010): *De que cor é o seu pára-quedas?*

Russian (Mann, Ivanov & Ferber Publishers, 2010): Какого цвета ваш парашют?

Indonesian (PT Gramedia Pustaka Utama, 2010)

Italian (Edizioni Sonda, 2008): *Ce L'hai il Paracadute?*

Complex Chinese (Faces Publications, 2006): 你的降落傘是什麼顏色?

Coming Soon

Hungarian (HVG Kiado)

Japanese (Tatsumi Publishing)

Serbian (Carobna Knjiga)

Spanish (Gestion 2000)

Vietnamese (TGM Books)